KU-215-220

IMMIGRATION
SERVICE
- 4 OCT 1988
DEPARTED
(1095)
HONG KONG

DEPARTMENT OF IMMIGRATION
PERMITTED TO ENTER
AUSTRALIA.
24 APR 1986
on
For stay of 12 Month
SYDNEY AIRPORT 54

IMMIGRATION DIVISION BANGKOK - THAILAND
A
72
DEPARTED
- 9 FEB 1987
SIGNED

IMMIGRATION ... ETHNIC AFFAIRS
.... Person
30 OCT 1989
DEPARTED
AUSTRALIA
SYDNEY 32

T R A V E L E R ' S

FLORIDA

C O M P A N I O N

上陸許可
ADMITTED
15. FEB. 1986
Status: 4-1-   4
Duration: 90 days
NARITA(N)
Immigration Inspector

U.S. IMMIGRATION
160-LOS C-4125

MAY 23 1998

ADMITTED_____
UNTIL   (CLASS)

ADMITTED
20 OCT. 1988
Status: 4-1-16
Duration   180 days
Port: HANEDA
Signature

USED
Narita Air Port

HONG KONG
(1038)
- 7 JUN 1987
IMMIGRATION
OFFICER

The 1998–1999 Traveler's Companions
ARGENTINA • AUSTRALIA • BALI • CALIFORNIA • CANADA • CHINA • COSTA RICA • CUBA •
EASTERN CANADA • ECUADOR • FLORIDA • HAWAII • HONG KONG • INDIA • INDONESIA •
JAPAN • KENYA • MALAYSIA & SINGAPORE • MEDITERRANEAN FRANCE • MEXICO • NEPAL • NEW
ENGLAND • NEW ZEALAND • PERU • PHILIPPINES • PORTUGAL • RUSSIA • SPAIN • THAILAND •
TURKEY • VENEZUELA • VIETNAM, LAOS AND CAMBODIA • WESTERN CANADA

Traveler's FLORIDA Companion
First Published 1998

World Leisure Marketing Limited
Unit 11, Newmarket Court
Newmarket Drive
Derby, DE24 8NW, England
Web Site: http://www.map-world.co.uk

ISBN: 1-84006-057-3

Published by arrangement with Kümmerly+Frey AG, Switzerland
© 1998 Kümmerly+Frey AG, Switzerland

Created, edited and produced by Allan Amsel Publishing
27700 Les Andelys, France. E-mail: aamsel@aol.com
Editor in Chief: Allan Amsel
Editor: Laura Purdom
Original design concept: Hon Bing-wah
Picture editor and designer: David Henry

Printed by Samhwa Printing Co. Ltd., Seoul, Korea

TRAVELER'S
FLORIDA
COMPANION

by Donald Carroll
Photographed by Nik Wheeler

Kümmerly+Frey

Contents

MAPS

Florida	8–9
Miami and Miami Beach	80
Fort Lauderdale	108
The Gold Coast	122
The Atlantic Coast	130
Orlando and Disney World	163
Central Florida	171
The Panhandle	178–179
The Gulf Coast	196
Tampa and St. Petersburg	203
The Everglades and Florida Keys	224
Key West	239

TOP SPOTS 11

St. Augustine	11
The Everglades	13
Ybor City	13
Tarpon Springs	14
Florida's Secret Beaches	15
Key West	16
Miami	16
Blue Spring State Park	18
St. Petersburg-Clearwater	18
Sanibel Island	19
Fort Myers	20
Daytona Beach	20

YOUR CHOICE	23
The Great Outdoors	23
Sporting Spree	28
The Open Road	31
Backpacking	34
Living It Up	37
Family Fun	40
Cultural Kicks	42
Shop Till You Drop	44
Short Breaks	50
Festive Flings	51
Galloping Gourmet	56
Special Interests	60
Taking a Tour	62

WELCOME TO FLORIDA	65

THE STATE AND ITS PEOPLE	69
Historical Background	71
Geography and Climate	75

MIAMI AND ENVIRONS	79
Miami	81
Background • General Information •	
What to See and Do • Where to Stay •	
Where to Eat • How to Get There	
Miami Beach	96
Background • General Information •	
What to See and Do • Where to Stay •	
Where to Eat • How to Get There	

THE GOLD COAST	103
Fort Lauderdale	106
Background • General Information •	
What to See and Do • Where to Stay •	
Where to Eat • How to Get There	
Palm Beach and Boca Raton	115
Background • General Information •	
What to See and Do • Where to Stay •	
Where to Eat • How to Get There	

THE ATLANTIC COAST   **125**
The Space Coast   127
   Background • General Information •
   What to See and Do • Where to Stay •
   Where to Eat • How to Get There
Daytona   132
   Background • General Information •
   What to See and Do • Where to Stay •
   Where to Eat • How to Get There
St. Augustine   138
   Background • General Information •
   What to See and Do • Where to Stay •
   Where to Eat • How to Get There
Jacksonville   145
   Background • General Information •
   What to See and Do • Where to Stay •
   Where to Eat • How to Get There

CENTRAL FLORIDA   **151**
Background   153
Walt Disney World   153
   General Information • What to See
   and Do • Other Things to See in
   Disney World • Where to Stay •
   Where to Eat • How to Get There
Greater Orlando   164
   Background • General Information •
   What to See and Do • Where to Stay •
   Where to Eat
Other Attractions In Central Florida   171
   South of Orlando • North of Orlando

THE PANHANDLE   **175**
Tallahassee   177
   Background • General Information •
   What to See and Do • Where to Stay •
   Where to Eat • How to Get There
Panama City   181
   General Information • What to See
   and Do • Where to Stay • Where to
   Eat • How to Get There
Pensacola   186
   Background • General Information •
   What to See and Do • Where to Stay •
   Where to Eat • How to Get There

THE GULF COAST   **193**
Tampa   195
   Background • General Information •
   What to See and Do • Where to Stay •
   Where to Eat • How to Get There
St. Petersburg   202
   General Information • What to See
   and Do • Where to Stay • Where to
   Eat • How to Get There
Sarasota   206
   Background • General Information •
   What to See and Do • Where to Stay •
   Where to Eat • How to Get There
The Shell Coast   211
   General Information • What to See
   and Do • Where to Stay • Where to
   Eat • How to Get There

THE EVERGLADES	**217**
Everglades National Park	218
Background • General Information •	
What to See and Do • Where to Stay •	
Where to Eat • How to Get There	
THE FLORIDA KEYS	**227**
Key Largo to Long Key	229
General Information • What to See	
and Do • Where to Stay • Where to	
Eat • How to Get There	
Grassy Key to Stock Island	233
General Information • What to See	
and Do • Where to Stay • Where to Eat	
Key West	237
General Information • What to See	
and Do • Where to Stay • Where to	
Eat • How to Get There	
TRAVELERS' TIPS	**243**
Getting There	244
By Air • By Rail • By Bus • By Car	
Tourist Information	245
Consulates	246
In Florida • In New York	
Travel Documents	246
Customs	246

When to Go	246
What to Take	247
Getting Around	247
Basics	248
Health	248
Money	248
Accommodation	248
Prices	249
Eating Out	249
Tanning	250
Tipping	250
Driving	250
Camping	251
Tennis	251
Golf	251
Fishing	251
Cruises	252
Public Holidays	252
Mail	253
Telephones	253
Radio and Television	253
Newspapers and Magazines	255
Buying Property	255
Recommended Reading	256
QUICK REFERENCE **A–Z GUIDE**	**257**
To Places and Topics of Interest with	
Listed Accommodation, Restaurants	
and Useful Telephone Numbers	

T R A V E L E R ' S
F L O R I D A
C O M P A N I O N

TOP SPOTS

St. Augustine

ST. AUGUSTINE, AMERICA'S OLDEST CITY, IS A TIME CAPSULE CAPTURING NEARLY 500 YEARS OF HISTORY and offering a welcome relief from the theme parks and modern-day attractions that abound elsewhere in the state.

Horse drawn carriages clip clop along narrow cobbled streets, red tile roofs overhang walled courtyards and guitar music wafts out of historic buildings made from crushed seashells and coral.

Founded by the Spanish in 1565 — 42 years before the English colonized Jamestown — St. Augustine is a living museum with 144 blocks of historic buildings listed on the National Register of Historic Places.

You can stroll down narrow lanes in the Spanish quarter past coquina stone

houses with their overhanging balconies and intimate walled gardens, meander along the waterfront with its ancient gnarled trees festooned with hanging Spanish moss, or just laze the day away on the miles of nearby white sand beaches.

Animated yet accurate tour guides lead visitors through the centuries by horse and carriage, trolley trains, river cruises and walking tours.

Take in **Castillo de San Marcos** ((904) 829-6506, built in 1672, and the nation's oldest stone fort, and **Fort Matanzas**, constructed half a century later, which can only be reached by boat.

The city boasts the nation's **oldest wooden schoolhouse**, the **oldest store** and the **oldest surviving house** (1727), as well as other architectural masterpieces including Henry Flagler's nineteenth-century **Ponce de León Hotel** now a college, the Venetian Renaissance Revival **Memorial Presbyterian Church**, and the **Bridge of Lions** carved of Carrera marble.

There is the **Lightner Museum** with one of the world's most impressive cut glass displays, the candy striped **Lighthouse Tower and Museum**, **Government House Museum** and nearby **Fort Mose**, established for free slaves and the first black settlement in North America.

And when you have had your fill of antiquity, visit America's first **Alligator Farm** ((904) 824-3337, established in 1893,

ABOVE: St. Augustine's beautiful buildings span five centuries of history. OPPOSITE: Locals believe this is the site of Ponce de León's legendary fountain of youth.

and the world's original **Oceanarium** ((904) 471-1111, or discover the 24 miles (38 km) of unspoiled beaches on nearby Anastasia Island.

The Everglades

THE EVERGLADES NATIONAL PARK IS THE LARGEST REMAINING SUBTROPICAL WILDERNESS in North America, covering more than one and a half million acres (600,000 hectares) and it is home to scores of threatened and endangered species of plants, animals and birds.

The Everglades is really a vast slow-moving, freshwater river up to 50 miles (80 km) wide and often only a few inches deep fed by Lake Okeechobee to the north. More than half the park is covered by shallow water although wading is not a good idea because of the large number of poisonous snakes and tens of thousands of alligators, some more than 20 ft (six meters) long.

Everglades City on the Gulf Coast is one of the most popular access points and offers a wide choice of water tours, from sedate glass bottom craft to air boats which hurtle across the surface. The National Park also has guided boat tours which leave from the ranger station, one mile (one and six tenths kilometers) south of Everglades City.

The **E. J. Hamilton Observation Tower**, on State Road 29, with its 180 steps, offers panoramas over the Everglades and Ten Thousand Islands; while the **Tamiami Trail** (State Road 41) runs almost coast to coast along the northern edge of the park providing a number of access points.

Much of the vegetation is similar to that found in Cuba and the West Indies and in addition to the several species of palms and other tropical and subtropical plants, almost 300 species of birds and 600 species of fish can be found within the park. It is one of the few areas where the docile manatee, or sea cow, is assured a permanent sanctuary, and you can also spot alligators, turtles, snakes and on occasion, porpoises.

The park is open year round and apart from the boat trips, there are four marked canoe trails. It is advisable to file your trip with the ranger office before leaving and to report back on your return. There are also a number of well-signposted scenic drives and conducted tram tours which leave from **Flamingo Lodge**. The best trails are **Shark Valley** which can also be done on hired bicycles, and the Anhinga Trail which starts at the **Royal Palm Interpretive Center**.

There is a lot to see and do in the Everglades so allow as much time as possible — and don't forget your insect repellent.

Ybor City

THIS LIVELY CUBAN QUARTER OF TAMPA IS FAMOUS FOR CIGAR MAKING and bustles with craftsmen who work from their close packed houses and small factories that have changed little over the decades.

OPPOSITE: An anhinga or snake bird, dries its wings. RIGHT: The Columbia restaurant, a renowned tourist haunt since 1905.

craft centers along 15th Street, including a glass studio and the **Florida Center for Contemporary Art**, opposite El Encanto Cleaners, an Ybor City family business that has survived for three generations. **Las Novedades**, built in 1917 and once an award-winning restaurant, now houses the Tracks nightclub. There are organized tours around **Villazon & Co.** on Armenia Avenue, a mechanized cigar factory — although the traditional methods of hand rolling are still demonstrated.

Tarpon Springs

There are still cobblestone streets, intricate wrought iron balconies and Spanish tiles in abundance. The Cubans brought their cigar making skills with them when they emigrated in their thousands in the mid-nineteenth century, and soon Ybor City became home to many other immigrant groups including Germans, Jews and Italians. The history of the city, now part of Tampa, is told in the **Ybor City State Museum**, and it makes a useful first port of call as you can pick up a map and self-guided walking tour of the area. The museum on the corner of 9th Avenue and 19th Street is dedicated to the city's founder, Don Vicente Martinez Ybor. His settlement attracted thousands of immigrants and their special skills; Ybor City quickly established itself as the cigar capital of the world. The rich history of the city is preserved at the museum, once the town bakery, and you can visit nearby **La Casita**, a restored cigar worker's home. The first cigar factory was in Ybor Square, 8th Avenue and 13th Street, now a shopping mall specializing in antiques and memorabilia.

Many of the restaurants reflect the ethnic traditions of the early settlers. The **Don Quixote restaurant** specializes in authentic Cuban cuisine. Try the fresh baked Cuban bread at **La Segunda Central Bakery** on 15th Avenue, which will give you a conducted tour of the premises if you ask in good time. There are a number of interesting shops and

TARPON SPRINGS IS "THE SPONGE CAPITAL OF THE WORLD" and Florida's "Little Greece". The Greek influence is very strong as Greek fishermen and sponge divers helped settle the area in 1876. By the 1890s there was a thriving port and there is still a Mediterranean atmosphere as you wander round the picturesque sponge dock. The sponge boats are anchored along the quay and the other side of the road is packed with shops selling more sponges than you have ever seen, as well as Greek restaurants, bakeries and the imposing Orthodox church.

Most people who visit the town believe it is on the coast although it is some way inland on the Anclote River. One of the highlights of a visit is to take a boat cruise down the river, past luxury waterside homes, the many islands and secluded beaches to the sea and back. You can also go out on a sponge boat and watch the divers at work wearing the traditional rubber suit, lead boots and screw-on helmet with its pipe connected to an air pump on board.

Visit **St. Nicholas Greek Orthodox Church**, built in 1943 and a replica of St. Sophia's in Constantinople, and an example of New Byzantine architecture. The **Konger Coral Sea Aquarium** has a simulated coral reef with marine life in a 100,000-gallon (380,000-liter) tank and tidal pool, and the **Spongeorama Exhibit Center** traces the history of sponge diving.

The **Anclote Keys** are three miles (five kilometers) off Tarpon Springs and only accessible by boat. You can be dropped off in the morning, spend the day swimming and sunbathing and be picked up in time for dinner.

Florida's Secret Beaches

FLORIDA BOASTS MANY OF THE FINEST BEACHES IN THE UNITED STATES but the beaches of the Panhandle remain some of its best kept secrets.

This stretch of coastline from Pensacola, close to the state's border with Alabama, east to Panama City, runs for almost 100 miles (160 km) and contains one sweeping, spectacular sugar white sand beach after another.

The unspoiled beaches of **Pensacola** run for 25 miles (40 km) and span two long and narrow barrier islands which form part of the Gulf Islands National Seashore. Much of Pensacola Beach is protected from development while high rise condos, holiday homes and old time night spots are to be found on Perdido Key.

The **Navarre**, **Fort Walton** and **Destin** area has 24 miles (38 km) of beaches

known as the **Emerald Coast** because of the brilliant emerald green waters. Navarre was a sleepy fishing village until outsiders discovered its beaches and now it is one of the fastest growing communities along this coast. The pace of life is still gentle, however, and the beaches are still unspoiled. The two towns of Fort Walton and Destin are noted for their southern hospitality and excellent fish restaurants. Almost two-thirds of their beaches are protected and the safe waters make them ideal family holiday destinations. While there are lots of land- and water-based sporting opportunities available, the main activities are swimming, sunbathing and seashell collecting.

South Walton boasts 26 miles (42 km) of undisturbed beaches with Grayton Beach voted the best beach in the continental United States in a recent survey. There are 18 small beach communities in South Walton and no fast food outlets, amusement parks or

OPPOSITE: Greek boys dive for the white cross to mark the start of Greek Orthodox Epiphany on January 6. ABOVE: Hand in hand, a sunset stroll along a Gulf Coast beach.

large hotels but the area is popular with families with young children who just want to enjoy mile upon mile of 40-ft (12-m)-high sand dunes and crystal clear, warm water.

Panama City Beach is the last and largest stretch of beach along the Panhandle running for more than 27 miles (43 km). It is rated the number three sports beach in the United States and is noted for its fishing — thus its claim to be the seafood capital of the world. While the beaches attract visitors during the day, there are a wide range of entertainments and activities to keep them amused at other times.

Key West

KEY WEST IS THE SOUTHERNMOST CITY IN THE CONTINENTAL UNITED STATES. Its unique atmosphere is partly because it is only 90 miles (145 km) from Havana — closer than Miami — has a strong Caribbean influence, and its relative isolation has long attracted groups who for one reason or another in the past, were considered rather eccentric.

Over the years it has been the home of Spanish conquistadors, pirates, New England mariners and European royalty. Today, it has a strong gay population, many artists and writers, and attracts about 1.5 million visitors a year.

It is most famous as the home of writer Ernest Hemingway; there must be something in the air that stimulates writers to greatness. Ten Pulitzer Prizes have been awarded to writers who have lived on Key West, and more than 100 published authors live full- or part-time on the island. It is still popular with writers, artists and the famous, and celebrity-spotting is an island pastime.

The eclectic architecture is just one of the many pleasing aspects of Key West. Many of the wooden buildings are built in a style referred to as Conch, or Bahamian. The town adopted West Indian gingerbread decorations in the 1850s, and it became very fashionable to incorporate elaborate scroll-cut work on

balconies, under eaves, and under gables. Wrought iron railings were also popular, and these features continue to add a special Caribbean charm.

Sights to see include the beautifully restored 1812 **Audubon House and Gardens**; the **Curry Mansion**, a Victorian home packed with antiques, rare Tiffany glass and other furnishings; the **Old Customs House** now the Museum of History and the Arts; the **Mel Fisher Maritime Heritage Society's Treasure Museum**; and the **Ernest Hemingway Home and Museum**. When Hemingway and his wife moved in, they built the city's first swimming pool in the spacious grounds, where peacocks and scores of cats roamed.

Finally, no visit is complete without watching the sun set from **Mallory Market** on the waterfront. The place comes alive as the sun goes down with street artists, musicians and jugglers out in force to entertain the hundreds, and sometimes thousands of people who gather for this nightly Sunset Celebration ritual.

Miami

GREATER MIAMI HAS GOT TO BE ONE OF THE ULTIMATE TOURIST DESTINATIONS WITH MILE AFTER MILE OF WHITE SAND BEACHES, PALMS AND LUSH TROPICAL VEGETATION, accommodation from vast hotel resorts to charming intimate inns and hundreds of restaurants and nightclubs, plus elegant shops, historic buildings and Art Deco mansions, museums and galleries, more than 800 parks and nature areas, and sporting opportunities galore. The area is the home of scores of celebrities from film stars to sporting greats, it is the playground of the rich and its cosmopolitan nature which attracts visitors from around the world, has been enhanced by the influx of large numbers

OPPOSITE TOP: A street performer amuses the crowd which gathers nightly in Mallory Market, Key West. BOTTOM: A bottle-encrusted fence in Key West, one of the islands many eccentricities.

racing and a wealth of water sports from windsurfing and scuba to sailing and jet-skiing, or you can battle with a marlin or spot alligators in the nearby Everglades. It really does have something for everyone.

Blue Spring State Park

FOR HUNDREDS OF YEARS THIS LAGOON AREA OF NATURAL SPRINGS ALONG THE ST. JOHNS RIVER WAS THE HOME OF THE TIMUCUAN INDIANS. Their staple food was snails gathered from sandbars in the river and huge mounds of discarded shells can still be seen. In 1766, three years after England acquired Florida from Spain, John Bartram, a British botanist explored the St. Johns River and landed at Blue Spring. By the middle of the nineteenth century it was at the heart of a large citrus estate with steamships navigating up river to pick up the fruit. The pilings of the old dock, as well as the restored estate house, can still be seen.

Today, the main attraction of this state park is that every winter it is the home of large numbers of manatees, one of Florida's gentlest and most endangered species. Between November and March they leave the cold waters of the St. Johns River and surrounding waterways for the safety and comfort of the year-round 22°C (72°F) springs. Not only does the amazing clarity of the water allow you to see these docile creatures, you can even swim in the water among them.

There is a boardwalk along the river bank which can have changed little since the days of the Timucuan Indians. There are also areas where you can camp, fish, canoe and backpack if you want to get a taste of the real Florida.

of Hispanics, many of them refugees from Cuba, which explains why most street signs are given in both English and Spanish. In some areas — like Little Havana — Spanish is the predominant language. Their arrival has had a major impact on the culture, traditions and cuisine of the area. The area features conch fritters and black beans and rice, cowbells and castanets, salsa and compas, and jig and rumba. There is theatre and ballet, art groups and opera, and galleries galore.

Miami is the world's largest cruise ship port and Miami International Airport handles 28 million passengers a year from around the world, most of whom head for the 13 miles (21 km) of tropical beaches.

Greater Miami is also one of the nation's major sporting centers with the NFL's record-breaking Miami Dolphins, baseball's new major league team the Florida Marlins, the Miami Heat professional basketball team, and the National Hockey League's Florida Panthers. There is championship golf, international tennis, Grand Prix motor

St. Petersburg-Clearwater

THIS IS THE MOST POPULAR HOLIDAY SPOT ON FLORIDA'S GULF COAST ATTRACTING FOUR MILLION VISITORS A YEAR — 90 percent of whom say they will

return. The twin cities occupy the Pinellas peninsula, the most densely populated area in all Florida. **St. Petersburg** is largely a resort city, connected by a series of bridges with Tampa and by causeways to the Holiday Isles to the west. It claims the title "Sun Capital of America", because of a one-time record 768 consecutive days of sunshine. Between 1910 and 1986 the St. Petersburg *Evening Independent* was given away free on days when the sun did not shine, and in 76 years, the newspaper was given away free only 295 times, less than four times a year. It is very much a resort city with its palm-lined streets, bustling waterfront and pier, shops and restaurants, and three fine museums — the **Museum of Fine Arts**, **Salvador Dali Museum** and the **Great Explorations** children's museum.

Clearwater and **Clearwater Beach** offer excellent swimming and long stretches of sandy beaches for sunbathing. There is a bustling sport fishing fleet based at the **Clearwater Marina** which is also the home of **Sea-Orama**, a museum and aquarium opened in 1954 and concentrating on the wildlife of the Gulf. There are all sorts of sea trips on offer from deep sea fishing, dolphin spotting and dinner specials to watching the sun set at sea. Concerts and Broadway shows are staged at the **Ruth Eckerd Hall**, and you can spend an interesting and educational afternoon at the **Clearwater Marine Science Center**. Clearwater Sunset is a nightly open air celebration staged at **Pier 60** featuring magicians, musicians, jugglers and other entertainers who perform as the crowds gather to watch the sun set over the Gulf. Top sights include the reconstructed 1890s **Boatyard Village**, on Fairchild Drive, Clearwater; **Largo Heritage Park and Museum**, 125th Street, with restored residences and buildings on a 20-acre (eight-hectare) wooded site; and the **Marine Aquarium and Science Center**, Windward Passage, Clearwater, a research and rehabilitation facility.

Sanibel Island

SANIBEL IS AN IDYLLIC ISLAND GETAWAY REACHED BY A TOLL CAUSEWAY WHICH HELPS TO LIMIT CROWDS. The island's beaches are consistently voted as among the best in the world, and Sanibel is also world famous for its shelling and wildlife. More than 200 different types of shell have been found along its beaches. As the light starts to fade, you can wade through the water with manta rays swimming around your legs and ibis and egrets following you along the sand and watch the most stunning sunsets.

Periwinkle Way is the main thoroughfare and on either side, hidden among the lush tropical vegetation, are interesting shops, galleries and fine restaurants. The best way to get around the island is to hire a bike from one of the many outlets. The **Old Schoolhouse Theater**, formerly a one room schoolhouse built in 1894, is now a cozy community

OPPOSITE: Cuban expatriates play dominoes in Miami's Little Havana. ABOVE: Taking to the water is one of the best ways to explore Sanibel Island.

theater, while the **Pirate Playhouse** is the island's professional theater, staging major productions and attracting big name stars to this intimate venue where no seats are more than 15 ft (five meters) from the stage.

The **J.N. "Ding" Darling National Wildlife Refuge** is one of Florida's best wildlife spots and occupies 5,400 acres (2,160 hectares) on the north side of the island. It is named after Pulitzer Prize winning cartoonist Jay Norwood "Ding" Darling, the first environmentalist to hold a presidential cabinet post (in Franklin Roosevelt's administration). There are driving, walking and cycling trails and you can hire a canoe or kayak and paddle your way along the coast through the tiny offshore mangrove islands. The **Sanibel-Captiva Conservation Foundation** is another delightful nature center covering 1,100 acres (440 hectares) just south of the island's main road. The **Bailey-Matthews Shell Museum** is the only dedicated seashell museum in the United States.

Fort Myers

FORT MYERS IS THE MAIN CITY ALONG THE SOUTHWEST COAST AND IT IS PACKED WITH HISTORY, FINE OLD HOMES AND MUSEUMS.
In the mid-1800s there were many Seminole Indians (*seminole* is the Creek word for "free" or "runaway"), and

runaway slaves in the area, and in 1865 Fort Myers (formerly Fort Harvie) was reopened as a Union Fort manned by all black regiments of former slaves. Today it is known as the City of Palms because McGregor Boulevard, originally a cattle trail, which runs for 15 miles (24 km) through Fort Myers, is lined with towering royal palms, the first 200 of which were imported from Cuba by Thomas Edison. The **Thomas Edison Winter Home and Museum** is one of the city's major attractions and was the inventor's winter home for 46 years. The house on a 14-acre (six-hectare) river front estate was built in 1866. It was donated to the city by his widow Mina Miller Edison and opened to the public in 1947. His first light bulbs had such rugged elements that some of the originals are still in use today. The huge banyan tree in the garden was a gift to Edison from industrialist Harvey Firestone. The tree is the largest specimen of banyan in the United States and the aerial roots have a circumference of more than 400 ft (122 m). The **Henry Ford** home is next door. Ford and Edison were close friends and there was a gate between the two properties which is still known as the Friendship Gate. The city has many other fine historic downtown homes and a rich cultural life, while **Fort Myers Beach** on Estero Island, is one of the world's safest beaches because of its gently sloping shoreline, soft sand and warm, clear waters.

Daytona Beach

THE REPUTATION OF DAYTONA BEACH HAS BEEN BUILT ON ITS BEACHES AND RACING CARS, earning it the titles of "World Center of Racing," and "World's Most Famous Beach". It has an historic downtown district and one of the premier beaches in the world, but between 1902 and 1935 it was more famous for speed trials than sunbathing and swimming. Between those years, 13 world speed records were set on the sands by motoring aces such as Barney Oldfield, Sir Henry Seagrave and

Sir Malcolm Campbell, while Louis Chevrolet and Henry Ford used the beach to test their early racing cars. While you can still take your vehicle on the sands, you must stick to the 10-mph (16-kph) speed limit. The racing tradition continues at the **Daytona International Speedway** which presents top racing events throughout the year, including the SunBank 24-hour race in January, the Daytona 500 in February and Bike Week in March, which attracts thousands of bikers from around the world. **Daytona USA**, is a new interactive motorsports attraction allowing visitors the chance to take part in a pit stop, design their own race car, and become a television race commentator.

The very lively Daytona Beach area actually encompases seven communities along the Atlantic Coast. Daytona Beach is the largest municipality. The others are Ormond Beach, South Daytona, Daytona Beach Shores, Holly Hill, Ponce Inlet and Port Orange. There are 23 miles (37 km) of beaches, in places more than 500 ft

(150 m) wide. Cars can be driven along the hard packed sand from the Ormond Beach exit to the Ponce de León Inlet in the south for a small charge. Alongside the beach is the bustling promenade with the palm-lined **Boardwalk** amusement area near the fishing pier, sightseeing tower and a sky ride which carries visitors high over the half mile long (eight-tenths of a kilometer) **Main Street Pier**. Offshore is a Mecca for water sports activities from sailing, canoeing, surfing and jet-skiing to power boats, scuba and fishing. Daytona Beach is also noted for its museums and year round program of cultural events including world class visiting symphony orchestras at the **Peabody Auditorium**, the **Daytona Playhouse**, and summer season at the **Seaside Music Theater**.

OPPOSITE: All the wildlife on Sanibel Island is protected, making it one of the world's top bird-watching centers. ABOVE: Cars and pedestrians mingle on Daytona's famous beaches.

22   YOUR CHOICE

YOUR CHOICE

The Great Outdoors

FLORIDA HAS WORLD CLASS BEACHES, THEME PARKS AND ATTRACTIONS, but it also has a vast great outdoors which few visitors take time to enjoy.

In the north there are forests with cycle and walking trails, lakes and waterways for canoeing and boating, and a wealth of wildlife, including the Florida black bear and endangered Florida panther.

The center of the state from coast to coast, is farming and ranching land, with citrus groves and cattle farms and thousands of lakes. Most of these lakes are connected by navigable rivers and waterways, on which it is possible to travel hundreds of miles south to the Everglades and the Atlantic Ocean.

The Everglades, of course, dominate the southern part of the state, and while it is not advisable to penetrate too deeply without an experienced guide, there are lots of opportunities to canoe, cycle and walk by yourself among the lush vegetation and surrounded by exotic wildlife.

Florida has five national parks, the largest and the most famous of which is the **Everglades** (see TOP SPOTS), which is now well on the way to recovering from the extensive damage caused by Hurricane Andrew in 1992. It is a naturalists, walkers and canoeists paradise, and even if you do not get out of your car, you can see the most exotic wildlife at close hand. The various visitors centers and ranger stations have free brochures about nature walks and what to see along the way, and you should experience at least one of the trails, most are on boardwalks so you do not get your feet wet.

The other national parks are the **Canaveral National Seashore and Merritt Island**, which runs along the coast by the Kennedy Space Center, and is an internationally important wader and wildfowl habitat; the **De Soto National Memorial**, on Tampa Bay, which commemorates De Soto's landing in Florida in May 1539; the mostly

OPPOSITE: A boardwalk allows visitors to safely explore the Everglades Cypress Swamp Reserve. ABOVE: The shy green heron can be found in marshes throughout the state.

underwater **Biscayne National Park** in Miami Bay; and the **Gulf Islands National Seashore**, a chain of sandy barrier islands running from Pensacola east towards Panama City.

There are more than 100 state parks and recreation areas, as well as ornamental gardens. Most offer campsites, picnicking facilities, swimming, fishing, hiking trails, nature walks and boat ramps. Many also have distinctive features — you may be able to watch manatees at close quarters, take a guided tour through caverns, or snorkel among colorful coral and tropical fish.

A state park is defined as "an area of regional or statewide significance established to preserve the natural setting, while permitting a full program of compatible recreational activities".

A major advantage of Florida's great outdoors is that it is so flat. Trails may be a little uneven in places but they are rarely steep, so they are accessible to almost everyone. In areas where the ground is marshy, boardwalks allow easy and dry access. Many trails are also wheelchair accessible. The main disadvantages are that Florida is semitropical so insects abound, and it is usually very hot and humid. If you are planning to go hiking or cycling in one of the state parks, use an insect repellent, wear a hat and carry drinking water.

The other problem is deciding just where to go because the choice is so great. Even if you are vacationing in central Florida be adventurous and travel around as you can almost always find a motel or hotel room if you need to stay overnight.

Places worth visiting, by area:

NORTHWEST

Florida Caverns, three miles (five kilometers) north of Marianna on State Road 167, has a network of caverns with eerie limestone formations and offers guided one-hour tours from the interpretive center. There is a campground, as well as nature and hiking trails, swimming, fishing and boating.

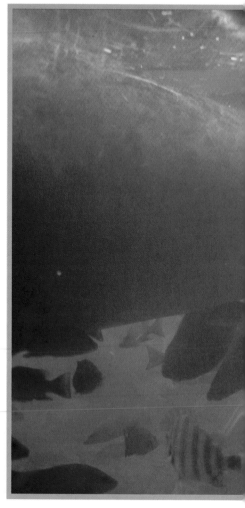

Manatee Springs, six miles (10 km) west of Chiefland on State Road 320, has hiking trails and canoe rentals, and manatees do make occasional appearances near the mouth of the springs where 117 million gallons (443 million liters) of crystal clear water flow daily.

St. George Island in the mouth of the Apalachicola River, is reached by a toll bridge off US 98, 10 miles (16 km) southeast of East Point. It offers some of the most pristine beaches and shoreline in the state with good shelling and birdwatching along nature trails and observation platforms. The oyster industry is based here.

St. Joseph Peninsula, near Port St. Joe off State Road 30, is noted for its white sand beaches and huge barrier dunes. It is also a major birdwatching area with 210 species recorded in a small area. It is one of the best observation points in the autumn in the eastern United States to spot migrating hawks.

Torreya, between Bristol and Greensboro, is mountainous by Florida's standards, with canyons and steep bluffs, some rising 150 ft (46 m) above the Apalachicola River. In the autumn, the surrounding hardwood forests provide one of the best foliage displays in the state. There are nature and hiking trails, guided tours and campfire programs.

YOUR CHOICE

Wakulla Springs, on State Road 61, is one of the world's largest and deepest freshwater springs. There are glass bottom boat tours, plus hiking and nature trails, wildlife observation boat trips, and overnight accommodation in a 27-room Spanish-style lodge, built in 1937, and featuring marble floors, ornate ceilings and antique furnishings.

NORTHEAST
Ichetuckee Springs, four miles (six kilometers) north of Fort White, is a good place for nature watching, hiking and snorkeling. There are nine springs

Gentle manatees graze in the warm waters of Homosassa Springs.

and the average flow of water is about 233 million gallons (845 million liters) a day at a constant temperature of 23°C (73°F).

Little Talbot Island, on State Road A1A, 17 miles (27 km) northeast of Jacksonville, is an area of sand dunes, pristine beaches and important as a nesting site for sea turtles. There are guided walks.

O'Leno, 20 miles (36 km) south of Lake City on US 441, is a popular camping area, offering hiking, canoeing, horse back riding, guided walks and nature trails. One of its main attractions is the river sink, where a stretch of the Sante Fe River disappears underground for more than three miles (five kilometers) before re-emerging. It is a good place for alligator and turtle spotting.

The Suwanee River, 13 miles (21 km) west of Live Oak on US 90, is the state river and subject of the state anthem, although most people mistakenly refer to it is the Swanee. The state park has nature and hiking trails, and is the site of the former town of Columbus. Parts of the old stage road which ran from Pensacola to Jacksonville in the early 1800s, can still be walked.

CENTRAL EAST
Blue Spring is off French Avenue in Orange City, and a winter gathering ground for manatees seeking shelter from the colder waters of the nearby St. Johns River. The mammals can be clearly seen from a number of observation platforms over the water, and you can even swim with them in the spring. There are nature and hiking trails, canoe rentals, boat tours of the St. Johns River, camping areas and vacation cabins.

Bulow Creek, just north of Ormond Beach, on Old Dixie Highway, is famous for the Fairchild Oak, believed to be more than 800 years old. This is a 5,000-acre (2,000-hectare) area of coastal hardwood forest, *hammocks* — raised, tree-clad mounds in the swamps which serve as observation points and campsites — and salt marsh, with hiking and nature trails.

Hontoon Island, six miles (10 km) west of DeLand, can only be reached by private boat or public free ferry which runs from 9 AM to one hour before sundown although you can stay overnight in the campground or one of the basic cabins. The island is interesting because it was an Indian settlement for many centuries and there is a replica of a large owl totem carved more than 600 years ago and Indian mounds.

Tomoka, three miles (five kilometers) north of Ormond Beach on North Beach Street, is another ancient Indian settlement, with guided tours, nature and hiking trails and canoe rentals. In the late 1700s, the land was granted to Richard Oswald, a wealthy English merchant and statesman, who helped negotiate the accession treaty with England after the American Revolution.

CENTRAL
Highlands Hammock, six miles (10 km) west of Sebring on State Road 634, is one of Florida's four original parks and was created when local residents became

alarmed at plans to clear the hardwood forests for farmland. There are walking, cycling and horse riding trails, an interpretive center, guided tours, picnic areas and campsites.

Lake Kissimmee, 15 miles (24 km) east of Lake Wales on Camp Mack Road, and a long way from Kissimmee City, offers a taste of Florida past and present. Observation platforms, hiking, nature and canoe trails allow you to see how the area's environment and wildlife are being managed today, while you can see what life used to be like in a recreated 1876 cow camp.

CENTRAL WEST

Caladesi Island is reached by ferry from Honeymoon Island off the Dunedin Causeway, and is one of the few undisturbed barrier islands in the state. It has nature and hiking trails and offers swimming, fishing and more than two miles (three kilometers) of white sand Gulfside beaches.

Egmont Key, southwest of Fort DeSoto Beach, can only be reached by boat. The island has the only manned lighthouse remaining in the United States. It was used as a camp for captured Indians during the Third Seminole War, and was Union navy base in the Civil War. Now it is a wildlife refuge.

Homosassa Springs, on Fish Bowl Road, in the town of the same name, combines state park, wildlife park and the Florida Nature Museum, which has a collection of artifacts and fossils found in the region. The 55-feet (17-m)-deep springs are the headwaters of the Homosassa River, and you can descend into the underwater observatory to view the fish, manatees and other wildlife. The springs are important because they are home to both freshwater and saltwater species of fish. There are nature trails and guided boat tours.

SOUTHWEST

Cayo Costa, south of Placida and

OPPOSITE: Spanish moss festoons these Kissimmee trees but does no harm. BELOW: Wildflowers can be found in profusion along most of Florida's beaches.

offshore from Boca Grande, is one of the largest undeveloped barrier islands along the coast and only accessible by boat. It is noted for its wildlife and Indian relics, and there are nature and hiking trails. Both osprey and bald eagles nest on the island, frigate birds are regularly spotted and it has one of the largest brown pelican rookeries in the state. It is also a good place for shell collectors, especially during the winter months.

Collier-Seminole Park, 17 miles (27 km) south of Naples, is special as it features a tropical hardwood hammock of trees more commonly found in the West Indies and Mexico's Yucatan peninsula than in southwest Florida. It also has an extensive mangrove swamp. There are hiking and nature trails, observation platforms, fishing, swimming and camping.

Myakka River Park, 14 miles (22 km), covers 28, 875 acres (11,550 hectares) and has an extensive network of hiking, nature and horse riding trails, with interpretive center, campsites, cabins, fishing, guided tours, boat trips along Upper Myakka Lake and canoe rentals. It is noted for its scenic panoramas and rich wildlife, including deer, alligators and wading birds.

SOUTHEAST
Bahia Honda, on Bahia Honda Key at Mile-Marker 37, is a wildlife reserve containing many rare species of plants

and birds, such as the white crowned pigeon, great white heron, roseate spoonbill, reddish egret and least tern. The nearby offshore waters offer some of the best tarpon fishing in the state. There are a number of hiking and nature trails, with campground, cabins and swimming in both the Atlantic Ocean and Florida Bay.

John Pennekamp Coral Reef, around Key Largo, is the state's only underwater park and the first to be designated in the nation. On land there is an interpretive center, campsite, hiking and nature trails, but it is the water that mainly attracts the visitors. It is the only area of living coral reef in the continental United States and the park covers 178 sq miles (463 sq km) of reef, seagrass beds and mangrove swamps. You can explore by boat and canoe, snorkel or scuba. An attraction is the 10-ft (three-meter)-high bronze statue of Christ of the Deep, which stands in 20 ft (six meters) of water in the Atlantic Ocean. It is one of the state's top diving and snorkeling areas.

Sporting Spree

FLORIDA IS IN A LEAGUE OF ITS OWN WHEN IT COMES TO SPORTING OPPORTUNITIES. No other state can boast as many tennis courts, golf courses — more than 1,200 at last count — or as many pleasure boats.

Whether a spectator or a player, the great thing about Florida is that the year-round good weather means you can enjoy your favorite recreation whenever you want.

Florida offers endless opportunities for water sports of all kinds. There are more than 1,000 miles (1,600 km) of beach, more than 7,700 natural lakes of 10 acres (four hectares) or more, as well as 1,700 rivers and waterways navigable by small boats and canoes.

As soon as the sun breaks the horizon, the surfers are crouched over the boards waiting to catch the first waves of the day. Beneath the sparkling blue waters of the Florida Keys, snorkelers explore the only living coral reef in the continental United States, while a freshwater fisherman settles down beside a central Florida lake hoping to catch a record breaking largemouth bass. Daily bag limits for each species have been imposed to conserve stocks, and an honor system is in place whereby small fish are returned to the water to grow so they can be caught another day. There are 24 species of game fish in Florida's lakes and waterways, and state records include a 20-lb (nine-kilogram) largemouth bass, 38-lb (17-kg) striped bass, and 40-lb (18-kg) carp. If you are 16 or over and plan to fish, you must have a valid fishing license, issued at fishing camps, bait shops and sporting good stores.

Anglers can also try their luck at reeling in a marlin, sailfish or shark on a sportfishing excursion in the Atlantic Ocean or Gulf of Mexico. SCUBA divers can explore the more than 4,000 shipwrecks that lie off the coast. The Florida Association of Dive Operators ((904) 222-6000, 335 Beard Street, Tallahassee, FL 32303, can supply details about dive resorts and courses. Water-skiing, parasailing and jet-skiing can also be enjoyed throughout the state.

Boating is a year round activity because of the good weather. Florida has 8,426 miles (13,481 km) of tidal shoreline, 4,500 sq miles (11,707 sq km) of inland water, and 750,000 registered boats. Any boat over 16 ft (4.9 m) has to be registered with the Florida Department of Natural Resources. There are at least again as many smaller, unregistered boats in the state. Powerboats are more popular than sailboats mostly because they operate better in shallow waters and distances are so great. It is one of the reasons why Florida is one of the main venues for international power boat racing, including grand prix races. Both sail and power boats can be hired throughout the state, while more sedate house boats are available for cruising some of the larger lakes and waterways.

Canoeing is still one of the best ways to explore the state's hundreds of miles of inland waterways. The great advantage of canoeing is that it enables you to

silently explore many areas not accessible on foot, and to see the varied wildlife at close quarters. There is good canoeing throughout the state but best locations include the Blackwater and Suwannee Rivers in the northwest and the Myakka and Peace Rivers near Arcadia. Local operators provide equipment rentals and transportation for visitors. In Kissimmee, only a short distance from Disney World you can rent a canoe by the main road and within a couple of minutes be in a different world as you explore backwaters where the only sounds are the calls of the birds and the croaking frogs. Canoeing is great fun especially for families. It takes a few minutes to get the hang of paddling and it is best that a grown-up sits at the back to control the direction of the canoe; otherwise there is a tendency to go round in circles! This also allows grown-ups to keep their eyes on the children in front.

If planning a canoe trip remember to keep your bearings at all times as it is possible to get disoriented, especially

OPPOSITE: A pelican waits for a catch on New Cedar Key. ABOVE: Boating is the best way to explore the Everglades and its rich wildlife.

when paddling among mangrove islands. Wear a hat and sunscreen, liberally apply insect repellent and always carry water or another drink because it is easy to dehydrate when exercising in the heat. For more information contact the Florida Association of Canoe Liveries and Outfitters ((813) 494-1215, PO Box 1764, Arcadia, FL 33821.

Florida is world famous for its golf courses, both public and private, which attract avid golfers from around the globe. There are resort courses where you can take a holiday villa or an apartment alongside the fairway and play all day long. There are golf passes which allow you to play at a number of courses in the area you are staying, and at fees well below those you would normally pay. The Florida Sports Foundation ((904) 488-8347, 107 West Gaines Street, Tallahassee FL 32399, can provide more details about the wealth of golfing opportunities in the state.

Tennis is another of Florida's most popular sports with thousands of tennis centers and tens of thousands of courts, with clay, grass and hardcourt surfaces — many of them floodlit. There are tennis hotels and training schools where you can take lessons from the pros and scores of professional and major amateur tournaments. If newly arrived in Florida on holiday, book your court for early in the morning or late in the afternoon when the sun is not so intense.

There are also lots of opportunities to watch a wide range of sports, and for non-Americans, the chance to learn something of the national sports of baseball, basketball and American football. Twenty of the nation's 28 top baseball teams have spring training camps in Florida where you can watch some of the nation's best players in action.

The Sunshine State has a home team in every major spectator spot with National Football League teams in Miami, Jacksonville and Tampa playing from September to December; National Basketball Association teams the Miami Heat and Orlando Magic, whose season runs from October to April; two National

Hockey League teams in Orlando and Tampa; and the Fort Lauderdale-based Florida Marlins, the state's first national franchise baseball team.

If you get the chance you should try to attend at least one of these fun-packed games. A basketball game may consist of only four 12-minute quarters, but the match with time outs and stoppages can last three hours or more, and with the pre-game show and snacking you can add another hour. Any of these games makes a great family occasion with every second, both on the court and off, packed with things to keep you entertained.

Daytona Beach is home to the world famous Daytona 500 motor race where racing fans can also enjoy the Sebring 12-hour endurance race, and the Gainesville annual Gatornationals, the largest drag racing event on the Atlantic seaboard.

Polo is played from mid-November to the end of March at the Palm Beach Polo and Country Club, where Prince Charles is a regular guest, as well as at the Royal

ABOVE: The Sunshine State boasts more golf courses than any other region on earth. RIGHT: Roadside vegetable stand in central Florida.

Palm Polo Club in Boca Raton and the Windsor Polo Club in Vero Beach.

There is greyhound, horse and harness racing and the fast and furious game of jai alai, reputed to be the world's fastest ball game. The sport was introduced to Florida by Cuban immigrants and the ball reaches speeds of 175 mph (110 kph).

There are also college and amateur sporting events to be enjoyed throughout the state and year round. Regional convention and visitors centers can provide a wealth of information about sporting and recreational activities.

The Open Road

NOW THAT FLORIDA HAS RAISED THE SPEED LIMIT ON MOST OF ITS MAJOR HIGHWAYS to 65 mph (105 kph) or 70 mph (113 kph), especially in rural areas, it is now possible to get from one place to another a little quicker, but there is little point in rushing when there is so much to see and do along the way. And, if you want a glimpse of the real Florida it is better to avoid the interstate highways and turnpikes and stick to the country roads.

Florida has a number of scenic drives, the most spectacular of which, in my opinion, is along **State Road A1A** which runs beside the Atlantic Coast north from Daytona Beach for 105 miles (169 km) until the turn off for Fernandina Beach on Amelia Island, Florida's first resort and long before that a notorious haven for pirates and smugglers. For mile after mile you have huge stretches of near deserted sandy beach, and you can stop wherever you want to enjoy the views, laze in the sun or take a swim.

Almost as spectacular but generally much busier, is the drive from the Florida mainland to Key West. The **Overseas Highway** or US 1 is the only route through the Keys, and follows the path of the Overseas Railroad completed at huge cost in 1912 and destroyed by a hurricane in 1935. It crosses 43 bridges on its 113 mile (182 km) island leap-frogging route to Key West. Although it is an interstate, for most of its way through the Keys it is only a two-lane highway, but it offers wonderful scenery, passing emerald-green lagoons, turquoise seas, gently waving palms and olive-green

mangroves. You may see dolphins offshore as well as herons, pelicans, spoonbills and ospreys. Mile-Markers (MM) are positioned every mile along the Overseas Highway so that you always know where you are. They indicate the distance between Florida City on the mainland and Key West, and everyone uses them to give directions. If you stop to ask where your hotel is, you will be told it is just before MM 26, and all the brochures and guides use mile-markers as locator points. As you leave Florida City the marker bears the number 126, and when you get to the end of the road at the corner of Fleming and Whitehead Streets on Key West, the marker has the number 0. You are at the southernmost point in the continental United States. The journey between Miami and Key West can be traveled in less than four hours, but the whole idea of visiting the Keys is to slow down, so what's the hurry? Apart from the high season when most accommodation is fully booked, you can usually find a motel and hotel room along the way. If you are staying in central Florida and want to explore, this makes a good two- or three-day trip with the bonus of getting to visit Key West.

Another spectacular drive is the **Sunshine Skyway**, a roller-coaster of a journey from St. Petersburg. The road runs southeast from the city crossing Tampa Bay and rejoining the mainland north of Bradenton. The route consists of mile after mile of causeway joined by soaring bridges which rise to 175 ft (53 m) above the water — high enough to let the largest ocean going craft pass beneath. The longest bridge is modeled on the Brotonne Bridge which spans the Seine in France, although it is a little longer — running for almost 15 miles (24 km). There are places to stop along the way for sightseeing, fishing and even swimming, and the toll of $1 is well worth it. If staying in central Florida the Sunshine Skyway can easily be included as part of a long day trip to the Gulf.

Other scenic drives include: **Bayshore Boulevard,** in Tampa, which offers scenic views of Hillsborough Bay and some of the area's most exclusive homes. The drive allows you to take in Davis Island, one of Tampa's most beautiful neighborhoods, and built on three man-made islands constructed in the 1920s.

Indian River Scenic Drive, in Fort Pierce, follows the river's west shore towards Jensen Beach past native trees, exotic flowers and a rich birdlife. The farming community grew on the site of a United States Army post built in 1838 during the Indian Wars. The St. Lucie County Historical Museum on Seaway Drive, highlights the history of the area focusing on the Seminole Indians and the first Spanish colonists. Take time during the drive to stop and cross the footbridge over to Jack Island, a bird and wildlife refuge where you can enjoy a swim and a picnic.

There are a number of scenic drives in the Miami and Miami Beach area, the best of which are the **Main and Ingraham Highways** and **Old Cutler Road**, the section which runs south from Coconut Grove and takes in exclusive Coral Gables. Old Cutler Highway passes Matheson Hammock Park and the Fairchild Tropical Gardens. **South Miami Avenue** between 15th Road and

Dixie Highway, is lined with royal poinciana trees, which are a blaze of red flowers during late May and June. The tree is known locally as the tourist tree — because the flowers arrive in the summer and immediately turn bright red!

Another interesting drive in Miami Beach is along **Collins Avenue**, with its huge hotels and nearby luxurious island homes, which range in style from Spanish Colonial to ultra-modern. While the houses are not open to the public you can drive round and view them from the road.

The **Tamiami Trail** (US 41) skirts the northern borders of the Everglades National Park. A memorable drive is to take **State Road 9336** which runs to the park's main entrance and then south to Flamingo. Locals tend to speed along the road but just slow down and let them pass. If you rush you will miss so much. As you drive through this area, you will also see signs alerting you to watch out for the rare Florida panther which may suddenly appear on the

road. Apart from the drive itself through the heart of the Everglades, there are a number of walking trails along the road that can be explored, and in Flamingo there are restaurants and all variety of wildlife, fishing and sightseeing boat tours.

In the Panhandle, **US 98** offers a scenic drive along the Gulf of Mexico for almost 100 miles (160 km) from Panama City to Gulf Breeze, just south of Pensacola. The road follows the coast, or is never far from it, and there are lots of opportunities to find your own near-deserted stretch of beach or explore among the huge dunes. This coastline has some of the highest and most extensive dunes in the southeast, which the onshore winds are constantly changing and re-sculpting. If the winds have been strong, sand does get blown across the road and can be quite deep in places, so always drive carefully.

OPPOSITE: A custom car in Clearwater. BELOW: The Sunshine Skyway Bridge is a roller-coaster of a ride.

Backpacking

THERE ARE ABOUT 1,744 MILES (2,800 KM) OF HIKING TRAILS IN FLORIDA, about 120,000 conveniently placed picnic tables along the way, and more than 120,000 campsites in official campgrounds, so backpackers have a lot of options. Florida is still a relatively new state and most settlement has taken place in the last 100 years, so there is still a strong pioneering spirit with hunting, fishing and camping very popular.

The Florida Trail Association is actively promoting new trails and connecting existing ones to the statewide network. They can be contacted at PO Box 13708, Gainesville, FL 32604, ℂ (904) 378-8823.

The best backpacking trails are in the national and state parks and forests, where maps showing trails and campgrounds are available from the ranger stations. Most drive-in campgrounds offer a high degree of comfort with toilets, washrooms, laundry, picnic tables and benches and barbecue grills. There are usually electric and water hook ups for motor caravans, known as recreational vehicles (RVs) in the United States. Many of the larger parks also have wilderness campsites, which are more remote and have few or no facilities. These are true backpacking campsites where you have to carry in

everything you need, including water, and carry out all evidence of your stay. Primitive camping is usually free, although some parks levy a small charge, but the number of sites is restricted both on environmental grounds and so that you actually feel you are alone in the wilderness and not surrounded by scores of other campers. If heading for a primitive campsite, let the visitors center or ranger station know where you are going and how long you plan to be away, and report back on your return so they can cross you off their list and not institute a search party.

The state's longest trail is the 1,300-mile (2,094-km)-long Florida National Scenic Trail. It runs the length of the state, and connects with many other trails along the way.

You can get a good flavor of what this long distance trail is like in the **Ocala National Forest** which covers 430,000 acres (172,000 hectares). The forest is crisscrossed by hiking, cycling and canoe trails, while the Ocala Trail runs the length of the forest. The 65-mile (105-km)-long Ocala Trail is part of the Scenic Trail and you should plan to spend at least four days to walk it comfortably, and you should add an extra day if you have the time. The paths are good and well signposted, but there are plenty of distractions along the way, and a gentle pace is advisable because of the heat and humidity. The forest's wildlife includes alligator, black bear, armadillo, raccoon, skunk, porcupine, wild pig and the rare Florida panther. There are lots of opportunities to take a swim in the many lakes, or you can hire a canoe for a few hours from one of the many concessions.

As with all the parks, there are always other trails to explore. In the Ocala National Forest at Alexander Springs, for instance, you can detour on to the Timucuan Indian Trail, a self-guided interpretive walk explaining the plants used by the early Indians for culinary and medicinal purposes.

Another good day's walk is in the **Lower Wekiva River State Reserve**, the entrance of which is on State Road 46, off I-4 east of Orlando. There is a 10-mile (16-km) walk through the reserve to Rock Springs Run and then along the St. Johns River. The spring run is formed

OPPOSITE: A wood stork, one of the rare visitors to Florida. ABOVE: The Everglades Swamps are threatened by man's encroachment.

by several artesian wells and wilderness camping is allowed. Along the way you may see black bear, white-tailed deer, river otter, alligator and snakes — the most common of which is the long, black and non-poisonous indigo snake. Because of the fresh water, this area was settled by the Indians long before the Spanish arrived, and some mounds remain. (Although Indian artifacts are still found, it is an offense to touch or remove them.) From St. Johns River, you can then follow another trail which leads into the Wekiva Springs State Park where there is are family camping grounds.

The **Tosohatchee Trail** runs through the Tosohatchee State Reserve. Take State Road 50 east through Christmas and then Taylor Creek Road to the reserve entrance. The trail, through stands of slash pine — some of which are more than 250 years old — follows old logging roads in places. There are three wilderness campsites at the end of a three-mile (five-kilometer), 10-mile (16-km) or 25-mile (40-km) hike in. You must telephone the ranger station in advance to reserve a campsite ℭ (407) 568-5893.

Some of the best hiking on the west coast is in the **Withlacoochee State Forest**, where the Florida Trail Association has marked out and maintains a 30-mile (48-km) trail in the Croom area. Florida's state forests are often not as well signposted as either state parks or national forests but they are worth seeking out because they all have well maintained trails, are rich in wildlife, and are usually far less busy. The Croom Wildlife Management Area runs for about 16 miles (26 km) along the Withlacoochee, the Indian word for "long and winding river", and is reached on State Road 50 and Rital Croom Road, which runs just east of I-75. The trail starts at the Tucker Hill Tower just off Croom Road, where you can pick up a free trail map. The route is divided into three loops for those who do not want to overnight, but there is a campsite for those who do.

Living It Up

WHILE MOST PEOPLE GO TO FLORIDA FOR THE HOT WEATHER, THERE IS MORE THAN ENOUGH TO KEEP THEM BUSY ONCE THE SUN HAS GONE DOWN. The major resort hotels offer their own restaurants, night clubs and floor shows, and there is never a shortage of choice if you want to go out.

There are concerts, ballet and opera for classical music lovers, and bluegrass, jazz, reggae, rock and roll and country and western music clubs for the rest. There are comedy clubs, discos and dancing to live music. There are dinner shows featuring Arabian horsemen, Wild West shoot-outs or medieval jousting and minstrels, and if you feel hungry at the end of the evening, there are always some restaurants and cafés that never close. Tourist offices can give you the latest information about new attractions, and there is a mass of free information available throughout the state. Look for

OPPOSITE: The warm waters of Sanibel Island teem with an amazing array of fish. ABOVE: An immature eagle is displayed in the Everglades National Park.

free magazines such as *Enjoy Florida* and *The Best Read Guide* which not only list all the attractions and current prices and times, but are packed with discount vouchers. Don't ignore these give-away magazines; over the course of a two-week holiday, they can save a family hundreds of dollars off the price of restaurant bills and attraction tickets.

Central Florida offers a wide choice in evening entertainment with venues such as Pleasure Island and Church Street Station.

Pleasure Island is part of Walt Disney World, and features themed nightclubs in a six-acre (two and a-half-hectare) entertainment, shopping and dining complex. There is the Adventurer's Club, decorated with outrageous artifacts reminiscent of the 1930s, while 8TRAX offers Seventies music. There is also the Comedy Warehouse, Mannequins Dance Palace featuring contemporary music, the Neon Armadillo Music Saloon featuring country music, and the Rock and Roll Beach Club.

Church Street Station is one of the most popular night spots in downtown Orlando and caters for all tastes with dozens of bars, restaurants and specialty shops. Rosie O'Grady's features Dixieland jazz; you can rock and roll in the Orchid Garden, enjoy country and western in the Cheyenne Saloon, and disco to the early hours in Phineas Phogg's Dance Club.

Generally, the finest dining in central Florida is in the major resort hotels, especially within Walt Disney World. Non-guests are welcome to dine in these restaurants but reservations are essential.

Among the best gourmet restaurants in central Florida are **Arthur's 27** ((407) 827-3450, on the top floor of the Buena Vista Palace; **Chatham's Palace** ((407) 345-2992, on Dr. Phillips Boulevard, Orlando; **Gran Cru** ((407) 859-1500, in the Sheraton Plaza, Florida Mall; **Hemingways** ((407) 239-1234, at the Hyatt Regency Grand Cypress Resort; **Hemisphere** ((405) 825-1234, at the Hyatt Regency Orlando International Airport; **Manuel's** ((407) 246-6580, on the 28th floor of the Barnett Bank building on North Orange Avenue, Orlando; and the excellent **Victoria and Albert's** ((407) 824-3000, at the Grand Floridian Beach Resort, Walt Disney World.

In the Greater Miami area, there are even more hotels and an even greater choice of restaurants and night spots. When the sun goes down in Miami, the stars really do come out — along with world famous models, musicians and other celebrities who live nearby. Star spotting is a sport in Miami whether in a dance club, jazz café or more exclusive night spot. The South Beach's club scene rivals that of New York and Los Angeles; Coconut Grove and Coral Gables offer some of the area's finest, and most expensive restaurants, while downtown Miami has a vast range of regional and inter-national cuisines to tempt you. For the finest dining, try **Victor's Café** ((305) 445-1313, 2340 Southwest 32nd Avenue, Miami; **Café Sci Sci** ((305) 446-5104, 3043 Grand Avenue, Coconut Grove; **Monty's Seafood Restaurant** ((305) 858-1431, 2550 South Bayshore Drive, Coconut Grove; and **Casa Juanaho** ((305) 642-2452, at 2436 Southwest 8th Street, Miami, for Cuban cuisine.

ABOVE: This South Walton course is just one of the reasons Florida is the golfing capital of the world. OPPOSITE: Fountains, palms and tropical flowers decorate this Turnberry Isle property.

For culture buffs there is the Ballet Flamenco La Rosa and Florida Classical Ballet, as well as a number of contemporary dance troupes. There is a wide choice of theater and music, including the Florida Grand Opera.

St. Petersburg-Clearwater also offers a wide range of evening diversions from dinner theaters to vast entertainment complexes. The Coliseum Ballroom, on 4th Avenue, St. Petersburg, is one of the largest in North America and features a variety of live entertainment, as does the Tierra Verde Resort Ballroom, on Madonna Boulevard, Tierra Verde. Most of the liveliest nightspots are in the large beach hotels and resort complexes, but exceptions are Cha Cha Coconuts at The Pier, and Woody's Waterfront in St. Petersburg. The Crow's Nest Supper Club at the St. Petersburg Beach Holiday Inn offers dinner with a Las Vegas-style review, while there is nightly entertainment in the Grog Shoppe, an English-style pub at the Bilmar Beach Resort. There are many fine restaurants and the best specialize in seafood, such as Kingfish on Kingfish Drive, Treasure Island, and Shells, at 17855 Gulf Boulevard in Redington Shores. Jesse's Landing, overlooking Lake Seminole at 10400 Park Boulevard North, offers elegant dining.

Family Fun

FLORIDA IS THE IDEAL DESTINATION FOR CHILDREN OF ALL AGES WITH ITS SAFE, SANDY BEACHES AND WARM SHALLOW WATERS; spacious affordable accommodation and cheap eating places; and enough attractions to keep even the most active child amused for weeks on end.

Most people head for the theme parks of central Florida which can easily swallow up every minute of a two-week holiday, but there are lots of other things to keep families amused, and many of them are free.

There are, of course, the **beaches**. The Gulf Coast generally offers the safest paddling for young children; the surf and riptides can sometimes be a problem on the Atlantic coastline. Most of the popular beaches are patrolled by lifeguards but you should always keep an eye on your children while they are in or near the water.

It is great to spend time lying around in the sun and swimming; however, be especially careful if you have young children. Until they become acclimatized to the sun, keep them covered. They should wear a hat and T-shirt with their swimsuit, and sunscreen with a protection factor of at least 20 is recommended.

Florida's beaches, especially on Sanibel and Captiva Island, offer another great free attraction. They are among the best places in the world to find seashells. There are hundreds of different varieties to be collected and many of the larger shells make attractive souvenirs. The best time to collect is just after high tide, especially if there has been a strong onshore breeze.

Take time as a family to discover the real Florida away from the attractions and theme parks. Spend a day walking and picnicking in one of the many state parks and see how many new plants, animals and birds you can spot.

Canoeing is another fun and affordable family pastime, and great for younger children. Canoe rentals are available throughout the state, and you can take a canoe out for an hour or two or the whole day provided you take a picnic and drinks with you. The advantage of canoes is that they are silent and as you drift up backwaters, you will see a wide range of wildlife that would normally be frightened away. Again, with canoeing, it is important to wear a hat, sunscreen and insect repellent, and to have drinks to replace the fluids lost through the (even modest) exertion of paddling. It is also vital that young children and non-swimmers wear the life vests that are provided.

Children and parents get a close-up look at Florida's marine life at this Key West aquarium.

If you don't want the effort of canoeing, take the family on one of the hundreds of boat trips available around the state. There is a huge selection from wildlife trips in glass bottom boats up the quiet St. Johns river or through the Everglades, to game fishing trips into the Gulf. For a little more action, hire an air boat, the sort of craft made famous in James Bond's Everglades chases, which zoom across the water. It does take a little while to get the hang of steering.

Cycling can be fun but not on the highways if you have children. Escape to the car-free trails of the state and national parks where you can hire bikes and pedal in safety. There are already 2,000 miles (3,600 km) of bicycle trails in

Florida, and the state has embarked on an ambitious program of developing new trails, many following the old railroad tracks.

A great number of Florida's cultural and scientific attractions are specially geared for children. There is Orlando's new **Science Museum**, a hands-on, interactive learning and fun experience. There is **Frannie's Teddy Bear Museum** in Naples, the **Miami Youth Museum**, **Museum of Discovery and Science** in Fort Lauderdale, Orlando **Toy Train Museum**, and the **Young at Art Children's Museum** in Fort Lauderdale.

In Kissimmee you can pet young farm animals at **Green Meadows Children's Farm**, swim with dolphins at a number of marine attractions, watch lions from the safety of your car at West Palm Beach's **Lion Country Safari**, and go horse riding along the beach or through the forest.

Cultural Kicks

WITH THE EXCEPTION OF ST. AUGUSTINE, WHEN YOU TALK ABOUT HISTORIC BUILDINGS IN FLORIDA you are talking about structures generally dating back 100 or 150 years. It is perhaps one reason why the state protects so fiercely what culture and heritage it has both in its museums and its historic sites.

There are world class museums in Miami, St. Petersburg, and Orlando, which now has a new hands-on **Interactive Science Museum**. Of particular importance are the **Boca Raton Museum of Art**, the **Lowe Art Museum** in Coral Gables, Daytona Beach's **Museum of Arts and Science**, Fort Lauderdale's **Museum of Art**, the **Cummer Gallery of Art** in Jacksonville, Miami's **Center for the Fine Arts** and **Museum of Art**, the **Henry Morrison Flagler Museum** at Palm Beach, the St. Petersburg **Museum of Fine Arts** and **Salvador Dali Museum**, **John and Mable Ringling Museum of Art** in Sarasota, Tampa's **Museum of African American Art**, and Winter Park's **Cornell Fine Arts Center**.

There are also a few slightly more offbeat museums, such as the **John Gorrie Museum**, in Apalachicola. Gorie was the inventor of the first artificial ice machine in 1851, an invention that eventually led to air-conditioning and refrigeration, two essentials without which life in Florida might not be bearable. The **Forest Capital**, just south of Perry, is a museum dedicated to the state's forestry industry, which after tourism, remains one of Florida's biggest earners. In the grounds you can explore a Cracker homestead, the traditional log cabin built by the first settlers. The first Floridians were known as "crackers" because of the sound their whips made as they drove their ox-driven carts. In Port St. Joe off US 98, you can also visit the **Constitution Convention** where the details of the state's constitution were hammered out. St. Joseph was one of Florida's most prosperous towns until hit by a yellow fever outbreak in 1841 which killed or drove away all the residents. The new town of Port St. Joe dates from 1900.

Florida has many historic and archaeological sites, some of which are living museums with costumed guides re-enacting life in bygone times. The most interesting of these include:

Fort Clinch, at Fernandina Beach, was built in the mid-1800s and was captured by stealth by the Confederates in 1861 during the Civil War. A year later it was retaken by Union troops. Today, the life of the Union soldier in 1864 is recreated with role-playing soldiers at Fort Clinch State Park.

Natural Bridge Battlefield State Historic Site, six miles (10 km) east of Woodville, recreates the battle between Union and Confederate forces which took place on March 6, 1865. Union troops had landed south of Tallahassee with the task of disrupting Confederate war supplies and taking the capital.

OPPOSITE: At Kissimmee's Gatorland TOP, a giant reptile has a leisurely meal; and alligators BOTTOM get acquainted with visitors to Miccuosukee Indian Village. ABOVE: A blacksmith re-creates daily life in Spanish colonial St. Augustine.

After 12 hours of fighting, the Union troops were forced to withdraw and Tallahassee was the only uncaptured Confederate state capital east of the Mississippi River. The battle is re-staged on the Sunday nearest March 6.

Kissimmee Cow Camp, at Lake Kissimmee State Park, has something for all ages. It is a recreated 1876 cattle camp, typical of those set up along the route of the annual Florida cattle drive. The scrub cows which can be seen today are directly descended from the Spanish Andalusian cattle. Each spring the cattle would be rounded up and driven to Punta Rassa near Fort Myers where they were shipped to Cuba. The roleplaying cowboys show what life was like on a cattle drive more than a century ago.

Fort Foster, at Hillsborough River State Park, six miles (10 km) southwest of Zephyrhills, also has costume-clad, role-playing, musket-carrying rangers re-enacting the lives of soldiers during the 1830s Indian Wars.

Interesting archaeological sites include **Lake Jackson Mounds**, just north of Tallahassee, which contains Indian mounds dating back to 1200 AD, and the **Fort George State Cultural Site**, 16 miles (26 km) east of Jacksonville on State Road A1A, an island that has been occupied continuously by man for more than 5,000 years. Traces of each occupation period have been found. Also at this site, Mount Carnelia at 65 ft (20 m) is the highest point along the Atlantic Coast south of Sandy Hook, New Jersey. The **Crystal River** complex, off US 19-98, also has traces of Indian settlement dating back to 200 BC, including burial mounds, temple and hundreds of graves.

There are also a number of state run ornamental gardens such as **Ravine**, at Palatka. The gardens of azaleas and camellias are planted inside a ravine which creates its own micro-climate along the west bank of the St. Johns River. The flowers are in full bloom in March and April. **Washington Oaks,** two miles (three kilometers) south of Marineland on the A1A, are formal

gardens planted with exotic species, including azalea, camellia and many species of roses. About 100 species of camellia and 50 species of azalea, together with some 160 species of other exotics, can be seen at the **Alfred B. Maclay Gardens** in Tallahassee, where there are guided tours, nature and hiking trails and canoe rentals.

Shop Till You Drop

WHEN YOU PACK TO GO TO FLORIDA IT IS A GOOD IDEA TO INCLUDE AN EMPTY CARRY-ALL TO BRING BACK VACATION PURCHASES. Because of low taxes, intense competition and millions of free-spending consumers, Florida offers some of the best shopping opportunities in the country. Antique shops, department stores, discount malls, boutiques and flea markets abound. Flea markets come in all shapes and sizes. Most have hundreds of stalls — usually indoors — offering everything from surplus army gear to high fashion and antiques to the latest CD systems. Some stores even offer their own theme park-like thrills. The Fort Lauderdale Swap Shop, for example, features fairground rides and daily circus performances, while Old Town, Kissimmee, offers rides on an antique carousel and Ferris wheel.

While there are few true Florida specialties other than local arts and crafts and bags of citrus fruit that can be mailed worldwide, there are real bargains to be had, especially for European visitors, because there is no VAT and everything from clothing to cameras, and luggage to lingerie is much cheaper than at home.

My advice here is the same as my advice on eating out: look for what the natives do best, for what you can't get elsewhere. This means, if you are like me, you will come back with a whole suitcase stuffed with cigars and an innocent smile on your face as you pass through customs. Florida, especially Tampa, is God's gift to budget-conscious cigar-lovers.

It is also God's gift to kitsch-lovers: if you like deliciously vulgar, outrageously colorful, unbelievably silly, totally useless things, you have come to the right place. Remember, only a relative handful of the pink flamingos in Florida exist outside the souvenir shops.

Of the items that you might want to bring back as gifts, the lightest and most beautiful are the seashells you can buy almost anywhere, but especially along the southwest coast. The heaviest and tastiest are the sacks and/or crates of Florida citrus, which any store will be happy to ship back home for you. Florida is also the place to buy any leisure wear that you might need for the beach, as well as any accessories such as suntan oil or beach towels, because the competition to provide these things in a beach-fringed state is so intense that the prices are correspondingly low.

When it comes to things that are typically Floridian, aesthetically appealing, and attractively priced, your best bet is the range of handicrafts still produced by the Seminole Indians. These include colorful hand-sewn garments and wall hangings, leather goods, and turquoise jewelry.

The best bargains, however, if you are coming from outside the United States, are indisputably to be found in the mouth-watering array of electronic gadgetry (well, it makes *my* mouth water). Everything you could possibly need — as well as everything you *couldn't* possibly need — for the home or office, is available here, usually at a fraction of the prices these things sell for overseas. But do remember that American electrical items run on 110 volts; if your home voltage is 220 volts, you will need an adapter, or you will need to run the appliance of batteries.

Another thing that might cause problems is Florida's sales tax which varies from county to county, but generally hovers around six percent. This tax does not appear on the price tag but is automatically added by the cash register which can cause misunderstandings.

Finally, and unfashionably, I would like to put in a good word for the American shopping mall. If you want

Genuine cowboy boots LEFT make good souvenirs, while sponges RIGHT in Tarpon Springs can be bought for a fraction of the price elsewhere.

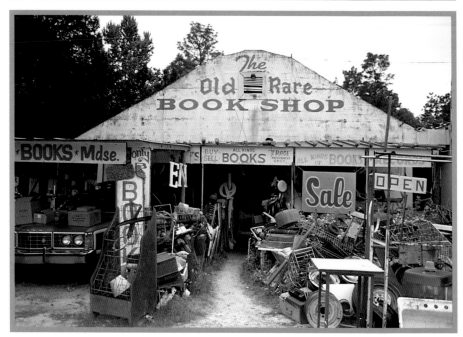

quality and value for money and convenience, plus a good return on your investment of time and effort, I would direct you to any of the thousands of shopping malls scattered around Florida. They are all — or almost all — open until 9 PM, seven days a week, and all are worth a visit, regardless of what you are looking for. The following outlets offer some of the best shopping opportunities around the state.

NORTHWEST

ANTIQUE DEALERS AND SHOPS

The Antique Cottage ((904) 769-9503, 903 Harrison, Avenue, Panama City, FL 32401.

The Brown Pelican ((904) 785-7389, 3213, West Highway 98, St. Andrews, FL 32401.

Galleria Gifts of Distinction ((904) 769-4906, 2303 Winona Drive, Panama City, FL 32405.

Gorman's Antiques ((904) 265-9705, 1205 Ohio Avenue, Lynn Haven, FL 32444.

The Rast Gallery ((904) 769-2962, 571 Harrison Avenue, Panama City, FL 32401.

Shady Oaks ((904) 785-3308, 3706 West Highway 98, Panama City, Florida 32405.
Specialists of the South ((904) 785-2577, 3706 East 6th Street, Panama City, FL 32401.

FLEA MARKETS

Cob Web Corner ((904) 872-8321, 2417 Highway 231, Highland Park, FL 32405.

Music Barn Flea Market ((904) 233-1616, 20520 Back Beach Road, Panama City Beach, FL 32413.

Redwood Flea Market ((904) 872-9290, 1517 East 11th Street, Panama City, FL 32401.

15th Street Flea Market ((904) 769-0137, 2233 West Highway 98 and 15th Street, Panama City, FL 32405.

Springfield Flea Market ((904) 769-4999, 3500 Highway 22, Panama City, FL 32401.

OUTLET MALLS

Russell Mills Outlet Store ((904) 243-3425, 127 Miracle Strip Parkway, Unit N7, Fort Walton Beach, FL 32548.

SPECIALTY SHOPS

Seaside ((904) 231-4224, County Road 30A, Santa Rosa, FL 32549.

The Shores Shopping Center
((904) 837-3600, 853 East Highway 98,
Dunedin FL 32541.

NORTHEAST
FLEA MARKETS
ABC Flea Market ((904) 642-2717,
10135 Beach Boulevard, Jacksonville,
FL 32216.
Jacksonville Market Place Flea and
Farmers Market, 614 Pecan Park Road,
Jacksonville, FL 32218.

MALLS
Orange Park Mall ((904) 269-2422,
1910 Wells Road, Orange Park, FL 32073.
Regency Square Mall ((904) 725-1220,
9501 Arlington Expressway, Jacksonville,
FL 32225.

SPECIALTY SHOPS
Jacksonville Landing ((904) 353-1188,
Two Independent Drive, Jacksonville,
FL 32202.

CENTRAL EAST
FLEA MARKETS
Daytona Beach Flea Market, 1425
Tomoka Farms Road, Daytona Beach,
FL 32119.

Frontenac Flea Market ((407) 631-0241,
5601 North US 1, Cocoa, FL 32922.

SPECIALTY SHOPS
Historic Cocoa Village ((407) 690-2284,
301 Brevard Avenue, Cocoa, FL 32922.

OUTLET MALLS
Daytona Outlet Mall ((904) 756-8700,
2400 South Ridgewood Avenue,
South Daytona, FL 32119.

CENTRAL
ANTIQUE DEALERS AND SHOPS
Antique Mall ((813) 293-5618,
3170 Highway 17 North,
Winter Haven, FL 33881.
Attic Gallery ((813) 967-2267,
205 Bartow Avenue, Auburndale,
FL 33823.
Biggar Antiques ((813) 956-5113,
140 West Haines Boulevard, Lake Alfred,
FL 33850.
The Peach Magnolia ((813) 956-5113,
1070 South Lake Shore Way, Lake Alfred,
FL 33850.

OPPOSITE: Treasures can be found at quaint shops
and flea markets. ABOVE: Shopping malls like this
one in Miami are often open round the clock.

Potpourri Antiques ((813) 956-5535, 144 West Haines Boulevard, Lake Alfred, FL 33850.

FLEA MARKETS

Bartow Outdoor Drive-in Theater and Flea Market ((813) 533-6395, 2850 US 17 South, Bartow, FL 33830.
Flea World ((407) 647-3976, Highway 17-92, between Orlando and Sanford, one mile (one and six-tenths kilometers) from exit 50 on I-4.
King Flea ((813) 688-9964, 333 North Lake Parker Avenue, Lakeland, FL 33801.
Lakeland Farmers Market ((813) 682-4809, 2701 Swindell Road, Lakeland FL 33801.
International Market World ((813) 665-0062, 1052 US 92, West Auburndale, FL 33823.
192 Flea Market ((407) 396-4555, 4301 West Vine Street, Kissimmee, FL 34746.
Osceola Flea and Farmers Market ((407) 846-2811, 2801 East 192 Highway, Kissimmee, FL 32742.

OUTLET MALLS

Belz Factory Outlet Mall ((407) 352-9600, 5401 West Oakridge Road, Orlando, FL 32819.
Kissimmee Manufacturers Mall ((407) 396-8900, 2517 Old Vineland Road, Kissimmee, FL 34741.

SPECIALTY SHOPS

Church Street Station Exchange ((407) 422-2434, 129 West Church Street, Orlando, FL 32801.
Mercado Mediterranean Village ((407) 345-9337, 8445 South International Drive, Orlando, FL 32819.
Old Town Shopping ((407) 843-4202, 5770 West Irlo Bronson Memorial Highway, Kissimmee, FL 34741.

CENTRAL WEST
ANTIQUE SHOPS
South Tampa and Ybor City are packed with antique shops and galleries.

FLEA MARKETS
Gunn Highway Flea Market
((813) 920-3181, 2317 Gunn Highway, Tampa, FL 33637.
The Big Top Flea Market
((813) 986-4004, 9250 East Fowler Avenue, Tampa, FL 33637.
North 301 Flea Market ((813) 986-1023, 11802 North US 301, Tampa, FL 33637.
Oldsmar Flea Market ((813) 855-5306, 180 North Race Track Road, Oldsmar, FL 33626.
Top Value Flea Market ((813) 884-7810, 8120 Anderson Road, Tampa, FL 33634.
University of South Florida Flea Market
((813) 974-5309, 4202 East Fowler Avenue, Tampa, FL 33612.

SPECIALTY SHOPS
Old Hyde Park Village ((813) 251-3500, 1517 Swan Avenue, Tampa, FL 33606.
St. Armands Circle ((813) 388-1554, off Boulevard of Presidents, Sarasota, FL 34236.
The Shops on Harbour Island
((813) 229-5093, 601 South Harbour Island Boulevard, Tampa, FL 33602.
Ybor Square ((813) 247-4497, 1901 North 13th Street, Tampa, FL 33605.

SOUTHWEST
ANTIQUE SHOPS
Third Street South ((813) 649-6707, 1262 Third Street South, Naples, FL 33940.

SPECIALTY SHOPS
Bell Tower Shops ((813) 489-1221, 13499 US 41 South, Fort Myers, FL 33919.
Coastland Center ((813) 262-7100, 1900 North Tamiami Trail, Naples, FL 33940.
Fifth Avenue South (no telephone), 1700 North Tamiami Trail, Naples, FL 33940.
Old Marine Marketplace
((813) 262-4200, 1200 Fifth Avenue South, Naples, FL 33940.
Royal Palm Square ((813) 939-3900, 1400 Colonial Boulevard, Fort Myers, FL 33907.
YOUR CHOICE

Springs Plaza ((813) 992-7770, US 41 and Bonita Beach Road, Bonita Springs, FL 33923.

SOUTHEAST
ANTIQUE SHOPS
The Esplanade ((407) 833-0868, Palm Beach, FL 33417.

FLEA MARKETS
New Opa Locka-Hialeah Flea Market
((305) 688-8080, 12705 Northwest 42nd Avenue, Opa Locka, FL 33054.
Thunderbird Swap Shop ((305) 791-7927, 3501 West Sunrise Boulevard, Fort Lauderdale, FL 33311.

OUTLET MALLS
Palm Beach Square Factory Outlet
((407) 684-5700, 5700 Okeechobee Boulevard, West Palm Beach, FL 33417.
Sawgrass Mills ((305) 846-2300, 12801 West Sunrise Boulevard, Sunrise, FL 33323.

SPECIALTY SHOPS
Bal Harbour Shops ((305) 866-0311, 9700 Collins Avenue, Bal Harbour, FL 33154.
Bayside Marketplace ((305) 577-3344, 401 Biscayne Boulevard, Miami, FL 33132.
Galleria ((305) 564-1015, 2414 East Sunrise Boulevard, Fort Lauderdale, FL 33304.
Haitian Art Company ((305) 296-8932, 600 Frances Street, Key West, FL 33040.
Key West Aloe ((305) 294-5592, 524 Front Street, Key West, FL 33040.
Key West Handprint ((305) 294-9535, 201 Simontown Street, Key West, FL 33040.
Las Olas Boulevard, Fort Lauderdale, designer shops, galleries and boutiques.
Mayfair Shops in the Grove ((305) 448-1700, 2911 Grand Avenue, Coconut Grove, FL 33133.
The Partridge Christmas Shop
((305) 294-6001, 120 Duval Street, Key West, FL 33040.

OPPOSITE: Conch shells and T-shirts are offered as souvenirs at the southernmost point in the continental United States— on Key West.

Short Breaks

No matter where your holiday base is in Florida you should aim to see as much of the state as possible during your stay. From Orlando and the major central Florida attractions, it is only an hour or so to either Cocoa and the Kennedy Space Center on the Atlantic Coast, or Tampa, Clearwater and St. Petersburg on the Gulf. It is three hours or so north to St. Augustine and an overnight trip if you want to explore the Panhandle. From Orlando, allow just over three hours to drive south to Miami on the Atlantic Coast, or Everglades City on the Gulf and the gateway to the Everglades National Park.

Your options don't end there, however. Just north of the Kennedy Space Center is Port Canaveral, one of the country's main cruise ship terminals, and from here you can sail off on a three-day mini cruise to the Bahamas. And if you have visited Florida before, you might decide to fly out from one of the many airports and spend a couple of days in New Orleans, Boston, New York — or whatever strikes your fancy.

As most visitors stay in the central Florida area, either inland in the Orlando region or on the Gulf or Atlantic coasts, the following suggestions are places to visit either as a long day out, or involving an overnight if you want to take your time. Apart from the height of the tourist season (over Christmas and August), you should be able to find a hotel or motel bed, but it is always advisable for peace of mind, to have made a reservation.

Ocala and Horse Country. Historic, downtown Ocala with its pre- and post-Civil War houses, has a traditional 1800s city square, and is just over an hour from Orlando. Get a self-guided walking tour brochure from the Chamber of Commerce and see the sights and then explore the surrounding countryside. Ocala is surrounded by horse farms where you can see thoroughbred Arabians, Quarter Horses, Tennessee Walkers, Morgans and many other breeds. Many farms welcome visitors; watch for signs.

Gainesville is a two-hour drive north of Orlando and deserves a visit for its well-preserved historic district. Although most of the properties are little more than

100 years old, more than 700 are protected. There are nineteenth-century Queen Anne-style homes along Northeast Third Street and Third Avenue. On University Avenue there are Italianate style houses, and the curbside blocks used to step in and out of horse drawn carriages can still be seen. There are other historic buildings in the Southeast and Pleasant Street districts and downtown, including the Hippodrome Star Theatre, converted from the old post office, and one of the finest examples of Florida's Beaux Arts Classical style. The University campus also boasts 19 red brick buildings built between 1905 and 1939 in the collegiate Gothic style of Yale and Princeton, with intricate tracery, fan-vaulted ceilings and gargoyles.

St. Augustine really deserves a longer visit as there is too much to see and do in one day. It is the oldest city in the United States and one of the most delightful. It has many charming bed and breakfast establishments where an overnight stay and southern hospitality can add to your enjoyment, although it is best to book in advance. It is a good two-hour drive from Orlando. The fastest route is to take I-4 and then I-95 north until the US 1 or State Road 214 exits, both of which lead into the historic area. The best way to see the city is on foot but you can catch the tram which runs between all the main sights. The ticket allows you to get on and off as often as you like, and as there are regular trams throughout the day, you can spend as long as you like in one area before moving on. Opening times and prices vary according to the season, so your first stop should be the Visitors Center on the corner of Castillo Drive and San Marco Avenue, where you can pick up free brochures and maps and watch a 15-minute video to familiarize yourself with the area. Parking is a problem, so park away from the Center and either walk in or catch the tram.

Sights that you must visit include the Castillo de San Marcos National Monument, where park rangers dressed in seventeenth century Spanish uniforms re-enact fort life and demonstrate how the old weapons were used. The restored Spanish quarter of St. George Street is also a must. Many buildings have been restored to show how Spanish settlers and soldiers lived 300 years ago, and craftsmen, dressed in period costumes, recreate daily life in the eighteenth century. There are many good restaurants in the area so it is a good place to eat. Also take in the oldest house, oldest store and oldest schoolhouse, the old jail, the Moorish Zorayda Castle, and Lightner Museum.

For overnight accommodation try to stay at one of the 25 historic Victorian or Spanish Colonial-style bed-and-breakfast inns with their gingerbread trim and welcoming hot cider.

Festive Flings

WITH MORE THAN 40 MILLION VISITORS A YEAR TO FLORIDA, EVERY DAY IS A HOLIDAY, but there are a number of special occasions, both festive and sporting throughout the year, that are worth looking for.

JANUARY
The **Great Southern Gumbo Cook-Off** takes place in **Sandestin** when the restaurants vie with each other for the best gumbo title. If you eat, you get a vote.

The **Outback Steakhouse Gator Bowl** is held in **Jacksonville**. This is one of the major college football games of the year and brings together two of the nation's top teams. Similar plays-offs are held in Tampa and Orlando.

In **Kissimmee** there is **Warbird Weekend**, a two-day flying event held at the Flying Tigers Warbird Air Museum, and featuring aircraft from World War II.

In **Winter Haven** there is the 11-day **Florida Citrus Festival and Polk County Fair**. It comes at the end of the citrus harvest and is a typical old-time country

OPPOSITE: The impressive gardens surrounding the Castillo de San Marcos in St. Augustine.

fair with livestock exhibits, and traditional arts and crafts, including handmade quilts.

In **Miami Beach**, a seven-block **street festival** is held highlighting the city's historic Art Deco district, while in Marathon, you can enjoy the **Renaissance Faire**, a medieval theme festival with jousting knights, entertainment, bands and, of course, lots of food booths.

FEBRUARY

The **Battle of Olustee** was the largest Civil War battle in Florida and it saved Tallahassee from falling into the hands of Union forces. It is reenacted every year in **Lake City** with more than 2,000 participants, and is followed by a downtown festival with parades and arts and crafts displays.

Speed Week in **Daytona Beach** is one of the premier events in the North American motor racing calendar and features both road racing and stock car events. The Daytona 500 is the top event.

In **Tampa**, enjoy the **Florida State Fair**, a festival of food, country-western stars, agricultural exhibits and fun fair, or mingle with the stars in Miami at the annual film festival which showcases some of the world's finest new films.

Another historical insight can be discovered in **Tampa** at the **Gasparilla Pirate Fest Weekend**. Gasparilla was Florida's most notorious pirate and he is remembered by a mock pirate invasion which launches a huge street party and a month-long series of events ranging from a golf tournament to an arts festival.

A glimpse of African American history and culture can be gleaned from the **Sistrunk Historical Festival** held in **Fort Lauderdale**. Held along Sistrunk Boulevard, it features food, arts and crafts and entertainment.

A taste of the old Florida can be found at the **Silver Spurs Rodeo** in **Kissimmee**. Despite the world famous attractions nearby, central Florida is still predominantly a farming community producing citrus fruit and raising beef. The Silver Spurs Rodeo is one of the top 25 rodeos in the nation and you can

watch professional cowboys competing in events such as bull riding, steer wrestling and calf roping.

In **Fort Myers**, they remember the city's most famous resident with the **Edison Festival of Light**, and two weeks of events and parades.

MARCH

Another Civil War reminder takes places in **Tallahassee** with the **1865 Natural Bridge Battlefield Reenactment**. At **Gainesville**, there are the **Gatornationals**, a drag racing spectacle of speed, color and sound, and the largest event of its kind on the east coast.

In **New Port Richey**, the **Chasco Fiesta** commemorates the celebration of friendship between the Calusa Indians and the Spanish colonists. It features sporting events, coronation ball, Indian pageant, arts and crafts, and food and entertainment.

In **Plant City**, the winter strawberry capital of the world, country music's biggest stars gather for an 11-day festival,

OPPOSITE: Bahamanian dancer at Miami Pasco.
ABOVE: You can pick your own fruit at citrus farms like this one in Lake Wales.

while the **Floral City Strawberry Festival** is much more a family event with arts, crafts and food contests and children's activities and entertainments.

Bradenton stages **Manatee Heritage Week** which focuses on the county's heritage, and Sarasota holds its **Medieval Faire**, which takes visitors back to a time of jousting and medieval fun.

In **Kissimmee**, the annual **Bluegrass** music festival is held, while **Sanibel Island** hosts the **shell fair**. Sanibel is the nation's finest shelling area and number three worldwide. The fair features shell displays and arts and crafts using shells.

The nation's largest Hispanic celebration, reminiscent of Mardi Gras in Rio de Janeiro takes place in **Miami**, and culminates in the **Calle Ocho Festival**, a 23-block street party featuring food, dance, music, costumed revelers and top Latin entertainers.

APRIL

Panama City Beach hosts the **PGA Classic for Young Professionals**, while just up the coast, the huge Elgin airforce base opens its gates — and skies — with aerial acrobatics by the famous Thunderbirds display team. Coinciding

with the **Elgin Air Show** is the **Fort Walton Beach Seafood Festival**. **Pensacola** has a two-day **jazz festival** which attracts top performers, and **Tallahassee's Springtime**, has grown into a four-week-long celebration of spring with parades, contests, festivals and arts and crafts. The **Easter Parade** in downtown **St. Augustine** features horses and carriages, marching bands and floats. **Sunfest** in **West Palm Beach** has become one of Florida's largest jazz, art and water events festivals, while the **Seven Mile Bridge Run** in **Marathon** attracts runners from around the world.

MAY

Historic downtown **Grayton Beach** is the venue for a **fine arts festival** which features artists from around the United States, while **Fort Walton Beach** hosts the **Hog's Breath Hobie Regatta**. The annual **Flagler County Bluegrass Festival** is held in **Bunnell**, and downtown and riverfront **Jacksonville** stages **Heritage Days** featuring costume parades, street musicians and arts and crafts.

Shrimp lovers should head for **Fernandina Beach** and the **Isle of Eight Shrimp Festival**, a weekend filled with

54

the celebration of the birthplace of the shrimping industry, while the **Greater Daytona Beach Striking Fish Tournament** is the largest offshore fishing competition on the east coast with more than 250 boats taking part.

JUNE

The **Fiesta of the Five Flags**, a tribute to the five countries which at various times ruled Florida, is held in **Pensacola** with boat and street parades, music, ethnic festivals and sandcastle contests. At **Destin** and **Fort Walton Beach**, the **Billy Bowlegs Festival** celebrates another of Florida's famous pirates, with 500 boats taking part in an "invasion" of the Emerald Coast.

JULY

The **Fourth of July** is celebrated in every town and city throughout the state, but **Tallahassee** boasts the largest fireworks display, while **Flagler Beach** combines the festivities with the **Miss Flagler County Pageant**, and **Daytona Beach** celebrates it with **motorcar racing**, of course, and **jazz** and **country music**. At **Key West**, **Hemingway Days** is a week-long festival celebrating the life and work of the author, and at **Big Pine Key**, the **Underwater Music Festival** takes place when divers gather at the Looe Key National Marine Sanctuary to listen to an underwater symphony.

AUGUST

Panama City hosts the **Beach Fishing Classic** with prizes for anglers of all ages and at **The Pier** in St. Petersburg, the week long **Caribbean Calypso Carnival** is held featuring steel drum bands, Caribbean food and limbo dancing.

SEPTEMBER

Some of the country's best seafood is available in **Pensacola Beach** at the **Seafood Festival**, which also features music and arts and crafts. In **St. Petersburg**, it is **Sunsational Museums Month** with special events showcasing the city's world-class museums.

YOUR CHOICE

OCTOBER

In **Niceville**, about 11 tons of mullet are eaten during the **Boggy Bayou Mullet Festival**, while at **Destin**, known as the World's Luckiest Fishing Village, more than 1,000 competitors from around the world gather for the **Fishing Rodeo** which features inland, shore, offshore and bayou fishing. **Panama City Beach** hosts the **Indian Summer Seafood Festival**, **Madeira Beach** has its **John's Pass Seafood Festival**, **Jacksonville** is the venue for **The World's Greatest Free Jazz Concert**, and **Ocala** is home of the two-day **Florida Horse and Agricultural Festival**, showcasing the state's thoroughbreds.

In **Kissimmee** there is the **Florida State Air Fair**, while **Naples** stages the **Fifth Avenue Oktoberfest** with live performers, carnival rides, dancers, German bands and food.

NOVEMBER

Pensacola has the **Blue Angels Homecoming Show**, which welcomes the Navy's aerobatics team back after their year attending air shows around the world. It also hosts the **Arts Festival**. **Gainesville's Downtown Festival and Arts Show** features hundreds of artists, and **Lake City's Festival of Lights** sees downtown Olustee Park transformed into a Christmas wonderland. **High Springs** also lights up the town and stages special entertainment. Many other towns and cities have their own Festival of Lights as Christmas celebrations get under way after Thanksgiving in November.

Sarasota hosts the **French Film Festival** while **Greater Fort Lauderdale** is the venue for the east coast's largest **film festival** featuring entries from around the world. **Cypress Gardens** is the venue for the annual **Chrysanthemum Festival** featuring more than two million blooms, and you can try your hand at **sand sculpting** at the annual contest at **Fort Myers Beach**.

OPPOSITE : Rodeos are still very popular in the nation's largest beef-producing state.

DECEMBER

Tallahassee stages the month-long **Southern Accents of Winter**. It was the site of the first Christmas celebration in North America. There are **Christmas parades** in many towns and cities, but **St. Augustine's** is spectacular and followed by the **Grand Illumination**. **Fernandina Beach** has a month-long **Victorian Seaside Christmas** with tours of historic homes, ballet, Teddy Bear Teas and New Year's Gala. There is an **arts and crafts festival** at **Shady Hills**, and in **Fort Myers** the historic winter homes of Thomas Edison and Henry Ford are dressed up for Christmas week.

Galloping Gourmet

FINE DINING IS A RELATIVELY NEW PHENOMENON FOR MANY PEOPLE IN THE UNITED STATES. Until recently, sitting down to eat a leisurely meal with friends as a social event in itself was not a widespread practice. Instead, Americans ate on the run grabbing a quick burger or a hot dog and then got right back to what they were doing.

Fast food outlets still account for the vast majority of eating places in Florida and, for a family, they offer a fun and cheap way of eating out. Europeans, in particular, will find that most fast food outlet prices in Florida are about half those back home.

There are also amazing eat-all-you-can family buffet restaurants where you can help yourself to as much as you want. These make great breakfast stops where you can fill up for the day often for just a couple of dollars.

Don't dismiss these eateries as cheap and nasty; if they were, they would quickly go out of business in Florida where competition is intense and standards very high. They are certainly inexpensive but they offer outstanding value for the money.

The Sizzlers chain for instance, which has franchises throughout Florida, offers all-you-can-eat meals throughout the day, and there can be a choice of as many as 100 dishes for lunch and dinner. While you tuck in to salad, pasta, fish or meat from the carvery, your children can try anything they please. My boys used to

start with soup and then go straight on to the large selection of desserts. The meal price includes all the soft drinks you can drink, and a family of four can eat as much as they want for around $25.

The four overriding impressions one has of eating in Florida are price, portions, service and choice. In most places, eating out is even more pleasurable because you can enjoy good food, good service and good prices. Portions, in a word, are huge.

While there is a large choice of restaurants, most cater to the American preference for steak, chicken, pasta or fish and most meals are built around these. Remember that many restaurants include salad or soup in the price of the main dish so don't order too much or you may have trouble eating everything.

Choice really comes into its own if you are self-catering either in a motel room or rented holiday home. The food sections of supermarkets offer a huge variety from exotic fruits and live lobsters to ready-prepared meals. Whether eating in or out, the food is almost always good.

Local specialties include giant Gulf shrimps and Key lime pie but fresh produce is jetted in from around the world so there is a wide range of foods to enjoy. There are exotic fruits and juices, such as mango, papaya and carambola, and the freshest of fish and shellfish.

One of the great treats of Florida, especially on the coast, is being able to dine leisurely out of doors, enjoying both the sea views and the seafood. There is

OPPOSITE: Exotic fruit drinks on offer at a Key West stand. ABOVE: Enjoying the fruits of the sea.

yellowtail and mutton snapper, mullet, pompano, grouper, tiny grunt, dolphin (the fish mahi mahi, not the mammal), spiny lobster, oysters, conch, giant pink shrimp and delicious stone crab all from local waters. They come from the waters off the western side of the state, where the crab fishermen haul in the stone crabs, break off a large claw, and then — as required by law — throw the crab back into the sea, where it will grow another claw to replace the one you're eating. Stone crab claws are heavenly. Note, however, that during the closed season, mid-October to mid-May, there are only frozen ones available.

Seafood can be eaten grilled, boiled, baked or sautéed. It is used to make delicious soups, chowders and stews; and lobster and crab are delicious cold and served with a mayonnaise sauce.

Conch (pronounced "konk") are highly nutritious, and can be served in a variety of ways. They can be grilled, ground in conch burgers, fried in batter as fritters, or eaten raw in salads.

There is excellent beef, and the tenderest of steaks, which is not surprising as Florida is the nation's second largest beef producer after Texas.

Most steaks come in 8-oz and 12-oz (227-g and 340-g) sizes, but some restaurants specialize in 16-, 32- and even 64-oz (454-, 907-g and 1.8-kg) steaks! Southern cooking is represented by dishes such as Southern fried chicken, grits and hushpuppies (deep-fried balls of cornmeal and onion).

Most restaurants offer wonderful salad bars and all-inclusive specials which makes eating out both a pleasure and affordable. All-you-can-eat breakfasts, lunches and dinners are ideal for parents who have growing children with almost endless appetites, and if you want to dine a little early, most restaurants offer "early bird" specials with the same menu but lower prices.

A number of different ethnic cuisines are available from Cuban to Chinese, Caribbean to Italian and German to Japanese. You can try authentic Greek fare in Tarpon Springs, Spanish food in and around St. Augustine, Creole cuisine in the Panhandle, and Native American dishes such as fried breads and mashed cassava roots in the Everglades.

At the very least, you should sample the best of Old Southern, Cuban, and the Florida version of American cooking.

Among the dishes from the Old South that you should try are southern fried chicken (of course), hush puppies, ham steak, stuffed turkey, catfish, grits (granulated white corn), rice with giblet gravy, okra, collard greens, black-eyed peas, cornbread, and pecan pie. The mainstays of Cuban cuisine are black beans and rice, fried plantains, paella, *arroz con pollo* (chicken with rice), *picadillo* (ground beef with olives and onions in a piquant sauce), and a scrumptious variety of pork dishes. In Miami and elsewhere you can try Cuban-inspired *lechon*, roast pork flavored with garlic and tart oranges which give the dish a unique flavor. Other dishes include *ropa vieja* made from beef and which literally translated means "old clothes". All are usually served with boiled white or yellow rice, flavored with either saffron or bihol, and black beans. For the best of American cooking, Florida-style, I would recommend the steaks (Florida ranks second in the nation behind Texas as a producer of beef), anything barbecued (particularly spare ribs), anything that calls itself a salad, any delicatessen sandwich, and — yes, I know it's heresy — the fare at fast-food restaurants. *Haute cuisine* it isn't, but for something quick, tasty, convenient, and inexpensive, you cannot beat American fast food — which is why it has colonized taste buds all over the world.

There is probably not much point in raving about Florida's fruit; after all, you have probably been eating it all your life, given that 70 percent of the world's grapefruit and 25 percent of the world's oranges come from Florida, not to mention the tangerines, lemons, limes, and other citrus fruits which Florida bestows on the world's dining tables. But it's better here because it's fresher here. And citrus is only half the story; the sub-tropical half includes the most delicious mangoes, papayas, carambolas, lychees, guavas, zapotes, and coconuts.

Stop at a roadside stall and buy a large sack of oranges, grapefruit, lime or juicy tangelos for just a few dollars, but don't be tempted to stop and help yourself from a tree by the roadside, as it is a felony (for which you can go to prison) to steal fruit in Florida. If traveling around during the winter months, you will almost certainly see huge lorries filled with oranges, bound for the juice factories. The citrus season lasts over the winter and there are many types of fruits to be enjoyed. Growers are always developing new strains of seedless or juicier fruit. Towards the end of the season, look for late fruits such as Valencia oranges and seedless grapefruit. Even out of season, you should try some of the many citrus products, such as marmalade, orange wine and lemon jelly and candies. Roadside stalls also sell home grown peanuts, boiled or roasted, and pecans, while in the south you can buy locally grown sugar cane and the syrup and molasses it is turned into.

Desserts include "flans", such as baked and caramelized custard, guava shells stuffed with cream cheese, to fresh tropical fruits perhaps served with tropical fruit-flavored ice cream. Florida's winter strawberries are particularly succulent. And, of course, there is Key lime pie, made with condensed or evaporated milk and the juice and minced rind of the piquant Key limes. Florida's official dessert is so sacred to Floridians that it is often the subject of almost theological debates: what sort of lime juice is best, to what temperature should the pie be chilled, should it be served with a meringue or should the eggs be beaten into the pie itself, and so on. Anyway, two things are certain — the pie should be made with Key limes (which are small and yellow, not green), and it should have a graham cracker crust.

Two more comments about Florida restaurants: Except for the seriously upmarket eateries, restaurants in Florida tend to be very informal, and tend to open and close earlier (for all meals) than do restaurants in the rest of the world.

Citrus can be shipped worldwide if you want to take a taste of Florida home with you.

Special Interests

NATURALISTS

If you are interested in flora and fauna, a compact pair of binoculars, a camera, telephoto lens and lots of film are essential. The wildlife is prolific and in most areas, so accustomed to people that you can get amazingly close to it. Even in the Everglades and on Merritt Island close to the Kennedy Space Center, you can snap pictures of alligators from just a few yards away. The bird life is exotic with ibis and egrets feeding by the wayside, hovering humming birds and pelicans performing beachside aerial acrobatics. You will even find parrots and parakeets flying free.

Florida is exciting because its plants and wildlife are drawn from North and Central America as well as the Caribbean. For European naturalists, almost every species of bird seen will be a new experience.

More than half of Florida is covered by forests with more than 300 tree species and over 3,500 species of other plants. The hardwood forests of the north give way to the tropical forests and mangrove swamps of the south with Caribbean imports such a mahogany, gumbo-limbo, palms and palmettos.

For most of the year in the south, there is a blaze of tropical blooms including royal poinciana, poinsettias, gardenia, jasmine, bougainvillea, trumpet vine, oleander, hibiscus, orchids, flamboyant, morning glory and azalea. There are also trees bearing a wide range of edible fruits and nuts, from mango, papaya, carambola, banana and Key lime to coconut.

Few people realize that Florida's exotic wildlife includes panther, black bear and crocodile, not to be confused with the far more common alligator. There are about 100 species of mammals, 420 species of birds (the state bird being the mockingbird), 700 species of fish, 60 species of snake — the four poisonous types are rattlesnake, coral, cottonmouth moccasin and copperhead. You are quite likely to see armadillos, skunks and porcupines shuffling along roadsides late at night and squirrels, raccoons and opossums are all common. Otter and mink live close to inland waterways, white-tailed deer live in the woodlands, there are a dozen species of bat, and wild boar roam the swamps and woods the length of the state.

Graceful white cattle egrets can be spotted everywhere, and most holidaymakers take home with them memories of turkey vultures soaring effortlessly overhead and visions of pelicans posing on poles at the beach.

The warm waterways play host to the gentle manatee which needs all the protection it can get, while bottlenose dolphin are plentiful and can be seen in coastal waters.

SHELLING

There are rich pickings if you are a seashell collector. Pink conch shells up to 8 inches (20 cm) long are sometimes washed up on the beach; Triton's trumpets are rare but can measure up to nine inches (22 cm). Common shells include frog-shells, distorsios, volutes, tulips, murex, cones, olives, marginellas, cowries, augers and the Florida horse conch, the state's official shell, which can grow up to 24 inches (61 cm) long. Crown conch can be found near mangrove swamps and sheltered bays, and the smallest of the crown conch, melongena corona, can sometimes be found. There are more than 50 species of beautiful tree snails which grow up to two inches (five centimeters) long. Sanibel and Captiva Islands are the best shelling locations, but there are good areas along the Gulf Coast and throughout the Keys.

FLORIDA WINE

Florida is the home of American wine as the first grapes were harvested by French Huguenot settlers around 1562. They used the local Muscadine grape which is able to survive the very hot summers.

Today, the **Lakeridge Winery and Vineyards** in Clermont offers the chance to visit one of Florida's only two surviving wineries and sample its product — with gourmet grape juice available for children and designated drivers. The vineyard is undergoing expansion and will eventually cover 110 acres (44 hectares) growing several different grapes from classic varieties to experimental blends. The winery is open Monday to Saturday from 10 AM to 6 PM and on Sunday from noon to 6 PM. There is a museum featuring the state's winemaking history, including the boom period in the early 1900s, when more than 2,000 acres (800 hectares) of vines were cultivated in the Clermont area.

The most southerly vineyard in the United States is **Eden Vineyards Winery and Park**, on State Road 80, east of Fort Myers. It produces seven types of wine from American and French hybrid grapes and offers wine tastings and a tram tour of the winery.

GHOSTS AND SPOOKS
Many of the historic inns and bed-and-breakfast establishments of St. Augustine

lay claim to a resident ghost, and residents of Lake Wales insist a ghost is responsible for one of the most eerie phenomena in the state, which is certainly worth a visit.

Follow the signs for **Spook Hill**, off US 17 and at the junction of North Avenue and 5th Street. The idea is to drive a little way up the hill, stop at the mark on the road, put the car in neutral and take your foot off the brake after making sure there is nothing behind you. The car will start to roll slowly backwards down the hill, but if you look out of the rear window, you will be certain that you are going uphill. It is a very eerie illusion and locals will tell you it is all because of an old Seminole Indian Chief called Cufcowellax. He is said to have stalked for a month and then slain a huge alligator which had killed many members of his tribe. Ever since the spirit of the alligator has roamed the hill causing this bizarre occurrence.

This great heron is the largest of Florida's many species of heron.

Taking A Tour

MORE THAN A MILLION BRITONS HOLIDAY IN FLORIDA EVERY YEAR and it is an increasingly popular destination for the French, Germans and Scandinavians. South Americans, especially Brazilians, and the Japanese love it just as much.

With so many visitors, competition is fierce among travel companies to win their business. British Airways and Virgin are the major United Kingdom air carriers, primarily to Orlando but also to Miami and Tampa, while charter flights now also land at Sanford International Airport, a 30-minute drive north of Orlando. Air France, Lufthansa, SAS, KLM and Icelandair all offer regular scheduled services to Orlando.

Recent surveys show that most visitors stay in central Florida if it is their first visit, and go for a two-destination holiday if they have been before — spending one week near the attractions in central Florida and the second week or longer on the coast. More than 80 percent of visitors say they will return to the Sunshine State for another vacation.

The main United Kingdom tour operators are Virgin Holidays, British Airways Holidays, Thomson, Airtours, American Express and US Airtours, but there are literally scores to choose from. Some offer special interest holidays for golfers, birdwatchers or SCUBA divers. Your travel agent will be able to provide you with a wide selection of brochures from which to choose.

There are three types of holidays available: the package, those you arrange yourself before you leave, and those where you just fly out and decide what to do when you arrive.

Packages include air fares and accommodation, and often a rental car. Accommodation may be in a resort complex, a hotel or in a holiday home. More than 27,000 Britons own a holiday home in Florida and many of these are rented out to major tour companies for most of the year. They offer spacious accommodation, more freedom than a hotel, especially if you have children, and most have a pool.

For a do-it-yourself tour check out the small advertisements in the holiday pages of the nationals and you will see hundreds of ads offering holiday homes in Florida for rent. Competition is so fierce that a three-bedroom, two-bathroom holiday home with heated pool and close to the major attractions, which five years ago would have rented for about $750 a week, often commands less than half of this in the low season. Rented homes makes good economic sense, especially if you have a large family or are two couples with young children wanting to share. You cook in or eat out, and the houses have all the latest kitchen gadgets including dishwashers. Before you make a firm reservation to rent a house, make sure you can get a flight. Because of huge demand, air tickets for the peak periods over the summer holidays and at Christmas are often sold out a year in advance. If you can go at other times of the year, the flight will cost less and there will be fewer tourists around when you arrive.

The third option, and an increasingly popular one, is simply to take advantage of last minute, reduced air fares and to fix up accommodation when you arrive. If you choose this option, it is important to have a rental car waiting for you on your arrival. Florida, and especially central Florida, has more hotels and motel beds than any other tourist destination worldwide, so apart from the peak periods you can always find a bed. Drive down the main resort roads and the neon signs will tell you how much each establishment is charging and what else it is offering to entice you to stay with them. Many offer free breakfasts or free attraction tickets, so the savings can be substantial. Don't be hesitant to ask to look at the room before deciding whether to stay; everyone else does. And try haggling over the price if you're planning to stay for a few days as you might save a few more dollars.

Most hotels and motels offer two double beds in each room. Since you pay for the room and not per person, this can work out very reasonably if traveling with family or close friends. Rooms tend to be large; an extra bed or cot can usually be obtained for a small additional charge. Most rooms have en suite bathrooms and telephone, air conditioning and cable or satellite television. Many also have coffee- or tea-making facilities and motels offer rooms with kitchenettes for self catering.

Prices vary according to season and standard of service offered. Most hotel chains offer vouchers which if pre-paid, offer substantial discounts, so it is worth checking with your travel company. There are often also substantial discounts for senior citizens.

Many hotels and motels have their own restaurants, and offer American plan (full board) or Modified American (half board). If there is no restaurant, most hotels have free coffee in the lobby while ice machines and soft drink dispensers are available on each floor.

If you want to split your holiday between two destinations, spend the first week in the Orlando area, and the second on the Gulf, ideally between Clearwater and St. Petersburg in the north and Fort Myers Beach in the south.

A rental car is essential for your holiday. The distances between attractions, shopping malls and hotels is so great, that a car is the only viable option. If you are staying at a large resort hotel in central Florida, a free shuttle service will be provided to the attractions, but you will not be able to get out and explore. The public bus service in central Florida is irregular at best, and while taxis are plentiful, they are expensive on all but local journeys.

Most people have no trouble at all landing after a long trans-Atlantic flight, getting into their air-conditioned, automatic-shift rental car and driving to their final destination. Signposting is clear, the roads are wide, and most people stick to the speed limits in built up areas, so you have time to see the signs and make your turns in good time.

If you think you might be too tired to drive after the flight, get a taxi to your hotel or holiday home, and have the rental car delivered to you the next day.

Tropical vegetation adds to the charm of this Key West resort.

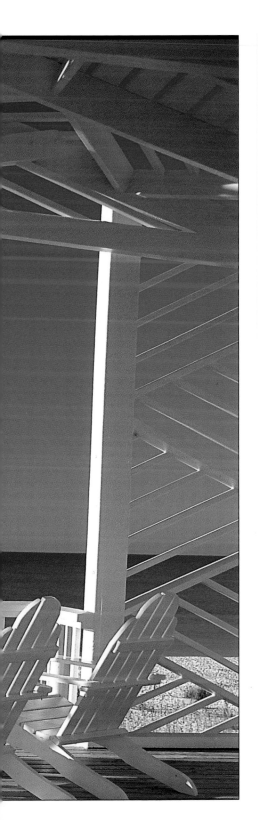

Welcome
to
Florida

IT IS FASHIONABLE — almost obligatory — to begin a travel guide by describing the area of one's travels as a land of contrasts. As a rhetorical device it's very handy; it allows the writer to gather up in a few sentences disparate phenomena that might otherwise require many paragraphs, if not pages, of laborious explanation. With contrasts one is able to envelop and summarize a place in one giant parenthesis, and then move briskly along.

Unfortunately — for the writer, that is — Florida is by no stretch of the imagination

a land of contrasts. It is a land of spectacular sameness. True, the oldest city in the United States, St. Augustine, is just up the coast from the headquarters of the Space Age, Cape Canaveral; while in the middle of ancient Indian territory is the 28,000-acre (over 11,600-hectare) reservation known as Walt Disney World. And no one has ever mistaken the antebellum Southern charms of Tallahassee for the Latin rhythms of Miami, any more than have the literati of Key West been confused with the glitterati of Palm Beach. And where other states have a generation gap, Florida has a generation chasm — between the young who flock there to live it up, and the elderly who migrate there to die.

Nonetheless, the overall impression is, if not of sameness, of minor variations on a few major themes. The principal theme, of course, is sunshine: Florida is very aptly nicknamed the Sunshine State. Another theme is flatness: Florida's highest point is only 345 ft (105 m) above sea level. Another theme is wetness: quite apart from the vast swampland of the Everglades, Florida has 30,000 lakes and 10,000 miles (16,130 km) of rivers and streams, and of course its 1,350 miles (2,177 km) of coast is lapped by the sea. Now, when you add to this the fact that most of the restaurants in the state (30,000 of them!) are distinguishable from one another only by their prices, or that most of the hotel rooms are distinguishable only by their addresses, or that most of the beaches are distinguishable only by their names, or that most of the roads are distinguishable only by their numbers, you can see why it would be difficult to speak convincingly of Florida as a land of great variety.

Why, then, with all this standardization and uniformity, do 40 million people visit Florida annually? Simple: because standardization is highly desirable if the standards are high, because uniformity is a good thing if things are uniformly good. That's Florida's secret. People know exactly what to expect. When you know that the weather will be sunny, and the beaches will be lovely, and the people will be friendly, and the service efficient, and the accommodation comfortable, and the prices reasonable, then you know why Florida is the most popular tourist destination in the world. No other place in the world can deliver all of this and Mickey Mouse, too.

However, while such consistency and dependability make Florida a very easy place to visit, they make it a difficult place to write about. When the level of quality is so evenly maintained, picking and choosing becomes even harder, and more subjective, than usual. And then there's the problem of quantity. Take hotels, for example. In Miami Beach, a narrow strip of land only seven miles (11 km) long, over 300 new hotels were built in one year alone! Or golf courses. In the vicinity of Fort Lauderdale, a city of modest size, there are 60 golf courses! With such a superabundance of tourist amenities, where does one begin the winnowing process?

Well, for better or worse, one begins with one's own set of preferences — all right, prejudices — as well as a sense of the sort of information I personally would have found valuable before going there.

A word about this information. While I have endeavored to make it as precise as I possibly could, there is one area of deliberate imprecision: hotel and restaurant prices. This is because each establishment's prices fluctuate enormously according to a number of factors. For instance, the price of the same hotel room could vary by as much as 100 percent depending on the time of year (summer is regarded as the off-season, except in the north), the number of occupants, the length of occupancy, whether special discounts are available, and whether sales tax (currently six percent) or tourist tax (currently two percent) is included. Restaurant prices are similarly variable; many restaurants, for example, offer substantial discounts to those willing to dine early in the evening. And none of this takes into account the fact that hoteliers and restaurateurs throughout the world have been known to change their prices without consulting me first. Thus, to try to be precise

about these prices would make this seem not so much a guidebook as the memoirs of a demented accountant.

I have therefore divided hotels and restaurants into three categories according to the *range* of prices you can expect. With hotels, **luxury** means you can expect to pay over — sometimes way over — $120 for a double room; **mid-range** hotels will tend to charge between $60 and $120; **inexpensive** hotels will cost under — sometimes way under — $60 for a double room. Restaurants listed as **expensive** will cost you over

$50 per person, excluding wine; **moderate** restaurants will generally charge between $20 and $50; **inexpensive** restaurants will be below $20, often well below. The categories are fuzzy, I know, but at least they are not misleading. When it comes to taking responsibility for the spending of your money, I would rather be vaguely right then precisely wrong.

One thing, however, I can predict with absolute certainty: you will find much to enjoy in Florida. In fact, if you can't enjoy yourself in Florida, don't bother to try anywhere else.

OPPOSITE: Greek girl at Tarpon Springs.
ABOVE: The pier at Naples reaches out into the Gulf of Mexico.

The
State and
Its People

It is perhaps appropriate that the world's most visited vacation spot should itself be populated mostly by new arrivals. Only about a third of Florida's nine million inhabitants were actually born there. And none of its inhabitants are descended from the native peoples who had been living there for over 10,000 years before the Europeans arrived in the sixteenth century and began the systematic extermination of the original Indian population.

Although Columbus claimed the territory for Spain, sight unseen, in 1492, the first European actually to lay eyes on Florida was almost certainly the English cartographer John Cabot, who sailed down the east coast of America on behalf of King Henry VII in 1498. The first European to set foot in Florida was the Spanish explorer Juan Ponce de León, who landed near present-day St. Augustine on April 2, 1513, while looking for the legendary Isle of Bimini, which according to folklore had a miraculous fountain of youth. Having arrived at Easter, he named the new land after Spain's Easter celebration, **Pascua Florida**, or Feast of Flowers.

Ponce then sailed down the coast, out around the Florida Keys (which he called **Los Martires**, because they appeared to him like kneeling martyrs in the water), and back up the west coast as far as Charlotte Harbor, near present-day Fort Myers. He returned to Florida in 1521 with 200 settlers and attempted to establish a settlement near Charlotte Harbor. However, the local Indians were in no mood to see the white man encroaching on their territory, and they launched a ferocious attack on the settlement, in the course of which Ponce himself was badly wounded. The entire party was forced to withdraw to Cuba, where Ponce died of his wounds.

Seven years later another Spaniard, Pánfilo de Narváez, landed at Tampa Bay with 300 would-be colonists. He led them on a march up to the Panhandle, where they were to rendezvous with his ships after conducting a search for the gold he was certain he would find en route. He found no gold, nor did he find his ships waiting for him. With his party now much reduced by the hostile attentions of the Indians they had encountered on their march, they decided to build their own boats and set sail for Mexico. They never arrived.

Undeterred by the fate of his two predecessors, Hernando de Soto sailed from Cuba in 1539 with 600 troops, landing at Tampa Bay and marching northwards more or less in the footsteps of Pánfilo de Narváez, searching for the same gold treasure that the Spanish were convinced was there somewhere. When he didn't find it, he just kept going and kept looking. He died on the banks of the Mississippi three years later.

In 1559 the conquistador Don Tristán de Luna arrived with 1,500 men at Pensacola Bay, where he attempted to establish a colony. After two years of struggle, he gave up and went home.

Ironically, it was the French who were indirectly responsible for the first Spanish success at colonization in Florida. In 1562, Jean Ribault explored the mouth of the St. Johns River and claimed the area for France. Within two years there was a colony of 300 Huguenots living there in the newly-built Fort Caroline. Not amused by the presence of these French squatters — and Protestant ones at that — on their territory, the Spanish dispatched a former smuggler, Pedro Menéndez de Avilés, to found a settlement nearby and to deal with the French. He accomplished both tasks.

After landing south of Fort Caroline on August 28, 1565, the feast day of San Augustin, Menéndez named his new settlement in honor of the saint and then led his men northward to sort out the French. Unfortunately for the little Huguenot community, Jean Ribault had the same idea with regard to the Spanish, and had set sail with his men to destroy the fledgling settlement of St. Augustine. Thus Menéndez found Fort Caroline virtually undefended and captured it easily, killing all but women and children. Meanwhile, Ribault's force had run into a storm at sea and were ship-

Replica of *HMS Bounty* moored at Miami.

wrecked before they could reach St. Augustine. The spot where Menéndez later found the survivors is known to this day as Matanzas — Spanish for "killings" — for he took no prisoners.

For the rest of the century the Spanish labored feverishly to consolidate and expand their hold on the peninsula. A chain of forts was established, along with a network of Franciscan missions to convert the Indians. Although Sir Francis Drake succeeded in burning down St. Augustine in 1586, two years before he

defeated the Spanish Armada, the English as well as the French were loath to challenge Spain's colonial supremacy in Florida throughout the seventeenth century. At the same time, Indian resistance to Spanish domination was crumbling rapidly. Those who weren't killed by Spanish firepower succumbed to the European diseases the Spanish brought with them — smallpox, diphtheria, and syphilis — while others were taken into slavery for the plantations in the West Indies. Thus for over a century the Spanish were the acknowledged overlords of Florida.

By 1700, however, there were signs that Spain's grip on Florida wasn't all that secure after all. To the north, English colo-

nies were proliferating — and flourishing. To the west, LaSalle had claimed the entire Mississippi River valley for France. Then the War of the Spanish Succession in 1702 brought English troops into Florida, where, with the help of the Creek Indians, they overran most of Spain's military outposts in the north and destroyed almost all of her missions. Then the French captured Pensacola in 1719. Although they handed it back soon afterwards, purely to keep it out of English hands, the writing was on the wall for Spain.

Finally, in 1763, after France's defeat in the French and Indian Wars left England as the undisputed master of the American continent, Spain ceded Florida to England in exchange for Havana, which the English had captured. By this time all of the native Indians had vanished, to be replaced by renegade Creeks from neighboring territories to the north and west. They were called Seminoles, from the Spanish words for renegades or runaways, *cimarrones*. The English got along well with the Seminoles, cultivating them as trading partners rather than exterminating them as savages, but England's ambitious plans for developing Florida had to be put on hold as the rebellion in the 13 colonies to the north approached revolution.

If the British colonial presence in Florida was brief — two decades, from 1763 to 1783 — it was also benign, as indicated by the fact that Florida did not join in the American Revolution, and indeed provided a haven for prominent English Tories fleeing the war. But when the war was lost, Britain traded Florida back to Spain in 1783 in exchange for the Bahamas.

In the years following the War of Independence citizens of the newly-sovereign United States of America began to develop a keen and acquisitive interest in this Spanish-owned territory dangling below the infant nation. The Seminoles, still loyal to their erstwhile British landlords, and (rightly) mistrustful of the intentions of the Americans who were buying up land in big chunks all around them, made violent nuisances of themselves to the new settlers — so much so that in 1817 Andrew Jackson led a small army into northern Florida to punish the Indians. This became known as the First Seminole War. Apart from teaching the Indians an unhappy lesson, it taught the Spaniards that they were manifestly incapable of protecting their territory. They sold Florida to the United States in 1821.

Andrew Jackson — an obvious choice — was created military governor of the newly annexed territory. Less obviously, Tallahassee was created its capital. It happened thus: because the British had divided the territory for administrative purposes into East Florida and West Florida, with capitals in St. Augustine and Pensacola respectively, the two settlements had rival claims to be the capital of a united Florida. To settle the issue, the territorial legislature came up with a novel solution. One man was dispatched from St. Augustine to Pensacola, and another man was dispatched from Pensacola to St. Augustine. Wherever they met up would be the new capital. They met in the forest at Tallahassee.

As the influx of new settlers from the north increased, the resistance of the Seminoles stiffened, prompting Congress in 1830 to pass the Removal Law, which required that all Indians be removed to the Arkansas Territory west of the Mississippi. Again the Seminoles resisted, and when Seminole warriors ambushed and wiped out a detachment of 139 United States troops under Major Francis Dade near Tampa in 1835, now-president Andrew Jackson had just the excuse he needed to go in and get rid of the Seminoles once and for all. But yet again the white man had underestimated the fighting spirit and determination of the red men. The Second Seminole War lasted for seven bloody years, even though the Seminoles' brilliant chief Osceola had been captured in 1837 while negotiating with the United States commander under a flag of truce.

In 1842, most of the surviving Seminoles were removed along the Trail of Tears to what is now Oklahoma. Even then, several hundred refused to capitulate, escaping into the Everglades where they and their descendants remained defiantly independent until the United States finally signed a treaty with them in 1934.

In 1845 Florida joined the Union as the twenty-seventh state, with a population of about 80,000, of which almost half were black slaves and almost none were Indians.

Unsurprisingly, given the state's geography and plantation economy, Florida sided with the Confederacy during the Civil War. Equally unsurprisingly, given the state's historical vulnerability to outside occupation, no major battles were fought there as the Union forces marched in and captured all the strategic spots without too much difficulty. The period of

Reconstruction was also less traumatic than in other southern states — and briefer, thanks to a wealthy Philadelphia industrialist named Hamilton Disston, who in 1881 was persuaded to buy four million acres (1.5 million hectares) of south-central Florida swampland for $1 million, thus erasing the state's debt burden in one stroke.

The next few years saw several developments which were to put Florida firmly on the road to becoming, a century later, the world's premier holiday playground. First, the American Medical Association

OPPOSITE: A typical sight in Pensacola's historic Seville Quarter. ABOVE: The Old Capitol in Tallahassee, now a museum.

The State and Its People

declared St. Petersburg to be the healthiest spot in the United States. Then the youngish but infirm inventor Thomas Edison forsook New Jersey for Fort Myers, where he built an estate with America's first modern swimming pool. Then along came Henry Bradley Plant, a Connecticut Yankee who built the Atlantic Coastline Railroad from Richmond, Virginia to Tampa — the single greatest attraction of which was Plant's Tampa Bay Hotel, a phantasmagorical hostelry stretching for a quarter of a mile (four-tenths of a kilometer) under

minarets, cupolas, and domes. Simultaneously, Henry Morrison Flagler, a retired Standard Oil executive, was building his Florida East Coast Railroad down the other side of the peninsula. He laid his tracks to St. Augustine, and then to Ormond Beach, and then to Palm Beach, and then to the little hamlet of Miami, and then, eventually, by way of a series of arched bridges, over the ocean and the Florida Keys to Key West. At every important stop along the way Flagler left behind at least one stunning hotel to accommodate the people his railway was transporting down from the north: the Ponce de León and the Alcazar in St. Augustine, the Ormond in Ormond Beach, the Royal Poinciana in Palm Beach,

and the Royal Palm in Miami. In the course of his triumphal march to the southernmost tip of the United States, Flagler also created two future cities: Palm Beach and Miami.

In 1912, the year before Flagler died, a millionaire from Indianapolis, Carl Fisher, discovered a barrier sandbar in Biscayne Bay, where he bought a large tract of land and then added to it with the help of a dredge. A few hotels and golf courses and tennis courts later, Miami Beach was in business. To the south of Miami George Merrick created Coral Gables, the nation's first fully planned city, while up the coast the eccentric architect Addison Mizner was putting up mansions in Palm Beach and buying up scrubland which was to become Boca Raton. At the same time, swampland in the Everglades was being drained to create rich farmland.

All of this activity led to a spectacular land boom in the early 1920s. People poured into the state from all over the country to get a piece of the action. As prices spiraled wildly upward, con-men sold the same parcels of land over and over. Others bought and resold real estate on the same day. Many bought land sight unseen, only to discover later that the land was in fact underwater. As a result of this feeding frenzy, by 1925 two and a half million people had invested in Florida land. But the following year the bottom fell out of what had come to be known as the "surreal estate market".

The boom was bound to go bust sooner or later, but its collapse was hastened by the fact that the railway companies simply couldn't satisfy the enormous demand for building materials, and many developers and builders went bankrupt as a consequence. Then one of the boats bringing materials to Miami capsized, blocking Miami's harbor and bankrupting more builders. The final blow, literally, came on September 17, 1926, when a savage hurricane blew into Miami, damaging over half the buildings and leveling nearby developments. The party was now over, and three years later when the stock market crash brought on the Great Depression, the lights were turned out.

74

They flickered back on again during World War II, when the United States military decided to take advantage of Florida's climate and use it as a year-round training ground. Not only did this give thousands of young soldiers their first tantalizing glimpse of this sunlit, sub-tropical land, but it also produced corollary benefits such as a much-improved system of roads and airports which made it possible for growers to ship their produce all over the country. Equally importantly for the state's economy, military research led to the develop-

There are, it is true, those who think that this growth has been achieved in part at the expense of the environment, that too little attention has been paid to the natural beauty that made the state so attractive in the first place. Others point to the paradox by which the state's glorious climate is starting to become a financial burden: by luring so many retirees from less hospitable climes, it ensures that the costs of health care and programs for the elderly will grow as well.

As of now, however, these are mere sunspots on the sun that shines on Florida.

ment of coolants that were to give Florida efficient air conditioning for its sweltering summers as well as a means of creating frozen concentrates out of its vast citrus crops. The war was definitely good for Florida.

So too, belatedly, was the land bust of 1926, because when people and prosperity began to return to Florida in the post-war years, the lessons of 1926 were remembered. Property transactions were regulated, developments controlled, subdivisions properly planned. Consequently, Florida is still enjoying the remarkable growth that was launched at roughly the same time as the first rocket was launched from Cape Canaveral in 1950.

The State and Its People

GEOGRAPHY AND CLIMATE

At first glance, it would seem rather pointless to write about Florida's geography and climate. After all, there must be very few travelers anywhere in the world who couldn't find Florida on a map or who wouldn't know what sort of weather they could expect to find when they got there. Nonetheless, there are aspects of Florida's geographical and climatic conditions that may still come as a surprise to the visitor.

By American standards the state is not very large — less than 60,000 sq miles

OPPOSITE: Sunset in Panhandle. ABOVE LEFT: The Panhandle town of Seaside. ABOVE: Rockets on parade at the Kennedy Space Center.

(97,000 sq km), about the size of England and Wales combined. Nor, as I have said, is it topographically very diverse. Most of Florida is either swampland or former swampland surrounded by coastal plains. Offshore these plains continue to surface intermittently as islands, sand bars, or coral reefs. At its edges, where Florida rejoins the sea whence it emerged some 20 million years ago, the beaches don't vary significantly in either texture or appeal. Along the northern Atlantic Coast they tend to be broad and the sand is rather tightly packed; along the southern Atlantic Coast they are still broad but softer; along the Gulf Coast they are narrower and softer still, and strewn with shells in the south; in the Panhandle, from Pensacola to Panama City, the beaches are sugary, almost powdery, both in color and consistency.

Within these sandy margins, there are over 300 species of trees, over 400 species and subspecies of birds, and at least 80 different land mammals. Florida's official state tree is the wonderful sabal palm, which can be found almost everywhere in the state, but in different regions its preeminence is challenged variously by pines, cypresses, magnolias, and live oaks. And of course there are the vast citrus groves in the central and south-central parts of the state.

Of the permanent bird population, the most exotic inland (and usually swampland) residents are the ibises, egrets, herons, ospreys, cormorants, cardinals, roseate spoonbills and flamingos. Along the shoreline you will find a somewhat less spectacular array of sandpipers, terns, and pelicans. Then there are those birds, such as ducks and geese, who just like wintering in Florida.

The most interesting mammals are, sadly but predictably, also the rarest: gray foxes, black bears, pumas, and wildcats. There is, however, one mammal that is both very interesting and very common: the friendly dolphin, which can often be seen disporting itself near the beach or beside the boat. Other familiar figures in the landscape, markedly less friendly, include those huge, waddling handbags called alligators (or, by Floridians, just 'gators).

Although Florida was named for the Easter Feast of Flowers in Spain, it could

just as appropriately have been named for the feast of flowers which it offers its beholders. This is especially true in the spring, when the bougainvillea, poincianas, orchid trees, geraniums, azaleas, trumpet vines, and tiger lilies conspire to incite a riot of color.

The climate — well, you already know about the climate or you wouldn't want to know about everything else. It is sunny all year round, with temperatures in most places ranging from fairly warm to very warm. In mid-winter in the northern parts of the state it sometimes, but rarely, plunges to 50°F (10°C); otherwise the thermometer tends to hover around 60°F (15°C). You add degrees as you move south: it can easily be 75°F (24°C) in Key West in January.

In the summer it is correspondingly warmer in different parts of the state, but — here's the good news — *not all that much warmer*. It seldom reaches 90°F (32°C) anywhere, and all the coastal areas are naturally air conditioned by the ocean breezes. (Every interior space untouched by the ocean breezes has been air conditioned by man.) And more good news: the waters around Florida, thanks partly to the Gulf Stream, are agreeably warm all year round.

And the bad news? You have to dial H to get any bad news: Humidity and Hurricanes. Neither, however, constitutes a serious inconvenience. The humidity can be avoided by staying indoors or in the water around midday in mid-summer; the hurricanes can be avoided by staying indoors.

Fortunately, hurricanes are relatively infrequent, even in the hurricane season (late July to mid-November) and their arrival is announced well in advance by the news media. Moreover, the buildings are reinforced to withstand high winds (as in California they are built to withstand earthquakes). As a result, Floridians have become so blasé about hurricanes that whenever a storm is imminent thousands of hurricane parties are organized, as it were, against the wind.

Basically, though, there is nothing in Florida that can come between you and the sea and the sun.

Sunset, soft sand and and serenity on the beach at Seaside, Florida.

Miami
and
Environs

ON JULY 28, 1890 the small fishing and farming community of Miami, with a population of 343 people, was incorporated as a city. By 1920 the population had grown to 30,000, and Miami's development as a major resort was well under way. Nowadays, nearly two million people live in the 26 municipalities which make up the Greater Miami area. These municipalities include Miami Beach, with its Art Deco hotels and miles of sand; the South Pacific-like Virginia Key and Key Biscayne islands below Miami Beach; Coral Gables, colloquially known as the Miami Riviera because of its Mediterranean-style buildings and High Society contingent; Coconut Grove, which is noted for the quality of its shops and its nightlife; and Little Havana, west of the downtown area, the city's Cuban district. Greater Miami now contains 2,040 sq miles (3,284 sq km) of land — of which 1,423 acres (58 hectares) are public beaches along a 15-mile (24-km) stretch of coast between Key Biscayne and Bal Harbour — and 354 sq miles (570 sq km) of water.

The area's ethnic mix is 36 percent white, 18 percent black, and 46 percent Hispanic. The majority of the Hispanics are of Cuban origin, but there are also considerable numbers from Panama, Colombia, El Salvador, and Nicaragua, as well as some 150,000 French-speaking Haitians. The influx of foreigners into Miami has given rise to the sobriquet "America's Casablanca," as some of the immigrants are political or economic refugees, particularly those from Latin American countries and the Caribbean.

Despite the tensions involved in such a racial mixture, and despite its (largely undeserved) reputation for crime and vice, the Miami area has just been judged the twentieth most desirable place to live in the United States among the 333 cities surveyed in Rand McNally's *Places Rated Almanac*. The almanac ranks cities according to the level of crime and the quality of such things as health care, the environment, public transportation, education, recreation, the arts, and the climate. By these criteria, Miami ranks among the best cities in the country.

The Miami International Airport is the second busiest in the nation, handling up to 850 flights a day, and the Port of Miami is indisputably the cruise ship capital of the world, welcoming more than two and a half million cruise passengers every year. But the crucial number — the number that attracts all these numbers of people — is 76°F (24°C). That's the average annual temperature in the Greater Miami area.

MIAMI

BACKGROUND

The first American settler in the area was a Carolina planter named Richard Fitzpatrick, who in 1826 brought a group of slaves to work the land on the banks of the Miami River. Fitzpatrick's Miami holdings were inherited by his nephew, William English, in 1842, the same year in which the Second Seminole War came to an end. English saw clearly the place's potential and began drawing up plans for a village by the mouth of the Miami River. He decided to call the new settlement Miami, a corruption of the Tequesta Indian word *mayaime*, meaning "very large," which is what the Indians once called Lake Okeechobee to the northwest.

Through newspapers in the state's northern cities, English advertised lots for sale at $1 each. Reassured that the Seminoles were no longer a threat, small but growing numbers of people were lured south by the bargain offer. Homesteads were established and the community grew steadily until 1855, when the Third Seminole War broke out.

During the Civil War the Miami area became a refuge for spies, deserters and blockade runners, but the actual battles were confined to the northern part of the state. New settlers arrived after the war, and the area's growth resumed: agricultural communities were established at Lemon City, Coconut Grove, Buena Vista and Little River, while a merchant named William Brickell set up a trading post near the mouth of the Miami River, which did a lively trade with the local Indians.

The "Mother of Miami," (so called because she is said to have "conceived" the city), a wealthy widow named Julia Tuttle, arrived in 1875. She set herself up in William English's old house and over the next 15 years became the area's most important landowner. She was persistent in her efforts to persuade Henry Flagler to extend his Florida East Coast Railroad to Miami, and even tried to tempt him with an offer of 300 acres (120 hectares) of land free, but to no avail. In 1895, however, freak weather conditions came to Mrs. Tuttle's aid. That was the year of the Great Freeze, which wiped out 90 percent of the state's citrus crop but left the Miami area relatively untouched.

The effects of the Great Freeze cut Flagler's railway profits and severely damaged the image of his resorts on the coasts to the north. Seeing her chance, Mrs. Tuttle sent a bouquet of Miami orange blossoms to Flagler as a little reminder that the Miami area had a climate dependable enough to produce citrus crops all year round. Flagler got the point, and his railway reached Miami the following year, 1896. Developers soon followed, building hotels and condominiums, and Flagler himself further invested in the new city by putting up the Royal Palm Hotel.

The real estate boom quickly accelerated and by 1910 the population had grown to 5,000, including some very rich people who had built some very fancy houses along Brickell Avenue overlooking Biscayne Bay. James Deering's elaborate Villa Vizcaya, still ogled at by tourists today, was probably the most impressive of these private palaces. By 1920 the planter John S. Collins and his partner, the businessman and speedway mogul Carl Fisher, had bought up most of the 1,600 acres (640 hectares) of mangrove island just off the coast, drained it, and developed it into Miami Beach. The decade of the Twenties was a major boom period for Miami: in the winter season of 1924–25, 300,000 tourists visited the city, and the city's population swelled to 100,000. In 1926, however, the boom came to an abrupt end and the financiers and developers who had fueled the boom rapidly began divesting.

Still, the development continued at a modest pace through the Depression years. George Merrick established Coral Gables as one of the most exclusive suburbs in the area, and Glenn H. Curtiss made Hialeah and Miami Springs into popular resort centers for winter vacationers. In Miami Beach, marvelous Art Deco hotels rose from the sands. In the 1937–38 winter season, more than 800,000 tourists came to Miami. The city expanded relentlessly to accommodate the ever-increasing numbers of visitors and new residents, until — like Los Angeles on the other coast — it became difficult to decide where the city stopped and the rest of the state began.

After the Cuban revolution in 1959 Miami began receiving waves of refugees: more than half a million over the next few years. The Cubans added a whole new dimension to the appearance and the sociocultural character of the city. Miami's architecture, food, music, politics, media, and of

course, language were all profoundly affected by these new arrivals. Cuban immigrants also brought considerable entrepreneurial skills with them, reinforcing the city's economic base and helping to establish it as one of America's most important financial centers. In addition to the hundreds of banks and insurance companies in Miami, many multinational corporations have set up their Latin American headquarters in the city because of its unrivaled airline connections to the Caribbean and South America.

Like all big cities, Miami has its problems. But I think it's fair to say that there are few cities in the world that wouldn't willingly swap their problems for Miami's — especially if the climate was part of the deal.

GENERAL INFORMATION

Comprehensive information on hotels, transportation, sporting events, festivals and special attractions in the Miami area can be obtained from the Greater Miami Convention and Visitors Bureau ((305) 539-3000, Barnett Tower, Suite 2700, 701 Brickell Avenue, Miami, FL 33131. For more detailed information on where to stay, contact the Greater Miami Hotel and Motel Association ((305) 371-2030, DuPont Plaza Center, Suite 719, 300 Biscayne Boulevard Way, Miami, FL 33131.

Downtown Miami's bold skyline reflects its status as one of America's most important financial centers.

For specific information on the most popular tourist areas, contact one or more of the following chambers of commerce: Greater Miami Hotel and Motel Association ((305) 371-2030; The Key Biscayne Chamber of Commerce ((305) 361-5207, 95 West McIntire, Key Biscayne; the Coconut Grove Chamber of Commerce ((305) 444-7270, 2820 McFarland Road, Coconut Grove; the Coral Gables Chamber of Commerce ((305) 446-1657, 50 Aragon Avenue, Coral Gables; the South Miami Chamber of Commerce ((305) 238-7192, 6410 Southwest 80th Street,

South Miami; and the Bal Harbour Chamber of Commerce ((305) 573-5177, 655 96th Street, Bal Harbour.

If you need still more information, you can find out what's happening and where to find it in Miami by checking the What You Can Watch and What You Can Do sections of the *Miami Herald*.

Useful phone numbers (all area code 305):

Miami International Airport	876-7077
Metro Taxicabs	944-4422
Yellow Cabs	885-5555
Central Taxicab Service	534-0694
Physician Referral Service	326-1177
Dental Referral Service	285-5470
Weather/Surf Information	661-5065

WHAT TO SEE AND DO

Sights

There are so many things to see in Miami that the best approach is to take one area at

ABOVE: The *Heritage of Miami* under full sail passes a cruise liner in Biscayne Bay. OPPOSITE: Getting around, Miami style.

a time. A good place to start is downtown, the commercial and business center of the city. Here you will find the **Center for Fine Arts** ((305) 375-3000, at 101 West Flagler Street, where 15 different national and international exhibitions of painting, sculpture, photography, and the decorative arts are mounted each year. Admission is $5 for adults and $2.50 for children.

The history of the region is brought into focus at the **Historical Museum of Southern Florida** ((305) 375-1492, which is in the same complex as the Center for Fine Arts at 101 West Flagler Street. The museum has displays which illuminate the lifestyles and culture of both the Indians and the nineteenth-century settlers; a photography and film exhibition shows how Miami emerged as a major city. Admission is $4 for adults and $2 for children aged three to 12.

Those who are more likely to be enthralled by modern technology than by art or history should head for the **Miami Museum of Science and Space Transit Planetarium** ((305) 854-4247, at 3280 South Miami Avenue. It has over 100 hands-on exhibits examining the natural sciences, biology, and human anatomy; there are also live scientific experiments, displays of advanced computer technology, and an Animal Exploratorium with a collection of rare natural history specimens. The Planetarium has a dome 65 ft (20 m) high which houses astronomy and laser shows, and the Weintraub Observatory for evening stargazing. The museum is open from 10 AM to 6 PM every day, with separate late night openings at weekends for the observatory. Admission is $6 for adults and $4 for children aged three to 12.

Another downtown attraction worth visiting is the **Vizcaya Museum and Gardens** ((305) 250-9133, at 3251 South Miami Avenue, where antiques, paintings, and Oriental decorations adorn the interior of James Deering's 34-room Italian Renaissance villa. The European-style formal gardens and fountains surrounding the villa are among the most beautiful in the country. Opening hours are daily from 9:30 AM to 5 PM, and admission is $10 for adults and $5 for children aged six to 18.

To reach Virginia Key and Key Biscayne take Rickenbacker Causeway from the mainland at Brickell Avenue and Southwest 26th Street, across Biscayne Bay. There are parks and beaches on both keys, with swimming and sporting facilities, and you can also see pockets of old mangrove swamp of the kind which once covered Miami Beach to the north. The first thing to see on Virginia Key is the **Miami Seaquarium** ((305) 361-5705, at 400 Rickenbacker Causeway, home to a performing killer whale called Lolita as well as Flipper

oldest structure in south Florida, the 95-ft (30-m)-high **Cape Florida Lighthouse**. You can climb to the top of the lighthouse and enjoy the view over Biscayne Bay and the Atlantic beyond.

Back on the mainland, to the southwest of the downtown area on Bayshore Boulevard is the bayside community of Coconut Grove, a haven for hippies during the Sixties but now home to an altogether more sophisticated set who enjoy the exclusive shops, French-style cafés, and trendy nightlife. The main sights in the Grove

the porpoise, veteran of films and a television series. There are regular dolphin shows, a shark pool, sea lions, and thousands of other sea creatures in dozens of aquariums at the Seaquarium, which is open from 9:30 AM to 6:30 PM every day. Admission is $18.95 for adults and $13.95 for children under 13.

On Key Biscayne you can take a look at the outside of **President Nixon's Home** at 485 West Matheson Drive, which was Nixon's holiday retreat for a number of years. The house is not open to the public. On the southern tip of the Key at 1200 South Crandon Boulevard is the **Bill Baggs Cape Florida State Recreation Area**, which has nature trails and beaches in addition to the

include **Silver Bluff**, which is a fascinating rock formation dating back thousands of years; it is on Bay Boulevard between Crystal View and Emathia Streets. The **Barnacle State Historic Site** ((305) 448-9445, at 3485 Main Highway, is a tranquil five-acre (two-hectare) estate which has in its grounds one of the region's oldest houses, built in 1870, where you can see authentic period furniture and historical photographs.

A few miles further down the coast is Coral Gables which is known as the "Miami Riviera" because of its Mediterranean-style architecture and well-heeled inhabitants. For a good example of the architecture, visit the **Coral Gables House** at 907 Coral Way, a coral rock structure built at the turn of the century as a home for George Merrick, the founder of the community. **Venetian Pool** ((305) 442-6483, at 2701 DeSoto Boulevard, is a lagoon carved out of rock, with caves, stone bridges, and a sandy beach. It is a delightful place to laze away an afternoon, and admission is only $4 for adults and $2 for children under 13.

The **Fairchild Tropical Garden** ((305) 667-1651, at 10901 Old Cutler Road, is the nation's largest tropical botanical garden, and offers hourly train rides through its

ful white Bengal tigers, koala bears, and over 300 exotic birds in a free-flight aviary. The animals live in natural habitats separated from the public by moats. Admission is $6 for adults and $3 for children; opening hours are from 10 AM to 5:30 PM daily. Still more exotic birds — over 1,000 of them — can be seen at **Parrot Jungle** ((305) 666-7834, 11000 Southwest 57th Avenue, where the birds fly around a sub-tropical jungle. It is open daily from 9:30 AM to 5 PM; admission is $10.95 for adults and $7.95 for children under 14. Caged walkways cross

83 acres (33 hectares) of exotic flora. The plant house contains rare specimens and a miniature rain forest. Admission is $7 for adults and free for children under 13. It is open daily from 9:30 AM to 4:30 PM. At the **Lowe Art Museum** ((305) 284-3536, 1301 Stanford Drive, there are several El Greco paintings among a fine collection of Renaissance and Baroque art.

Continuing along down the coast from Coral Gables, you arrive at the area of Greater Miami known as South Dade County, which has some of the most popular tourist attractions in the region. The largest cageless zoo in the nation, **Metrozoo** ((305) 251-0400, at 12400 Southwest 152nd Street, features very rare and very beauti-

Monkey Jungle ((305) 235-1611, at 14805 Southwest 216th Street, a unique colony of apes and monkeys living semi-wild in a natural tropical habitat. There are also daily shows featuring performing chimps. This primate enclave can be visited daily from 9:30 AM to 5 PM, for $10.50 adults and $5.35 children aged five to 12.

The **Weeks Air Museum** ((305) 233-5197, at 14701 Southwest 128th Street, is a new and increasingly popular attraction, housing 35 immaculately restored and preserved civilian and military aircraft dating from the

OPPOSITE: Villa Vizcaya, John Deering's Italian Renaissance villa, and ABOVE its sculptured stone barge.

earliest days of aviation. There are also exhibits and photographs depicting aviation history. The museum is open from Wednesday to Sunday, 10 AM to 5 PM, and admission is $6.95 for adults and $4.95 for children under 13. Another interesting collection of vehicles can be seen at the **Gold Coast Railroad Museum** ((305) 253-7834, 12450 Southwest 152nd Street, which has historic trains on display and features a ride around the museum's grounds in a steam locomotive. Admission is $4 for adults with children under 12 free.

Sports

Football fans can watch the Miami Dolphins of the NFL play between September and January in Joe Robie Stadium at 2269 Northwest 199th Street, Greater Miami North. There are tours of the 75,000-seat stadium. Call ((305) 623-6183 for details and for ticket information dial ((305) 620-2578. The Miami Heat **basketball team** of the NBA plays from November to April at the Miami Arena ((305) 577-4328, 721 Northwest First Avenue, Miami. Miami's new professional minor-league **baseball**

A good way to see a lot of the city in a little time is to take a ride on the **Old Town Trolley Tours of Miami** ((305) 374-8687. These tours leave on a two-hour narrated trip every half-hour from 14 different places in the city. There are numerous cruise lines offering a wide variety of cruises out of the Port of Miami, the most popular being the half-day cruises, evening dinner cruises, and full-day cruises to Bimini and the Bahamas. The prices are very reasonable, ranging from $50+ for half-day cruises to $100+ for full-day cruises. **Sea Escape Cruises** ((305) 379-0000, 1080 Port Boulevard, Port of Miami, sail from Pier 6; **Tropicana/Sea Venture Cruises** ((305) 477-5858, Port of Miami, leave from Pier 12.

team is the Miami Miracle, who play at the FIU University Park Campus ((305) 220-7040, Sunblazer Arena, 11200 Southwest Eighth Street, on the Tamiami Trail east of Miami. The baseball season runs from April to early October.

Horse racing takes place in the lovely surroundings of Hialeah Park ((305) 885-8000, at 105 East 21st Street, Hialeah, which has a French Mediterranean-style clubhouse and grandstand. There is a Metrorail station in the grounds of the park. For horsepower of a mechanical nature, go to the Hialeah Speedway ((305) 821-6644, at 3300 Okeechobee Road, off US 27, in Hialeah. Weekly **stock car races** are held in the winter season. The Miami Sharks of the

American Soccer League ((305) 477-2050, play from August to November at 11201 Coral Way, off Southwest 24th Street, Miami. Jai alai enthusiasts can watch the sport played at the Miami Jai Alai Fronton ((305) 633-6400, 3500 Northwest 37th Avenue, Miami. There are 13 games each evening, and it is legal to place bets on the games. You can see many of the world's top **tennis players** in action at the Lipton International Players Championship, which is the fifth richest two-week tennis tournament in the world, offering prize money totaling $3.1 million. The tournament is held in March at the International Tennis Center ((305) 361-5252, 7300 Crandon Boulevard, Key Biscayne.

For those who want to play rather than watch sports, there are 34 public **golf courses** in the Greater Miami area, including the Fontainebleau Golf Course ((305) 221-5181, at 9603 Fontainebleau Boulevard in Miami; the Country Club of Miami ((305) 821-0111, at 6801 Northwest 186th Street in Miami; the Key Biscayne Golf Course ((305) 361-9129, at 6400 Crandon Boulevard on Key Biscayne; the Biltmore Golf Course ((305) 442-6485, at 1210 Anastasia Avenue in Coral Gables; and the Palmetto Golf Course at 9300 Southwest 152nd Avenue in South Dade County. **Tennis players** are also well catered for in the Miami area. There are 11 public tennis centers to choose from, including the Biltmore Tennis Center ((305) 442-6565, at 1210 Anastasia Avenue in Coral Gables, which has 10 hard courts, and the International Tennis Center ((305) 361-8633, at 7300 Crandon Boulevard, Key Biscayne, which has 17 hard courts.

More information on tennis facilities in and around Miami can be obtained from the Florida Tennis Association ((305) 757-8568, at 9620 Northeast Second Avenue, Miami Shores. Miami's recreation department ((305) 579-6916, can give you information on both tennis courts and golf courses.

There is, as you might expect, terrific **fishing** in the waters off Miami. To arrange a fishing trip, contact Ocean Type Fishing Charters ((305) 446-8445, 4035 Southwest 11th Street, Coral Gables; or Sandskipper ((305) 361-9740, 4000 Crandon Boulevard,

Key Biscayne. **Sailing boats** can be rented from Easy Sailing ((305) 858-4001, Dinner Key Marina, Coconut Grove, where you can also rent powerboats and SCUBA diving equipment. **Diving charters** (and lessons) which go to various offshore reefs can be arranged through Diver's Paradise ((305) 361-3483, 4000 Crandon Boulevard, Key Biscayne, which also rents equipment. **Windsurfing equipment** and jet skis are available from Windsurfing Place ((305) 361-1225, 3501 Rickenbacker Causeway, Key Biscayne.

Shopping

For the widest range of choices in North Miami go to the **Aventura Mall** at 19501 Biscayne Boulevard, which contains several department stores and 150 shops selling just about everything. Another impressive shopping plaza is the **Bayside Marketplace** downtown at 401 Biscayne Boulevard. It is an open-air complex with brick walkways lined with tropical trees and plants; its 100 shops specialize in women's fashions, jewelry, gifts, African and Oriental arts and crafts, and personalized souvenirs. In Little Havana you can find Cuban arts and crafts

OPPOSITE: Some inhabitants of Parrot Jungle greet a visitor. ABOVE: The Bayfront Park in downtown Miami.

shops along the colorful **Southwest Eighth Street** between Route 95 West and 35th Street. For more upmarket shopping go to the **Mayfair Shops plaza** at 2911 Grand Avenue in Coconut Grove, or to the **Miracle Mile** between Douglas Road and Lejeune Road in Coral Gables. While you're there, go to the **Miracle Center**, a futuristic shopping mall at 301 Coral Way.

Nightlife

There are many cultural events to illuminate the Miami night. For comprehensive

listings you should take a look at the Arts Section of the *Sunday Miami Herald* and the monthly *Miami's Guide to the Arts*. Most of the major events are staged at the **Gusman Center for the Performing Arts** ((305) 372-0925, at 174 East Flagler Street, Miami, which is home to the **Miami City Ballet** ((305) 532-7713, and the **Philharmonic Orchestra of Florida** ((305) 945-5180, the state's foremost symphony orchestra. The center also hosts the **Miami Film Festival** every February. Opera lovers should know that the **Greater Miami Opera** is the seventh largest in the country, and regularly attracts the likes of Pavarotti and Domingo. Performances are at the Dade County Auditorium ((305) 854-7890, 2901 West Flagler

Street, Miami. The Florida Shakespeare Festival and the Hispanic Theatre Festival both take place at the **Minorca Playhouse** ((305) 446-1116, 232 Minorca Avenue, Coral Gables.

The liveliest popular nightlife in the region happens in downtown Miami, Little Havana, and in Coconut Grove. One of the oldest watering holes in Miami, **Tobacco Road** ((305) 374-1198, in the city center, at 626 South Miami Avenue, features live blues bands. For the samba sounds and tropical drinks of Brazil, you should head for the **Jardin Brasilien** ((305) 374-4748, in the Bayside Marketplace at 401 Biscayne Boulevard.

All the action in Little Havana happens along Southwest Eighth Street. At Nº 971 is **La Tranquera** ((305) 856-9467, where you can listen to Latin jazz and and dance to marengue music. At Nº 2235, flamenco dancing accompanies the mariachi music in **Cacharrito's Place** ((305) 643-9626. At Nº 3604, Latin jazz greats perform throughout the night at the **Copacabana Supper Club** ((305) 443-3801.

In Coconut Grove, a particularly lively venue is **Biscayne Baby** ((305) 445-3751, at 3336 Virginia Street, which features a dining area straight out of the 1950s as well as a disco. The **Hungry Sailor** ((305) 444-9359, at 3064 ¹/₂ Grand Avenue, is an English-style pub serving English food, ales, and beers along with its jazz, reggae, and folk music. **Regine's** ((305) 858-9600, in the Grand Bay Hotel, 2669 South Bayshore Drive, attracts the same trendies to its disco/lounge as its counterparts in other cities.

WHERE TO STAY

Luxury

It's a short taxi ride from the airport to the **Doral Resort and Country Club** ((305) 592-2000 TOLL-FREE (800) 327-6334, at 4400 Northwest 87th Avenue, Miami, which is one of the largest golf resorts in the world with five championship courses in its 2,500-acre (1,000-hectare) grounds. There are also

ABOVE: Golf is played year round in Florida's temperate climate. OPPOSITE: Palms and ponds decorate this course.

15 tennis courts, and you can receive instruction from the resort's resident tennis pro, Fabio Vasconcellos. Other exceptional facilities include the four-story Doral Spa, complete with steam rooms, saunas, Turkish baths, and gyms, and the 24-stable Doral Equestrian Center, which offers riding lessons. If you are still stuck for something to do, the hotel provides a regular shuttle service to the beach. Near the Bayside Marketplace downtown is the **Hotel Inter-Continental Miami** ((305) 577-1000 TOLL-FREE (800) 327-3005, at 100 Chopin Plaza, a

34-story triangular building with 645 attractive rooms and suites, a theater, and a rooftop recreation area with tennis and racquetball courts, a swimming pool, gardens and a jogging trail. In the hotel's lobby it is hard to miss the 70-ton sculpture by Henry Moore.

Downtown luxury can also be found at the **Crowne Plaza Miami International Hotel** ((305) 374-0000, 1601 Biscayne Boulevard, which has over 500 ultra-modern rooms many of them with stunning views of the Miami skyline and Biscayne Bay and its own leisure complex with expensive boutiques, bars, and night clubs. Over on Key Biscayne at 350 Ocean Drive, is the **Sonesta Beach Resort** ((305) 361-2021 TOLL-FREE (800) 343-7170, a popular hotel with families because it has a comprehensive program of activities for children. All the rooms and suites have balconies overlooking the island or the Atlantic, and the 28 villas in the grounds are full efficiencies with private swimming pools.

Two of the best hotels in the area can be found in Coconut Grove. The glamorous and extremely non-budget **Mayfair House** ((305) 441-0000 TOLL-FREE (800) 433-4555, at 3000 Florida Avenue, has its own shopping mall with designer boutiques, nine gourmet restaurants, and a central atrium festooned with fountains and plants. The hotel's 181 suites have Japanese hot tubs or Jacuzzis, and the rooftop facilities include a swimming pool and a solarium. Newspapers come with breakfast, and complimentary caviar is served in the Tiffany Bar. The elegant **Grand Bay Hotel** ((305) 858-9600 TOLL-FREE (800) 327-2788, at 2669 South Bayshore Drive, has English and French suites with baby grand pianos, and in every room new arrivals are greeted by flowers and complimentary champagne. The service is splendid, and you can arrange golf, tennis, or sailing through a very helpful concierge. The hotel's Grand Café is one of the best restaurants in Miami.

In Coral Gables is the Moorish castle-like **Biltmore Hotel** ((305) 445-1926 TOLL-FREE (800) 727-1926, at 1200 Anastasia Drive. The hotel's grand rooms with antique furnishings and vaulted ceilings adorned with frescoes are matched outside by the beautiful grounds featuring a golf course, tennis courts, and an enormous swimming pool.

Mid-range

Moderately priced and near the airport, the **Hotel Sofitel Miami** ((305) 264-4888, at 5800 Blue Lagoon Drive, offers a sauna, tennis courts, continental breakfasts, and soundproof rooms. In North Miami, the **Inn on the Bay** ((305) 865-7100, at Nº 1819 79th Street Causeway, is a family-oriented hotel with small but immaculate rooms, only a few minutes away from the beach. The **Everglades Hotel** ((305) 379-5461, downtown at 244 Biscayne Boulevard, has very comfortable, very modern rooms, while the rooftop has a swimming pool and a bar. Also downtown near the Bayside shops is the **Biscayne Bay Marriott Hotel and Marina** ((305) 374-3900, at 1633 North Bayshore Drive, where the marina has boating, fishing, and windsurfing facilities; the other amenities include five restaurants, a games room, and free in-room movies.

The **Doubletree Hotel** ((305) 858-2500 TOLL-FREE (800) 222-8733, at 2649 South Bayshore Drive, is one of the few in Coconut Grove which caters to the not-quite-so-wealthy. And it does it very well, with two excellent restaurants, tennis courts, a sauna, water sports facilities, and its own shops. In Coral Gables the best not-quite-expensive hotel is the **Hotel Place St. Michel** ((305) 444-1666, at 162 Alcazar Avenue. Every room is tastefully appointed, including European antiques, and apart from the complimentary continental breakfasts the

WHERE TO EAT

Expensive

Il Tulipano ((305) 893-4811, at 11052 Biscayne Boulevard in North Miami, is the creation of Filippo Il Grande, whose veal dishes and shellfish (especially the clams) are a delight. The **Pavillion Grill** ((305) 372-4494, at the Hotel Inter-Continental, 100 Chopin Plaza, should offer a map with its menu: the specialties include Key West tuna, Carolina pheasant, Texan cactus,

hotel's French restaurant is of a very high quality, as is the service throughout the hotel.

Inexpensive

Most of the budget-priced hotels in Miami are located in and around the downtown area, including the **Sunnyside Motel** ((305) 266-1727, at 6024 Southwest Eighth Street. But your best compromises between price and comfort can be found along Biscayne Boulevard, which at Nº 340 has the **Best Western Marina Park Hotel** ((305) 372-2862; at Nº 3400 the **Mardi Gras Motel Apartments** ((305) 573-7700; at Nº 3530 the **Bay Point Motel** ((305) 573-4444; and at Nº 6330 the **Economy Inn** ((305) 633-6916.

Wyoming rabbit, and Hawaiian sweet onions. Another excellent hotel restaurant downtown is **Veronique's** ((305) 374-3900, at the Biscayne Bay Marriott, 1633 North Bayshore Drive, where you should definitely order the Cajun-style seafood.

Southwest Eighth Street in Little Havana has two (among many other) distinguished restaurants. At Nº 740 the **Malaga** ((305) 858-4224, features such Cuban specialties as *arroz con pollo* (chicken with rice), spicy fried veal and pork, white bean and sausage soup, and other delicious concoctions. Located at Nº 2499 **El Bodegon de Castilla**

The huge swimming pool ABOVE in the Moorish castle setting of the Biltmore Hotel in Coral Gables and OPPOSITE its interior.

Miami and Environs

((305) 649-0863, specializes in Spanish cooking — mostly Castillian, obviously, but also some Catalan.

In Coconut Grove I would strongly recommend the **Mayfair Grill** ((305) 441-0000, in the Mayfair House Hotel, 3000 Florida Avenue. The star attraction on the menu — I'm not — joking is the grilled buffalo. In Coral Gables, go to **Chez Maurice** ((305) 448-8984, at 382 Miracle Mile, where Maurice Cambin runs a very good French Provincial restaurant.

Moderate

There is a selection of fine Italian restaurants spread along Biscayne Boulevard in North Miami, and among the best of them is **La Lupa** ((305) 893-9531, at 11220 Biscayne Boulevard, which features both northern *and* southern Italian cuisine. For authentic Nicaraguan food, you should go to **La Parilla** ((305) 553-4419, at 9611 West Flagler Street in Little Managua, about 10 miles (16 km) west of downtown Miami. The restaurant has a fascinating fried pork with yucca and red snapper in Creole sauce. For Spanish food try **Las Tapas** ((305) 372-2737, at 401 Biscayne Boulevard downtown at the Bayside waterfront. The house specialty is of course *tapas*, which can easily and infinitely be expanded into a wonderful main course.

For Cuban food I would single out **Centro Vasco** ((305) 643-9606, at 2235 Southwest Eighth Street, if only for their delicious stuffed squid in black bean sauce.

On Key Biscayne, I like **La Choza** ((305) 361-0113, an Argentinian steak house at 973 Crandon Boulevard. In Coconut Grove, I'm partial to **Señor Frog's** ((305) 448-0999, at 3008 Grand Avenue, which serves some of the best Mexican food in the Miami area. Also, if you order prudently, you can eat more or less economically at the splendid **Grand Café** ((305) 858-9600, in the Grand Bay Hotel, 2669 South Bayshore Drive in Coconut Grove. In Coral Gables, devotees of Thai food (and I'm certainly one) will be grateful for the presence of **Bangkok, Bankok** ((305) 444-2397, at 157 Giralda

Avenue, just as fans of Indian food (I'm one of those, too) sing the praises of the **House of India** ((305) 444-2348, at 22 Merrick Way in Coral Gables.

Inexpensive

In North Miami, **Nick and Maria's** ((305) 891-9232, at 11701 Northeast Second Avenue, is casual, welcoming, and serves some marvelous Greek dishes. If you are particularly health-conscious, the place to go to in downtown Miami is **Granny Feelgood's** ((305) 358-6233, at 190 Southeast First Avenue, where you can expect some wonderful salads, *inter alia*. At the other end of the spectrum — *fry! fry!* — is **The Big Fish** ((305) 372-3725, at 55 Southwest Miami Avenue Road. But for inexpensive, genuinely tasty meals, your best bet is simply to walk up and down Southwest Eighth Street in Little Havana: you will be amazed (and tantalized) by the number and range of budget-priced eateries.

On Key Biscayne, **The English Pub** ((305) 361-5481, at 320 Crandon Boulevard, is deservedly popular, mixing basic English and American cooking. In Coconut Grove, **Monty Trainer's Bayshore** ((305) 858-1431, at 2560 South Bayshore Drive, is a big local favorite, with its outdoor raw bar overlooking a marina, and its reggae and calypso bands at the weekend. In Coral Gables, you will find a very reasonably priced meal to your liking if you simply walk along Coral Way: it is crowded with many cheap and cheerful places to eat.

HOW TO GET THERE

More than 80 national and international airlines fly into Miami International Airport, which is only six miles (9.5 km) west of downtown. Numerous taxi and limousine companies serve the airport. A taxi takes about 20 minutes to reach the middle of Miami, and charges about $16. There is also a Metrobus station at the airport, which operates a shuttle downtown much more cheaply.

If you are traveling from the north by car you will have several options: I-95 and Route 1 come directly down the coast, and I-75 (Florida's Turnpike) comes through

OPPOSITE: Automotive and architectural reminders of the past in Miami Beach's Art Deco district.

central Florida and Orlando on its way to
the southeast. Route A1A, ocean-skirting
and island-hopping, is a slower and more
scenic way to approach Miami from the
north. From the west you will take Route
84, Everglades Parkway, also known as
"Alligator Alley".

MIAMI BEACH

Miami Beach is a narrow strip of land a little
over seven miles (11 km) long and only a
mile (1.6 km) wide at its widest point. It is
separated from mainland Miami by Biscayne Bay, and connected to it by three
causeways. It probably has more hotels than
any other comparable patch of land in the
world, and in a few blocks at the southern
end of the island it has the largest concentration of Art Deco buildings in America.
And then there is the beach itself, running
along the entire eastern side of the island.
Not only that, but it is getting bigger all the
time: at this writing there is a dredging
operation pumping offshore sand on to the
island to create a strip of beach over 300 ft
(91 m) wide at some points.

BACKGROUND

In 1912 Miami Beach was an offshore mangrove and palmetto swamp inhabited
mostly by crocodiles. The only inhabitant
of note was a horticulturist named John S.
Collins who had bought some land there
and established an avocado and citrus
plantation. He founded the Miami Beach
Improvement Company in 1912, initiated
some land sales on the island and began
the construction of a bridge to the mainland.

Collins ran out of money the following
year, and the unfinished bridge became
known as "Collins' Folly". Undaunted,
Collins set up a partnership with Carl
Fisher, who, in exchange for large areas of
land on the island, injected much-needed
capital into the company, enabling the
bridge to be completed and further devel-

opment to be launched. Fisher set about
clearing the swamps from his land and
creating new acreage by draining the shallow bays. What slowly emerged was a
tropical island with a wide swath of beach,
which Fisher and Collins immediately
recognized as a potential resort. They
spurred the development of the island into
the Twenties, building shopping plazas,
hotels, golf courses, and tennis courts.

Elderly people came here to retire, while
vacationers began to arrive in their thousands. Then, in the Thirties, after the worst
of the Depression was over, a new building
boom began at the southern end of the
island. Pastel, geometric, streamlined buildings started to appear: Art Deco had arrived
with a vengeance. Today over 100 Art Deco

Seven miles (11 km) of beach, the winter sun and a
lot of enterprise transformed a former mangrove
and palmetto swamp into Miami Beach, one of
America's leading resorts.

houses and hotels are to be seen in what is one of the most architecturally striking pockets in the country. Since the 1930s Miami Beach's story has been one of steady growth and development into one of the leading resorts in America, as hordes of tourists swarm in to enjoy the beaches and the winter sun. At the same time, more and more northerners are choosing to retire there, while from the south Latin Americans continue to arrive and to do their part to invigorate the island's growth.

GENERAL INFORMATION

The Miami Beach Chamber of Commerce ((305) 672-1270, is at 1920 Meridian Avenue, Miami Beach. For 24-hour information on hotels, car rentals, cruises, and the island's principal attractions, contact the Miami Beach Resort Hotel Association ((305) 531-3553, at 407 Lincoln Road, Suite 10G, Miami Beach.

WHAT TO SEE AND DO

Sights
Undoubtedly the main attraction in Miami Beach is the **Art Deco district**, which is a block north of Sixth Street between Lummus Park and the beach at the southern tip of the island. Each of the curved, multicolored buildings has its own unique character. If you would like to learn more about them you should get in touch with the Miami Design Preservation League ((305) 672-2014,

which organizes walking tours of the district. Three of the largest and most impressive Art Deco hotels in Miami Beach are found on **Collins Avenue**, which is more or less the spine of the island: they are the Delano, the National, and the Ritz Plaza, which resemble, respectively, a spaceship, a balloon, and a submarine. The most impressive hotel, however, is the majestic **Fontainebleau Hilton**, which is set among tropical vegetation, lagoons, and waterfalls, and has a expansive, wonderful mural on one of its exterior walls.

The only art museum of note on the island is the **Bass Museum of Art** ((305) 673-7533, at 2121 Park Avenue, which has Renaissance, Baroque, Rococo, and modern works in its collection, including especially interesting works by Rubens and Toulouse-Lautrec. The museum is open from 10 AM to 5 PM Tuesday to Saturday and from 1 PM to 5 PM on Sunday; admission is $5 for adults and $3 for children. The **Miami Beach Garden Center and Conservatory** at 2000 Garden Center Drive, is a place of great natural charm and beauty in which you can relax for no charge, seven days a week from 10 AM to 3:30 PM, or you can stroll along the **boardwalk** which runs beside the beach from 21st Street to 46th Street.

Different parts of the beach seem to have developed distinct personalities. The beach around **21st Street**, for example, has been colonized by young people and couples with small children; the beach at **35th Street** attracts a quieter, older group, and many of its beachfront hotel bars are open to the public; around **46th Street** you get the Very Important Tourists from the Fontainebleau and other top hotels; while up at **53rd Street** and **64th Street** you will find probably the quietest beaches on the island.

Sports

There are several public golf courses in Miami Beach: Normandy Shores ((305) 673-7775, at 2401 Biarritz Drive, the Bayshore Golf Course ((305) 673-7706, at 2301 Alton Road, and the Haulover Beach Golf Course ((305) 940-6719, at 10800 Collins Avenue in the northern part of the island. **Tennis players** should go to Flamingo Park ((305) 673-7761, at Michigan Avenue and 12th Street, where there are 17 public courts open from 9 AM to 9 PM; there are also public courts at North Shore Park ((305) 673-7754, Nº 350 73rd Street. The Miami Beach Recreation Department ((305) 673-7700, can give you further information on golf and tennis facilities.

If you are keen on **deep-sea fishing**, all sorts of cruises, from a few hours to a few days, can be chartered from the Kelly Fishing Fleet ((305) 945-0944, at 10800 Collins Avenue. For **scuba diving** enthusiasts, equipment rental, instruction, and chartered excursions are all available from Aquanauts ((305) 534-7710, at 677 Southwest First Street. If **boating** appeals to you, you can hire a boat from Beach Boat Rentals ((305) 534-4307, at 2380 Collins Avenue, from where you can cruise Biscayne Bay and the adjoining canals; yachts can be hired from Florida Yacht Charters and Sales ((305) 532-8600, at 1290 Fifth Street. The best place for **surfing** is at Haulover Beach at the north end of the island, but you shouldn't expect a major surfing experience as the area is not famed for its waves.

ABOVE AND OPPOSITE: Art Deco buildings in Miami Beach.

Shopping

There is no shortage of shops selling beach paraphernalia in Miami Beach. **Chocolate**, 119 Fifth Street, and **Tommy at the Beach**, 450 Ocean Drive, are as well-stocked as any of them. The best selections of more "serious" shops are in the **Bal Harbour Shops** at 9700 Collins Avenue. For antiques, arts and crafts, galleries and that sort of thing you should go to either **Española Way** or to the **Lincoln Road Mall** on Lincoln Road between Collins Avenue and Michigan Avenue.

Nightlife

Most of the after-dark action in Miami Beach takes place in the Art Deco district. New Wave music pounds through the night at **Joseph's on the Beach** ((305) 673-9626, 323 23rd Street, while at **Penrod's** ((305) 538-1111, One Ocean Drive, you can choose from various dance floors offering reggae, jazz, and rock music. For mellower sounds try the sidewalk café **The Tropics International** ((305) 531-5335, 960 Ocean Drive, which features live jazz on some nights. At the **Irish House Bar** ((305) 672-9626, 1430 Alton Road, a place full of character as well as characters, the odd song is played on the elderly juke box but the patrons mainly shoot pool and drink beer.

The bistro décor and the solo guitarist combine to give the **Café des Arts** ((305) 534-6267, at 918 Ocean Drive a whiff of Parisian nightlife. Another attractive, quasi-bohemian night spot is the **Wet Paint Café** ((305) 672-3287, at 915 Lincoln Road Mall, where the nicely decorated cellar reverberates with the sounds of live jazz and Caribbean music. Reggae features heavily at the **Club Bamboo** ((305) 538-5803, in the Eden Roc Hotel at 4525 Collins Avenue, while music from the Fifties tops the bill at **Chevy's on the Beach** ((305) 868-1950, 8701 Collins Avenue.

WHERE TO STAY

Luxury

There are 18 acres (seven hectares) of beautifully landscaped grounds surrounding the famous **Fontainebleau Hilton** ((305) 538-2000, at 4441 Collins Avenue, which also has 300 ft (91 m) of its own beachfront, seven hard-packed tennis courts, several swimming pools and waterfalls, and a giant spa with mineral baths, saunas, and Jacuzzis, not to mention 1,200 splendidly appointed rooms. There are also specially supervised programs and activities for children. At the **Doral Ocean Beach Resort** ((305) 532-3600, 4883 Collins Avenue, guests are welcomed with complimentary chocolates and a fruit basket in their rooms. The Doral's many amenities include the Aqua Sports Center offering water- and jet-skiing, snorkeling and scuba diving instruction, windsurfing, and sailing.

The luxury suites at the **Alexander Hotel** ((305) 865-6500, 5225 Collins Avenue, are elegantly (and antiquely) furnished, and each one has a private balcony overlooking the ocean and the hotel's 600 ft (183 m) of beach. Then there is the quirky and delightful old **Eden Roc** ((305) 531-0000, at 4525 Collins Avenue, with its 1950s furnishings, its New York deli with Israeli music, and its marvelous ocean-view restaurant. My favorite, though, is the **Hotel Cavalier** ((305) 531-6424 TOLL-FREE (800) 338-9076, in the Art Deco district at 1320 Ocean Drive. From the moment its limousine picks you up at the airport, it provides a joyful experience.

Mid-range

Although most of the hotels in the Art Deco district are as highly priced as they are highly desirable, there are some notable exceptions. One is the **Park Central Hotel** ((305) 538-1611, at 640 Ocean Drive, which has a ceiling fan in each room, and an excellent, uncomplicated restaurant, Lucky's. There is also the **Edison Hotel** ((305) 531-0461, at 960 Ocean Drive, where the rooms are modern and immaculate.

Moving away from the Art Deco district, you'll find the **Hawaiian Isle** ((305) 932-2121 TOLL-FREE (800) 327-5275, at 17601 Collins Avenue, which has lots of bamboo and tropical plants, as well as volleyball, tennis, and basketball courts, water sports facilities, and 400 ft (122 m) of beachfront. **Chateau by the Sea** ((305) 931-8800, at 19115 Collins Avenue, has, incongruously, a down-south country flavor to it. It also has a large swimming pool and its own shops. Even more incongruously, you will find a covered wagon and horses at 17201 Collins Avenue, which means you have arrived at the **Desert Inn** ((305) 947-0621 TOLL-FREE (800) 327-6362, a Wild West theme resort with a swimming pool and outside dining areas.

Inexpensive

The friendly, family-run **Beachcomber Hotel,** ((305) 531-3755, located at 1340 Collins Avenue, offers clean and comfortable accomodation in the Art Deco district. I would also recommend the **Beach Motel** ((305) 861-2001, at 8601 Harding Avenue, which has both rooms and efficiencies, in addition to the obligatory swimming pool, and the **Ocean Roc** ((305) 931-7600, at 19505 Collins Avenue, which has lovely, airy rooms with balconies, and a nice bar with its restaurant.

WHERE TO EAT

Expensive

If you are going to spend a lot of money for your dinner, you might as well do so at **Café Chauveron** ((305) 866-8779, 9561 East Bay Harbor Drive, where chef Roger Chauveron and his staff provide French cuisine and service of the highest standard. Another outstanding French restaurant is **Dominique's** ((305) 865-6500, located inside the Alexander Hotel at 5225 Collins Avenue, where chef Dominique D'Ermo specializes in nouvelle cuisine enlivened by the occasional American eccentricity such as wild boar sausage or sautéed alligator tail. **The Forge** ((305) 538-8533, at 432 Arthur Godfrey Road, having undergone a $2 million face-lift, now has a decor — chandeliers and stained glass and antiques — to match its rich menu and even richer wine list.

Two Art Deco restaurants well worth a visit are the **Carlyle Grill** ((305) 534-2135, at 1250 Ocean Drive, which features Americanized nouvelle cuisine, and **Joe's Stone Crab** ((305) 673-0365, at 227 Biscayne Street, where their specialty should be obvious (although for me the *real* specialty is their Key lime pie).

Moderate

There are two Italian restaurants in the Art Deco district well worth a visit: **Tiramesu** ((305) 532-4538, located at 500 Ocean Drive, and **Gino's Italian Restaurant** ((305) 532-6426, at 1906 Ocean Drive.

For excellent Chinese food go to **Christine Lee's Gaslight** ((305) 931-7700, at the Thunderbird Hotel, 18401 Collins Avenue. For cooking that can best be described as continental-Californian, with an ambiance and clientele to match, check out **The Strand** ((305) 532-2340, at 671 Washington Avenue. For eclecticism run riot, but deliciously so, try **Pineapples** ((305) 532-9731, at 530 Arthur Godfrey Road, where your grilled ginger dolphin (mahi mahi) could be preceded by a Chinese egg roll and accompanied by an Italian salad with Greek cheese.

Inexpensive

If you have finished a hard day's tanning on the beach near the Art Deco district, you can eat well and cheaply at **The Palace** ((305) 531-9077, 1200 Ocean Drive. It is anything but palatial, being a 1950s-style diner, but it *is* a treat. The **News Café** at 800 Ocean Drive is a bit more sophisticated, or at least tries to be, but is an equally good value. If you are feeling a bit piggish, but want quality with your quantity, probably the best place in town is **Wolfie Cohen's Rascal House** ((305) 947-4581, at 17190 Collins Avenue. Another good place for budget grub is **Pumperniks** ((305) 891-1225, at 12599 Biscayne Boulevard.

HOW TO GET THERE

First you have to get to Miami: see earlier section. Then from the mainland take the Broad Causeway to the Bay Harbour Islands and over to Bal Harbour, the John F. Kennedy Causeway to northern Miami Beach, the Julia Tuttle Causeway to central Miami Beach, and the MacArthur Causeway to southern Miami Beach.

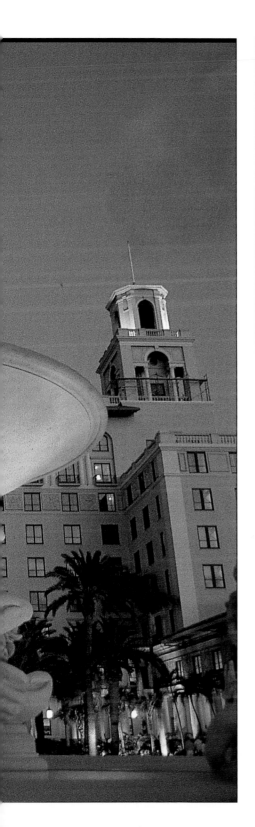

The Gold Coast

DRIVING along the 60-mile (97-km) stretch of coastline known as the "Gold Coast", where glittering resorts confront the ocean across golden sandy beaches, it is hard to believe that less than a century ago this was mosquito-infested swampland.

Indeed, the only mark left on the Gold Coast by earlier centuries is the name itself. It derives from the most lucrative business enterprise to occupy the inhabitants of this area in the nineteenth century: salvaging gold from the frequent shipwrecks offered up by Mother Nature on the rocks offshore. These salvage operations, known as "wrecking," proved to be so profitable that the wreckers are said to have taken not just to praying for shipwrecks but to praying for particular *kinds* of shipwrecks according to the demands of the market at any given time. And when Mother Nature failed to oblige, they were even known to indulge in a little do-it-yourself shipwreck-making, by luring passing vessels onto the rocks.

Wrecking largely died out towards the end of the century, with the advent of more sophisticated maritime navigational equipment and the arrival of Henry Flagler's Florida East Coast Railroad. Now it became the turn of the land to supply the riches. Flagler himself started the new gold rush in 1894 by erecting the enormous Royal Poinciana Hotel in Palm Beach, to which he enticed some of the richest families in America. The hotel, since demolished, had 1,150 rooms and a staff of 1,400. Two years later he built The Breakers in Palm Beach, which twice burned down but which now, in its third incarnation, stands as one of the most famous hotels in the world. That same year, 1896, Flagler extended his railway to Fort Lauderdale, and in 1902 built himself his own 55-room marble mansion in Palm Beach. Thus, by the turn of the century, the ground had been prepared for this once-inhospitable bit of coast to become one of the most popular and celebrated resort areas in the world.

Among the first to see the possibilities here was the flamboyant architect Addison Mizner, who arrived a few years later and decided that what the place needed was a lot of pastel stucco buildings designed by him. Whether it needed them or not, it got them as well as many more by other architects trying to imitate his style. That style has been variously described as "Italianate," "Pseudo-Spanish," "Mediterranean Revival," "Spanish-Moorish" and, my favorite, "Bastard Spanish-Moorish-Romanesque-Gothic-Renaissance Bull-Market Damn-the-Expense" style. Mizner's *chef d'œuvre* was the Cloister Inn in Boca Raton, now the Boca Raton Hotel and Club, a wonderful pink confection that remains one of the most expensive hotels ever built. To this palace Mizner lured as many of the rich and famous as he could attract, and they in turn attracted the multitudes. As Mizner had predicted, "Get the big snobs, and the little ones will follow."

Meanwhile, to the south, in Fort Lauderdale another visionary was doing his part to add luster to the Gold Coast. Charles Rodes, a property developer from West Virginia, suddenly came up with the "Venetian Solution" to the problem of what to do with all that swampland: he began dredging a series of finger canals that converted sodden, useless land into prime waterfront real estate. As a result, today the *soi-disant* "Venice of America" has almost 200 miles (322 km) of inland waterways to go along with its seven miles (11 km) of beautiful beach.

By the 1920s the allure of the Gold Coast had set off a feeding frenzy among property speculators, developers, investors, builders, prospective retirees, and would-be winter migrants from the north. There followed a land boom of incredible proportions, at the height of which over 2,000 people a day were arriving to stake their claim to a little bit of paradise. For most of them, however, that paradise was lost in 1926 when the boom abruptly collapsed.

For the next two decades, through the years of the Depression and the Second World War, some of the shine went off the Gold Coast (though none of the sunshine: there are 3,000 hours of it every year, with an average annual temperature of 75°F, or 24°C). Then paradise was regained after the war, and for the second half of this century it has been an irresistible magnet for countless millions of pleasure-seekers.

The Atlantic horizon, in a latticework frame.

FORT LAUDERDALE

Although sunny by disposition as well as by climate, Fort Lauderdale has long had an image problem. For decades it had to put up with being called Fort Liquordale, a sobriquet it earned during Prohibition when its bars and night clubs were awash in illicit alcohol smuggled in from the Bahamas. Then, in 1960, the old image was given a new twist in the film *Where the Boys Are*, which depicted the place as America's party headquarters for college students on their spring break. Although the new image had only a fractional basis in reality, the film succeeded in creating the phenomenon it was ostensibly portraying, so that for many years afterwards Fort Lauderdale was visited annually by migratory swarms of fun-seeking collegians. Now, to the manifest relief of the natives, most of the Eastertime action seems to have shifted north to Daytona Beach.

BACKGROUND

Fort Lauderdale's early history has vanished as completely as the fort which Major William Lauderdale built near the mouth of the New River in 1838 to protect settlers from attack by the Seminoles. What *is* known is that the first settler, Charles Lewis, arrived in 1793 and established a plantation by the New River. Exactly 100 years later another settler, Frank Stranahan, arrived and established a trading post for doing business with the Indians, as well as a general store and a ferry system. When he married a few years later, Stranahan converted the general store into a residence, which has since been restored and is open to visitors.

Although the arrival of Flagler's railway in 1896 opened up the area to accelerated settlement, there were still fewer than 200 residents when Fort Lauderdale was incorporated in 1911. It was not until the land boom of the Twenties that the city's spectacular growth began in earnest. Today, with upwards of 30,000 pleasure craft

A Fort Lauderdale welcome for yachts on the Round-the-World race.

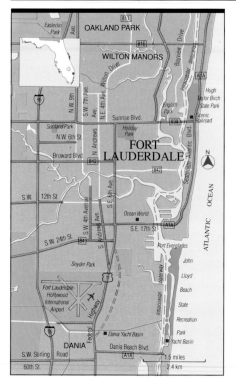

roaming its rivers and canals, and untold thousands of bodies from all over the world glistening on its beaches, the ghosts of Henry Flagler and Charles Rodes must be blinking in wonder.

GENERAL INFORMATION

The Greater Fort Lauderdale Convention and Visitors Bureau ((305) 765-4466, is located at 200 East Las Olas Boulevard, Suite 1500, Fort Lauderdale, FL 33301. The Greater Fort Lauderdale Chamber of Commerce ((305) 462-6000, is at 512 Northeast Third Avenue, Fort Lauderdale, FL 33301. The Broward County Hotel/Motel Association ((305) 462-0409, is at 701 Central East Broward Boulevard, Fort Lauderdale, FL 33301. The association is represented in Europe by Sastel International Ltd. ((0171) 630-5995, 18 Buckingham Palace Road, London SW1 0PQ.

For up-to-the-minute information on local events and attractions, check the listings in the *Fort Lauderdale News/Sun Sentinel*

OPPOSITE: Wearing big smiles: a bikini contest in Fort Lauderdale.

or in the free magazines, *See*, *Key*, and *Where*. For recorded information you can dial (305) 765-8068. The Broward Parks and Recreation Division also has a special-events number: ((305) 563-PARK.

Other useful telephone numbers (all in area code 305):

Fort Lauderdale/Hollywood International Airport	357-6100
Yellow Cabs	527-8600
Checker Cabs	485-3000
Broward County Medical Association	525-1595
Broward County Dental Association	772-5461
Physician Information Service	966-DOCS
24-Hour Doctors' House Calls	748-5900

WHAT TO SEE AND DO

Sights

It is not often that the most entertaining means of seeing the sights are themselves major tourist attractions, but this happens to be the case in Fort Lauderdale, where two large paddlewheel riverboats, the *Jungle Queen* and the *Paddlewheel Queen*, cruise the waters in and around the city.

The 550-passenger *Jungle Queen* ((305) 462-5596, has two three-hour cruises daily, at 10 AM and 2 PM, leaving from the Bahia Mar Yachting Center, 801 Seabreeze Boulevard. The cruise includes a stop at Indian Village where the sights include rare birds, monkeys, and alligator wrestling. In the evening there is a four-hour dinner cruise, which leaves Bahia Mar at 7 PM and features a vaudeville revue and other entertainment. The dinner, served on an exotic island in the New River, is an all-you-can-eat affair of barbecued ribs, chicken, and shrimp. Prices for the daytime cruises are $12.95 for adults and $7 for children; for the evening cruise $22.95 for everybody.

For sightseeing on your own by water there is available for rent just about every type of boat imaginable, though I'm partial to the **motorized gondolas** myself. They can seat up to six people, can be hired for any length of time you want, and are available from Gondolas of America, Inc. ((305) 522-3333, Bahia Mar Yachting Center, South Docks, 1007 Seabreeze Boulevard.

The best way to see Fort Lauderdale by land is on **Lolly the Trolley** ((305) 768-0700, a string of canopied, rubber-wheeled cars pulled by a little white Jeep. There are 90-minute conducted tours daily at 9:45 AM, 11:45 AM, and 1:45 PM, leaving from 419 South Atlantic Boulevard, and costing $10 for adults and $5 for children.

Among the sights particularly worth seeing I would put the **Museum of Discovery & Science** ((305) 467-6637, 401 Southwest Second Avenue, at the top of the list. It is a science and nature museum with hands-on exhibits that allow you to watch bees at work in a glass-fronted hive, go cave crawling, bend rays of light, and touch a star, among other things. Children love it. There is also an IMAX cinema with a 55-ft by 75-ft (17-m by 23-m) screen. Combination tickets for the museum and cinema are $8.50 for adults and $7.50 for children.

Also well worth a visit is the city's new multimillion-dollar **Museum of Art** ((305) 763-6464, at One East Las Olas Boulevard. It has an extraordinary collection of ethnographic art, including pre-Columbian, West African, Oceanic, and American Indian art; its Dutch and Flemish collections are quite strong as well. The museum stays open late on Tuesdays, and is closed on Sunday mornings and Mondays. Admission: adults $4, students $2.

The **Stranahan House** ((305) 524-4736, Fort Lauderdale's oldest remaining structure, is where Frank Stranahan traded with the Indians and sold to the settlers at the turn of the century before he converted it into a home. It has been lovingly and immaculately restored to its pre-World War I condition, and is open to the public on Wednesdays, Fridays and Saturdays from 10 AM to 3:30 PM, and on Sundays from 1 to 3:30 PM. The house is just off Las Olas Boulevard at the New River tunnel. Admission is $3 for adults and $2 for children.

To get an idea (but only an idea) of how some of the Indians lived with whom Stranahan did business, go to the **Seminole Okalee Indian Village** at the corner of Stirling Road and Route 7. The Indians support themselves by making and selling arts and crafts and believe it or not running bingo games.

For a close-up look at some of the native fauna, **Ocean World** ((305) 525-6611, at 1701 Southeast 17th Street, has continuous shows featuring trained dolphins and sea lions, plus a three-story-high aquarium for viewing all kinds of marine life. Tickets are $10.95 for adults and $8.95 for children. **Butterfly World** ((305) 977-4434, in Tradewinds Park, 3600 West Sample Road, is home to over 150 species of butterflies and features a screened-in tropical rain forest where thousands of exotic airborne flowers flutter by. Admission is $9.95 for adults and $6 for children. **Flamingo Gardens** ((305) 473-2955, at 3750 Flamingo Road, features a tram ride through its jungle, crocodiles, alligators, monkeys, tropical birds, a petting zoo and, of course, the obligatory pink flamingos. Admission is $8 for adults, $4.50 for young people under 18. Improbable as it may seem, Fort Lauderdale is one of the better places to see and experience the Wild West as it really (more or less) was. The suburban community of Davie has transformed itself into an authentic cowtown, complete with cowboys and cowgirls and, every Friday night, a rodeo in the **Davie Pro Rodeo Complex** ((305) 434-7062, at Orange Drive and Davie Road.

Sports

If you are a **baseball fan**, you should know that the New York Yankees hold their spring training here in February–March, during which they play exhibition games at Lockhart Stadium ((305) 776-1921, 5301 Northwest 12th Avenue. If you like more fast-paced action, combined with legal betting, you can see **jai alai**, at Dania Jai Alai ((305) 949-2424, 301 East Dania Boulevard, from late June until mid-April.

Golf enthusiasts will be very pleased to learn that there are no less than five dozen (yes, *dozen*) golf courses in the Fort Lauderdale area. There are 11 public courses within the city limits of Fort Lauderdale alone, not to mention the many private courses that welcome non-members. Among the most attractive and challenging courses are the American Golfers Club ((305) 564-8760, not far from the beach at 3850 North Route 1, the Bonaventure course ((305) 384-5020, located at 200 Bonaventure Boulevard, and the Deer Creek Golf and Tennis Club ((305) 421-5550, located at 2801 Deer Creek Country Club Boulevard, Deerfield Beach.

Tennis players are equally well catered to, with over 170 public tennis courts, including the lighted ones at George English Park ((305) 566-0664, 1101 Bayview Drive, and Holiday Park ((305) 761-5391, at 1400 East Sunrise Boulevard.

For comprehensive information about the availability of both golf courses and tennis courts, contact the Fort Lauderdale

Shopping

For maximum choice you should head for the **Galleria**, a huge shopping mall over one million sq ft (305,000 sq m) at 2500 East Sunrise Boulevard, a few blocks from the ocean. It has over 150 shops and restaurants, in addition to such department stores as Neiman-Marcus, Lord & Taylor, Dillards, Saks Fifth Avenue, and Brooks Brothers.

For maximum chic, palm-lined **Las Olas Boulevard** boasts an infinite variety of handsome (and occasionally offbeat) boutiques. For maximum craftsy shopping you

Parks and Recreation Department ((305) 761-2621.

Scuba diving and snorkeling can be enjoyed at more than 80 different dive sites along the bit of coast stretching about 12 miles (19 km) in each direction north and south of Fort Lauderdale. These include coral reefs, sunken wrecks, and ships that were deliberately scuttled to create artificial reefs. Of the many stores offering classes in diving and daily diving trips, as well as scuba and snorkeling equipment, are Force E ((305) 735-6227, at 2104 West Oakland Park Boulevard; Lauderdale Diver ((305) 467-2822, at 1334 Southeast 17th Street; and Pro Dive ((305) 761-3413, at the Bahia Mar Yachting Center.

should try the **Seminole Okalee Indian Village** at 5791 South Route 7. Here you will find the Anhinga Indian Museum and Art Gallery ((305) 581-8411; the Thunderbird Trading Post ((305) 585-2281; and the Flying Bird Gift Shop ((305) 792-3445.

Nightlife

The "in" place these days, or in any case, when I was last there is **Shooter's** ((305) 566-2855, at 3031 Northeast 32nd Avenue. What makes it "in" is not only that it is very attractive both inside and outside (where it sits beside the Intracoastal Waterway) but that, if you can't get in, it is also in between

Seaside promenade at sunset.

The Gold Coast

two other popular night spots, the **Bootlegger** ((305) 563-4337, which has its own swimming pool, and **Durty Nelly's** ((305) 564-0720.

Jazz fans won't want to miss the **Musician Exchange Café** ((305) 764-1912, at 200 South Andrews Avenue, which usually features regional performers during the week and more famous musicians at the weekend. If you like country-western, **Do-Da's** ((305) 791-1477, at 700 South Route 7, has four different theme rooms with dance floors, a Mexican restaurant, and a corral bar. The well-known bands play at the weekend.

If you want a good laugh, **The Comic Strip** ((305) 565-8887, at 1432 North Route 1, is a great place to catch comedians that haven't yet made it in addition to those that have. Note: Sunday and Monday nights are amateur nights. Further up the road is **Casey's Comedy Club** ((305) 491-4423, 6000 North Route 1, which often features well-known American comedians.

Those who would prefer to be entertained by the sights rather than the sounds of the night should go up to the **Pier Top Lounge** ((305) 525-6666, which rotates above the 17-story Pier 66 Resort and Marina at 2301 Southeast 17th Street. Although there is live music and a small dance floor, the main attractions here are views of the ocean and the sunsets. For sea-level imagery drop in at **Shirttail Charlie's** ((305) 463-3474, 400 Southwest Third Avenue, and watch the boats go by on the New River. The food is delicious.

WHERE TO STAY

Luxury

What do you say about a hotel with 1,100 ft (335 m) of beach frontage, 8,000 sq ft (2,438 sq m) of free-form swimming pool (with waterfall), five restaurants and five tennis courts, three boutiques and three lounges, and you-name-it? You say it is **Marriott's Harbor Beach Resort** and it is located at 3030 Holiday Drive and its telephone number is ((305) 525-4000 TOLL-FREE (800) 228-9290. The **Bahia Mar Resort and Yachting Center** ((305) 764-2233 TOLL-FREE (800) 327-8154, at 801 Seabreeze Boulevard, can also

boast some impressive statistics: a 40-acre (16-hectare) yacht basin, a 350-slip marina, a small fleet of charter fishing boats, but only (sigh) four tennis courts. The **Hyatt Regency Pier 66 Hotel and Marina** ((305) 525-6666 TOLL-FREE (800) 327-3796, at 2301 Southeast 17th Street, was Fort Lauderdale's first luxury high-rise hotel, and is still one of its finest, with a 142-slip marina and facilities for water sports rivaled only by Bahia Mar. Away from the beach — indeed, away from it all — is the **Bonaventure Resort and Spa** ((305) 389-3300 TOLL-FREE (800) 327-8090, 17 miles (27 km) west of Fort Lauderdale at 250 Racquet Club Road. Set in 1,250 acres (506 hectares), it has four restaurants, five swimming pools, 24 tennis courts, two 18-hole golf courses, a 160-seat amphitheater, a bowling alley, a roller-skating rink, riding stables, and a massive spa. Perhaps the most charming hotel in Fort Lauderdale — and certainly the one with the most charming and solicitous staff — is the **Riverside Hotel** ((305) 467-0671 TOLL-FREE (800) 325-3280, at 620 East Las Olas Boulevard. More Southern Comfortable than nouveau ritzy, it is in the heart of the city's most fashionable shopping area, with a swimming pool and gardens in the back beside the picturesque New River.

Mid-range

Some might argue that the **Lago Mar Hotel** ((305) 523-6511, located at 1700 Southeast Ocean Boulevard, belongs in the expensive category, above, but for what you get it is definitely not expensive. And what you get, most of all, is the peace and quiet that comes from being on the exclusive south end of the beach, far from the madding crowds. The hotel has a lagoon on one side and the Atlantic on the other, with two swimming pools, four tennis courts, and a putting green in between.

Just south of Fort Lauderdale there is another delightfully out-of-the-ordinary hotel, **DiVito by the Sea** ((305) 929-7227, at 3500 North Boardwalk, Hollywood. Known affectionately as the "Palace of Kitsch," it resembles a riverboat painted by someone who was both color-blind and in a hurry, and which is towing (or pushing) a replica of the Leaning Tower of Pisa. Among its other eccentricities is that it only likes letting rooms on a weekly basis, it only likes children from April to December, and it doesn't like any credit cards. Yet it's still a very likeable place. The **Holiday Inn Hotel and Conference Center (** (305) 739-4000, is at 5100 North Route 8.

Inexpensive
There is a stretch of North Birch Road, just two blocks away from the beach, that has dozens of inexpensive motels, with pools, side by side. Two of the nicest of these are the **Sea View Resort Motel (** (305) 564-3151, at 550 North Birch Road, and the **Sea Chateau (** (305) 566-8331, at 555 North Birch Road.

WHERE TO EAT

Expensive
Occupying the 12th-floor penthouse of the Four Seasons condominium at 333 Sunset Drive, just off Las Olas Boulevard, **Le Dôme (** (305) 463-3303, is one of the finest restaurants in Florida, with sensational views to match its dishes. Despite its name, the **Left Bank (** (305) 462-5376, at 214 Southeast Sixth Avenue, is more American than Parisian, and more romantic than bohemian; but no matter, owner-chef Jean-Pierre Brehier has created a superb restaurant. The cuisine inclines towards the nouvelle, and is memorably delicious. Visitors hungry for more traditional French cooking are advised to take their appetites to the corner of Route 1 and East Sunrise Boulevard, where they will find not one but two marvelous restaurants. **La Ferme (** (305) 764-0987, at 1601 East Sunrise Boulevard, is the creation of Henri and Marie-Paule Terrier, a delightful Lyonnais couple who will make you feel at home — that is, if you could get food like theirs at home. A few steps away from La Ferme is **La Coquille (** (305) 467-3030, at 1619 East Sunrise Boulevard, an enchanting little bistro run by Jean and Hélène Bert. **Casa Vecchia (** (305) 463-7575, at 209 North Birch Road, is just what the name says it is: an old house. And much more: in this beautifully redecorated old house beside the Intracoastal Waterway, restaurateurs Leonce Picot and Al Kocab have established a splendid Italian

restaurant specializing in the more subtle cuisine of northern Italy.

Moderate
To avoid praising the same people twice in one paragraph, I have decided to cheat and list as moderate the fairly expensive **Down Under (** (305) 563-4123, also the creation of Messieurs Picot and Kocab. The restaurant is "down under" the Oakland Park Boulevard Bridge, at 3000 East Oakland Park Boulevard, and offers a menu that is really an anthology of other restaurants' greatest hits. It works. Louis Flemati's **Café de Paris (** (305) 467-2900, at 715 East Las Olas Boulevard, is deservedly popular with the locals, as much for its cheery atmosphere (which includes strolling musicians) as for its tasty food. Just down the street, but half a world away, is the wonderful **Lagniappe Cajun House** at 230 East Las Olas Boulevard; the food is authentic Cajun/Creole, the decor is New Orleans Revival, and Saturday and Sunday brunches are accompanied by Dixieland bands. Equally if differently fun is the aptly-named **Sea Watch (** (305) 781-2200, a restaurant on the ocean at 6002 North Ocean Boulevard. Here, among lots of brass, wicker, and greenery, and within earshot of the waves, you can dine handsomely and reasonably on all kinds of fresh seafood.

Inexpensive
If you don't mind — or even if you do mind — eating off paper plates and using paper napkins, paper cups, and plastic forks, you should make for the **Southport Raw Bar (** (305) 525-2526, at 1536 Cordova Road, just off the 17th Street Causeway. Noisy and ugly, its only attractions are the most glorious oysters, shrimp, and clams you have ever tasted at prices you won't believe. If it's something meatier and spicier you're after, try **Ernie's Bar-B-Que (** (305) 523-8636, at 1843 South Route 1. Whatever you order here, you *must* try Ernie's conch chowder. Somewhat swankier and more specialized, **Bobby Rubino's Place for Ribs (** (305) 561-5305, at 4100 North Route 1, is, well, the place for ribs. If you are a devotee of Tex-Mex food, as I am, you can't do better than **Carlos and Pepe's 17th Street Cantina**

((305) 467-7192, at 1302 Southeast 17th Street. Celestial food at bargain-basement prices. A word of warning, however: I am not the first person to have discovered the cantina, so unless you go early you could have a bit of wait at the bar (not such a bad fate, actually).

HOW TO GET THERE

Fort Lauderdale/Hollywood International Airport is served by a large number of national and international airlines, although many people prefer to fly in to Miami's airport, about an hour's drive from the south. Taxi fares from the Fort Lauderdale airport to most of the beach hotels should be not more than $12. There are a dozen rental car companies with offices in or near the airport.

Approaching Fort Lauderdale by car from the north or south, drivers can take Florida's Turnpike (a tollway), or I-95, or Route 1 (also known as Federal Highway), or Route A1A, which snakes slowly and scenically along the coast. The main road from the west is Route 84, a toll road also known as Everglades Parkway or, more colloquially, "Alligator Alley".

PALM BEACH AND BOCA RATON

In a sense, Palm Beach is a mirage, because its special appeal is very much in the eye of the beholder. To some, it is an oasis of taste and style, a chic enclave for the upper classes, an island paradise for the mega-wealthy. To others, it is a 12-mile (19-km) long shrine to vulgarity and excess, an offshore game reserve where cash-laden social climbers and penniless aristocrats can prey on each other in peace. That globetrotting chronicler of high society, Taki, has called it, rather harshly, "a Gulag for the rich, the last refuge of the lifted, a Mecca for the monosyllabic."

To be honest, there is some merit to both views. But whichever view you take, there is no denying that the place *is* special, if not unique. Where else would you find flocks of (specially imported) parrots where you would normally find pigeons, or find an artificial reef offshore anchored by a Rolls Royce and a yacht, or find a city ordinance banning outdoor clotheslines because they are unsightly? Exactly.

BACKGROUND

The first settlers arrived in Palm Beach during (and probably because of) the American Civil War, but the palms didn't arrive until 1878, when a Spanish ship carrying a cargo of coconuts, the *Providencia* ran aground on the island. The coconuts were planted, and before long the place had a name as well as some distinctive flora.

Then in 1894 Henry Morrison Flagler arrived with his railway, built the Royal Poinciana and The Breakers hotels, and set about attracting the well-born and well-heeled. He succeeded. Not only did Vanderbilts, Wanamakers, Rockefellers, Guggenheims, Goulds, Astors, Posts, Huttons, Chryslers, DuPonts and other names out of the *Social Register* go there, but so did talented eccentric Addison Mizner, whose architectural creations were to give Palm Beach and Boca Raton their characteristic, pastel-tinted look.

ABOVE: Consuming is conspicuous along Worth Avenue in Palm Beach. OPPOSITE: The palms of Palm Beach.

During the Twenties Palm Beach became the place where anybody who was Anybody went for the winter season. Mansions sprouted among the palms. West Palm Beach was created, on the mainland, across from the island, by Flagler "for my help" — the army of servants required to staff the hotels and private homes. Since automobiles were prohibited as disturbers of peace, the gliterrati were ferried to and from by blacks in wicker rickshaws known as "Afromobiles". Palm Beach became the ultimate Fantasy Island for The Haves. Today

High Street, Croydon, Surrey CR0 0XJ. The Chamber of Commerce of the Palm Beaches ((407) 833-3711, is at 501 North Flagler Drive, P.O. Box 2931, West Palm Beach, FL 33401. The Boca Raton Chamber of Commerce ((407) 395-4433, is at 1800 North Route 1, Boca Raton.

Other useful telephone numbers (all in area code 407):

Palm Beach
International Airport   471-7400
Yellow Cabs   689-4222
Doctor referral service   433-3940

its social cachet may have been diluted somewhat by the infiltration of certain high-decibel, high-visibility *parvenus*, but it nonetheless remains a wonderful example of the happiness that money can buy.

GENERAL INFORMATION

The Palm Beach County Convention and Visitors Bureau ((407) 471-3995, is at 1555 Lakes Boulevard, Suite 204, West Palm Beach, FL 33401. The bureau has a European office ((069) 234098, at AM Hauptbahnhof 10, 6000 Frankfurt/Main 1, Germany, and is represented in Britain by Travel Markets International ((081) 688-1451, Wrencote House, 119–121 Croydon

WHAT TO SEE AND DO

Sights

Mansion-gazing is by far the most popular form of sightseeing in Palm Beach, and the best way to gaze at the mansions is from the water. Narrated sightseeing cruises go every day from Steamboat Landing — as do luncheon, cocktail, and dinner cruises with live entertainment. Ticket prices vary from $5 up to $50, so it's best to check in advance with Star of Palm Beach ((407) 848-7827, Steamboat Landing, 900 East Blue Heron Boulevard, Riviera Beach, FL 33404.

Among the mansions themselves, the two most noteworthy are **Mar-A-Lago** at 1100 South Ocean Boulevard, the 118-room

Moorish extravaganza built for cereal heiress Marjorie Merriweather Post in the Twenties and now owned by Donald Trump, and the 55-room marble palace built by Henry Flagler in 1902, which was originally called Whitehall but is now the **Henry M. Flagler Museum** ((407) 655-2833. As the Trump mansion is not open to the public, and only its 75-ft (23-m) tower is clearly visible from the road, the visitor's time is better spent inspecting Mr. Flagler's palatial edifice on Coconut Row. There are seven kinds of rare marble in the foyer

Dreher Park Zoo ((407) 547-9453, at 1301 Summit Boulevard in West Palm Beach. Among the zoo's more unusual animals are a 100-pound (45-kg) capybara, the world's largest rodent, and an endangered Florida panther. About 15 miles (24 km) further west on Southern Boulevard is the 500-acre (200-hectare) **Lion Country Safari** ((407) 793-1084, where you can drive along eight miles (13 km) of paved roads past African lions, elephants, zebras, giraffes, white rhinos, antelopes, and chimpanzees, to name only a few of the animals that roam free

alone, and each guest bedroom is decorated in the style of a different period in world history. Parked outside the mansion is Flagler's private railway car. The museum is closed on Mondays; admission is $5 for adults and $2 for children.

Considering that most of the expensive art in Palm Beach is in private homes, the **Norton Gallery of Art** ((407) 832-5196, at 1451 South Olive Avenue in West Palm Beach, has a surprisingly impressive collection, particularly of the French Impressionists and of twentieth-century American art. It also has a delightful outdoor sculpture garden. It is closed on Mondays.

Animal lovers and people with bored children will want to pay a visit to the

here. There is also a petting zoo as well as a number of free rides, games, and boat cruises. If you don't have a car, or if you feel a little uneasy about driving your own nice car past hundreds of wild animals, you can rent a car here for $5 an hour. Worth noting, too, is that there is an excellent campground right next to the park. The postal address of both the park and the campground is P.O. Box 16066, West Palm Beach, FL 33416. Admission is $11.95 for adults and $9.95 for children under 16 (under three, free).

OPPOSITE: "Italianate" buildings in downtown Palm Beach. ABOVE: Exterior and interior views of the Henry M. Flagler Museum.

The Gold Coast   *117*

Sports

Two major-league **baseball teams** hold their spring training in West Palm Beach, the Montreal Expos and the Atlanta Braves. They play at the Municipal Stadium ((407) 684-6801, Lakes Boulevard and Congress Avenue. You can watch **jai alai** from the first of the year until about the middle of May at the Palm Beach Jai Alai Fronton ((407) 844-2444, 1415 West 45th Street, West Palm Beach.

The spectator sport most closely associated with Palm Beach is, of course, **polo**. It is played from November until late April at the Palm Beach Polo and Country Club ((407) 793-1113, 13198 Forest Hill Boulevard, West Palm Beach; Gulfstream Polo Grounds ((407) 965-9924, Lake Worth Road; and Royal Palm Polo Club ((407) 994-1876, 6300 Clint Moore Road, Boca Raton.

With upwards of 80 **golf courses** in the area, golfers have plenty of choice. The first choice of most is the famous course at the PGA Sheraton Resort ((407) 627-2000, 400 Avenue of the Champions, Palm Beach Gardens.

Tennis players will find no shortage of courts, many of them free. The Lake Worth Racquet and Swim Club ((407) 967-3900, at 4090 Coconut Road, Lake Worth, will let you use one of their lighted courts for $10 an hour per player. For information on public courts near you in either Palm Beach or Boca Raton call the Palm Beach County Parks and Recreation Department ((407) 964-4420. There are countless opportunities for **scuba diving** and **snorkeling** along this coast. My advice would be to call or visit one of the half-dozen Force E stores in the Palm Beach-Boca Raton area. Not only do they rent the equipment you will need, but they also provide instruction if you need it as well as dive boats for charter. In West Palm Beach there is a Force E ((407) 471-2676, at 1399 North Military Trail; it has an office in Boca Raton ((407) 395-4407, at 7166 Beracasa Way; and another office ((407) 368-0555, at 877 East Palmetto Park Road.

Polo players in Boca Raton.

Shopping

If you know anything about Palm Beach, then you already know about **Worth Avenue**. It is to Palm Beach what Bond Street is to London, Rodeo Drive is to Beverly Hills, the Rue du Faubourg St. Honoré is to Paris, and the Via Condotti is to Rome. It is where beautiful objects go to find the Beautiful People who will want to own them.

Although it is only three blocks long, with the Atlantic at one end and Lake Worth at the other, the street is home to over 250 stores and boutiques, ranging in size from Saks Fifth

Theater ((407) 392-3755, at 303 Golfview Drive, presents Broadway musicals, with occasional guest stars, all year round. The **Top of the Bridge Lounge** ((407) 368-9500, at 999 Camino Real, gives you a lovely view of the Intracoastal Waterway along with the live music. Right on the Intracoastal Waterway is **Wildflower** ((407) 426-0066, at 551 East Palmetto Park Road. A restaurant as well as a lounge, it features spectacularly unconventional decor as well as a disk jockey playing dance music. **Tugboat Annie's** ((407) 394-9900, at 6909 Southwest

Avenue (30,000 sq ft or 9,144 sq m) to Tally Ho Antiques (25 sq ft or 7.5 sq m). For sheer, concentrated opulence, there is no street anywhere that can match it. Even the fire hydrant is chrome-plated. Worth Avenue is definitely worth a visit, if only for window-shopping.

Nightlife

Most Palm Beach nightlife revolves around private entertaining, not surprisingly, and therefore interesting night spots are in short supply. Apart from **Ta-Boo** ((407) 655-5562, a fashionable supper club at 221 Worth Avenue, the best places to go are the lounges at the big hotels, especially the one at The Colony. Boca Raton has rather more to offer after dark. The **Royal Palm Dinner**

18th Street, is your place if you like good rock and reggae in a relaxed atmosphere.

WHERE TO STAY

Luxury

Hotels don't get much more luxurious than these. To begin with, there is **The Breakers** ((407) 655-6611 TOLL-FREE (800) 833-3141, at One South County Road. This twin-towered, Italianate palace, modeled on the Villa Medici in Florence, was rebuilt (after two fires) in 1926. Ever since it has served as the unofficial community center for Palm Beach's glitterati, all the while retaining its reputation for graceful formality. In addition to almost half a mile (800 m) of beachfront, the hotel has 19 tennis courts, two 18-hole golf courses, and a swimming pool. Matching — some would say surpassing — The Breakers in upper-crustiness is **The Colony** ((407) 655-5430, at 155 Hammon Avenue, where the Duke and Duchess of Windsor usually stayed and John Lennon didn't (having been turned away on grounds of scruffiness). Although the hotel's *look* is distinctly, but tastefully, Floridian, it *feels* European: the service is excellent, understated, just right. Locals describe it admiringly as "a hundred rooms and a reputation".

One might think that the above hotels would be impossible acts to follow, but the **Brazilian Court Hotel** ((407) 655-7740, at 301 Australian Avenue in West Palm Beach, is right up there with them. Built in the same year as The Breakers, and extensively renovated a few years ago, it is the sort of place where you wouldn't be surprised to see Cary Grant or Gary Cooper — both of whom, in fact, did stay here. Like The Colony, it combines the best of New and Old World hospitality. The fourth member of this dazzling quartet is the **Boca Raton Resort and Club** ((407) 395-3000 TOLL-FREE (800) 327-0101, at 501 East Camino Real in Boca Raton also built in 1926. Originally named the Cloister Inn, this was undoubtedly Addison Mizner's masterpiece. It has since expanded outwards and upwards (only 100 of the hotel's 1,000 rooms are in the original building), and now includes four swimming pools, 22 tennis courts, a golf course, a 23-slip marina, seven restaurants, and over a mile (1.6 km) of beach. Yet its standards of excellence remain as high as ever, which explains why it is still one of the world's great hotels.

Mid-range

In the upper part of the middle range is the **Howard Johnson Motor Lodge** ((407) 582-2581 TOLL-FREE (800) 654-2000, at 2870 South County Road in Palm Beach. Nearby (in price as well) is the **Beachcomber Apartment Motel** ((407) 585-4648, at 3024 South Ocean Boulevard. A little further north in Riviera Beach there is the **Rutledge Resort Motel** ((407) 848-6621, at 3730 Ocean Drive, Riviera Beach, and the **Best Western Seaspray Inn** ((407) 844-0233 TOLL-FREE (800) 528-1234, at 123 Ocean Avenue. The **Best Western University Inn** ((407) 395-5255, at 2700 North Route 1, in Boca Raton is another good bet.

Inexpensive

The **Boca Raton Motel** ((407) 395-7500 TOLL-FREE (800) 453-4511, at 1801 North Route 1, is an excellent value. In the same area I also recommend the **Shore Edge Motel** ((407) 395-4491, at 425 North Ocean Boulevard. From here to Palm Beach there are dozens of economy motels to choose from. The best bargain I came across was the **Harbor Lights Apartments** ((407) 844-5377, on the water

at 200 Inlet Way in Palm Beach Shores. It has seven rooms, all very reasonably priced.

WHERE TO EAT

Expensive

Like the Casa Vecchia in Fort Lauderdale, **La Vielle Maison** ((407) 391-6701, at 770 East Palmetto Park Road in Boca Raton, is another old house restored and refurbished by the redoubtable Leonce Picot and Al Kocab. An elegant, two-story, artifact-filled honeycomb of alcoves and intimate spaces, the restaurant specializes in wonderfully imaginative French Provincial cuisine. Also in Boca Raton

ABOVE: The Breakers, a Palm Beach landmark since the turn of the century. OPPOSITE: Worth Avenue.

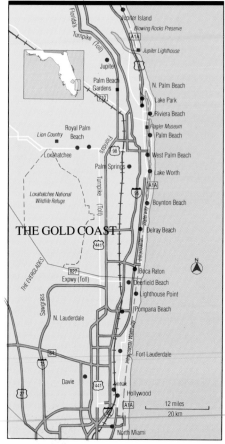

207 Royal Poinciana Way in Palm Beach, because most of the natives you meet will do it for me. For celebrity-spotting at all hours of the day or night, as well as for an amazing array of dishes in a splendid setting, plus live (and lively) music at night, you won't do any better than this. A few miles to the north on the Jupiter inlet is another local treasure, **Harpoon Louie's** ((407) 744-1300, 1065 Route A1A. Here you can enjoy a terrific view of the inlet and the famous Jupiter Lighthouse while gorging yourself on Louie's massive portions of seafood. For a completely different sort of atmosphere, and food, try the pub-like **Doherty's** ((407) 655-6200, at 288 South County Road in Palm Beach. It's very good, and very jolly. Finally, if you are as passionate about Thai food as I am, you are in for a treat at the **Siam Garden** ((407) 368-9013, in Oaks Plaza, 680 Glades Road, Boca Raton. Not only is it truly garden-like, but its food is authentic which means delicious.

Inexpensive

For your basic down-home cookin' with all the fixin's, go to **Tom's Place** ((407) 997-0920, at 7251 North Route 1 in Boca Raton. Ribs, fried chicken, stew, catfish, hush puppies — that sort of thing. Like Tom's, **Original Grandma Sarah's** ((407) 833-6369, at 1301 North Route 1 in West Palm Beach, provides hearty meals in a friendly atmosphere at friendly prices. **Hamburger Heaven** ((407) 655-5277, at 314 South County Road in Palm Beach, serves, yes, heavenly hamburgers. And **Toojay's** ((407) 659-7232, at 313 Poinciana Plaza in Palm Beach, serves scrumptious crab cakes and meat loaf.

is **Chez Marcel** ((407) 368-6553, in Royal Palm Plaza, Route 1 and Southeast Fourth Street. The creation of Marcel Wortman, from Strasbourg by way of Costa Rica, it is as unpretentious as its menu is rich. For classic French cooking with an intriguing twist, go to **Le Monegasque** ((407) 585-0071, at the President condominium, 2505 South Ocean Boulevard in Palm Beach. This utterly delightful restaurant is, both gastronomically and decoratively, an homage to owner Aldo Rinero's native Monaco. By contrast, **The Dining Room** ((407) 655-7740, which graces the Brazilian Court Hotel, celebrates many different cuisines, often in arresting new combination. For excellent taste wedded to excellence you can taste, The Dining Room is the place to go.

Moderate

It is probably a waste of space to recommend **Chuck & Harold's Café** ((407) 659-1440, at

HOW TO GET THERE

Although Palm Beach International Airport is only minutes away from Palm Beach itself, the Fort Lauderdale airport is served by many more airlines with many more flights into the area.

The principal north-south roads into Palm Beach and Boca Raton are the same as for Fort Lauderdale. The main road from the west is Route 98, which becomes Southern Boulevard as it approaches Palm Beach.

Facing the Atlantic: beach huts stand sentinel.

The Atlantic Coast

STRETCHING for over 300 miles (450 km) from Palm Beach to the Georgia state line, Florida's Atlantic Coast has attractions ranging from the oldest city in the country — St. Augustine — to the extremely High Tech marvels at the Kennedy Space Center on Merritt Island near Cape Canaveral.

Following in the wake of Columbus, the Spanish explorer Ponce de León led an expedition across the Atlantic in 1513 to try to discover the fabled waters of a "fountain of youth", rumored to exist somewhere near present-day St. Augustine. He was successful only to the extent that nowadays you can find a Fountain of Youth Discovery Park in the city's tourist guides.

By 1562 a small expeditionary force of French Huguenots had settled at what was to become Fort Caroline near the mouth of the St. Johns River, around which Jacksonville now stands. Responding to this challenge, King Philip II of Spain sent Pedro Menéndez de Avilés to Florida with orders to drive the French out of the northeast and establish a garrison town on the coast. At the end of August 1565 Menéndez spotted a strategic point overlooking a bay and some days later landed there. Thus began the long history of St. Augustine. Wasting no time, Menéndez marched against Fort Caroline and routed the garrison, and then destroyed what remained of the French forces on his way back to St. Augustine.

Although this confirmed Spain as the dominant power in the region, it by no means assured the Spanish of control for the long term. Indeed, Fort Caroline was retaken only two years later, and Amelia Island, just north of Jacksonville, has seen no fewer than eight different flags raised above it since 1562. The whole region was tossed back and forth between the Spanish, French, and English for a few centuries, and Mexico even laid claim to it for a brief period before the Union wrenched it away from the Confederacy.

In the years following the end of the Civil War the coast began to prosper from the north downwards. Jacksonville rose to prominence as a port, and the arrival of Henry Flagler's Florida East Coast Railroad in the 1880s secured the city's position as the state's shipping and industrial center.

As his railway crept further south Flagler dotted the coastline with luxury hotels to cater to the expensive tastes of the wealthy northerners who began spending winters in Florida. Resort towns soon developed to accommodate the increasing flow of tourists to the region. Nor were all the new arrivals tourists: it was the now-famous climate that attracted NASA to Florida's Atlantic Coast in the 1960s.

THE SPACE COAST

The Kennedy Space Center has become one of the most popular sightseeing destinations in Florida. Every year over 1.5 million people visit Spaceport USA (the name given to the public visitation program at the space complex), and many of them plan their visit to coincide with the launch of a spacecraft. Although the Space Center is clearly the main attraction, the coast also has resort towns with excellent beaches, and there is an abundance of wildlife including such rare species as the southern bald eagle and the West Indian manatee on Merritt Island itself.

BACKGROUND

Ais and Timucuan Indian tribes were the original inhabitants of the Cape area. The name "Canaveral" is derived from an Indian word meaning "canebearer", as the Indians' arrows were made from reed or cane. To this day, large areas of the region remain a wilderness of mosquito-infested swamp, savannah, and rugged coastline. In fact, most of Merritt Island is a national wildlife refuge; out of the 140,000 acres (56,000 hectares) of the island owned by NASA only seven percent has been developed for the space program. The rest is an extension of the wildlife refuge — a fact that NASA is keen to emphasize. Old Indian burial mounds have also been left untouched and lie next to the bunkers and buildings of the Space Center.

Hard on the heels of the Soviet Union's *Sputnik*, America's first satellite, *Explorer I*, was launched from Cape Canaveral on January 31, 1958. The National Aeronautics

A Saturn 5 rocket at the Kennedy Space Center.

and Space Administration (NASA) was created the following year, originally operating from the Cape itself but moving over to Merritt Island in 1964. By 1968 the Apollo program was well under way and came to fruition on July 20, 1969 with Neil Armstrong's first step on the moon. Such local towns as Cocoa Beach (which is opposite Cape Canaveral, unlike the town of Cocoa which is on the mainland across Indian River) were transformed by the influx of scientists, technicians, and workers from the Space Center.

GENERAL INFORMATION

The offices of the Cocoa Beach Tourism and Convention Council ℂ (407) 459-2200, are on Merritt Island at 400 Fortenberry Road, where you can get any needed information as well as free maps and brochures.

If you would like to be at the Cape for the launch of a spacecraft, call NASA TOLL-FREE (800) 432-2153 for information on launch dates and best vantage points. A limited number of passes, which enable you to drive into the grounds of the Space Center and park within five miles (eight kilometers) of a launch pad, are available for the shuttle launches. To make a reservation for a launch date, call ℂ (305) 452-2121 between

8 AM and 4 PM or write to: NASA Visitors Services Branch, PA-V1C, John F. Kennedy Space Center, FL 32899. (Do remember that there are plenty of vantage points outside the Space Center where you can park to watch a launch, especially along Route 1 in Titusville.)

WHAT TO SEE AND DO

Sights
The Kennedy Space Center's *Spaceport USA* promotional leaflet puts it like this: "Here you can experience it all. The excitement. The glory. The awe-inspiring achievements. What's more, you can relive it free. Free parking. Free admission. Free kennel facilities. Even free use of a camera." This breathless recitation of the FREEdoms at Spaceport USA is a little bit misleading, because not every service is free by any means.

Take Route 405 from Titusville to enter the Space Center at Gate 3, or take Route 3 from Cocoa Beach to enter at Gate 2; guards at each gate provide a pass for Spaceport USA. The **Visitors Center** is on the south side of the NASA Parkway on Merritt Island. Among the many exhibits you will be able to see in the Visitors Center are a piece of moon rock, the Astronaut Memorial, an Apollo capsule, a lunar module, and the flight deck of a space shuttle. The Hall of History contains a detailed account of the whole space program's history and two IMAX Theaters there (with giant five-story-high screens) show several half-hour films about the space shuttle and space exploration at an admission price of $4 for adults and $2.50 for children aged three to 12. It's advisable to make an advance reservation for the show as well as for the bus tour of the outlying grounds in order to avoid lengthy queues.

The **bus tour** takes two hours and costs $7 for adults and $4 for children under 12. A guide will answer any questions, ranging from the fuel consumption of the shuttle rocket thrusters at take-off (considerable) to the toilet procedures for an astronaut (problematic). You will get to visit the **Vehicle Assembly Building**, which is one of the largest buildings in the world, and the massive transporters which slowly carry the assembled rockets to the launch pad. The tour then moves on to the **launch pads** at Complex 39 and then to the **Astronaut Training Building**, where conditions of actual space flight are simulated. The cumulative effect of all these exhibits is, one has to agree, awe inspiring.

After visiting the Space Center you can come back down to earth with a driving tour through the island's wildlife refuge. Reservations for an official tour bus can be made by calling ((407) 867-0667, or you can guide yourself along the **Black Point Wildlife**

Lone Cabbage Fish Camp ((407) 632-4199, at Route 520, six miles (9.6 km) west of I-95, Cocoa.

Shopping

The best shopping in the area is at Cocoa Village in downtown Cocoa (not Cocoa Beach). More than 50 shops offer a variety of goods in an Old World market atmosphere that retains the charm and sense of ease that so many modern malls have lost. The Wine Experience, at 316 Brevard Avenue, has a good selection of Australian

Drive by entering the refuge via County Road 402, off Route 1 in Titusville. Birdwatchers will be particularly excited by the variety of species to be seen along the route, including a bird called the anhinga which swims underwater with its head above the surface.

If you really want to get away from it all, you can take the half-hour airboat ride up the St. Johns River and get a close-up look at the alligators hanging out on the riverbank. Despite their air of complete indifference, they have a way of giving the impression that they're really contemplating the next painful and inconsiderate thing they can do to something smaller and less toothy than they are. The boat leaves from the

and Californian wines. At Handwerk House, 206 Brevard Avenue, you will find a collection of beautifully-crafted stuffed animals and rag dolls. At the Indian River Pottery, 116-B Harrison Street, artisans produce a range of household utensils which go straight from the potter's wheel, via the kiln, into the shop window next to the caged singing birds. Not far away, at 4151 North Route A1A, is what is reputed to be the largest surf shop in the world, the Ron Jon Surf Shop, which sells and rents everything you might need in or on the water — and which never closes.

OPPOSITE AND ABOVE: Two views of the Rocket Garden at the Kennedy Space Center.

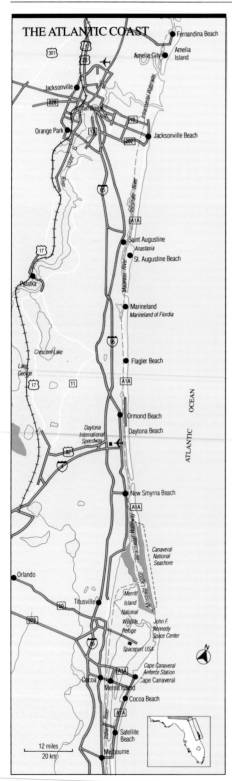

THE ATLANTIC COAST

Nightlife

The Cocoa Banana ((407) 799-3700, at 900 North Route A1A, Cocoa Beach, is one of the area's most popular night spots, featuring a disco, bar, electronic games room, and pool tables. Appealing to a slightly more mature crowd, Coco's ((407) 799-0003, at 1550 North Route A1A in the Hilton Hotel, Cocoa Beach, is a small disco lounge-bar playing the light soul sounds of the Sixties. At Dino's Jazz Piano Bar ((407) 784-5470, 315 West Route 520, Cocoa Beach, one can happily waste some after-dark hours in a relaxed atmosphere listening to good jazz.

WHERE TO STAY

Luxury

There are no surprises about the Cocoa Beach Hilton ((407) 799-0003 TOLL-FREE (800) 445-8667, at 1550 North Route A1A, Cocoa Beach. Its facilities are typically Hiltonesque, and many of its 300+ rooms overlook the sea. If you are lucky (or clever) enough to be there at the right time, you can witness space launches from the second-floor rooms at the Inn at Cocoa Beach ((407) 799-3460, 4300 Ocean Beach Boulevard, Cocoa Beach, a beautifully preserved residence which manages to combine luxury with a cozy atmosphere.

Mid-range

A good choice for families is the Crossway Inn and Tennis Resort ((305) 783-2221, at 3901 North Route A1A in Cocoa Beach, where children under 12 can stay free. The hotel has a games room, a swimming pool, and tennis and basketball courts. The Polaris Beach Resort Inn ((305) 783-7621 TOLL-FREE (800) 962-0028, 5600 North Route A1A, Cocoa Beach, has both a croquet lawn and a beach. Efficiency apartments are very well-equipped at the Polaris, as they are at Surf Studio Beach Apartments ((305) 783-7100, 1801 South Route A1A, Cocoa Beach, which has 11 moderately-priced units and personal, friendly service.

Inexpensive

As an alternative to staying in Cocoa Beach, and still only three miles (five kilometers) from the Kennedy Space Center, The Luck's

Way Inn ((305) 269-7110 TOLL-FREE (800) 228-2000, at 3655 Cheney Highway, Titusville, is a remarkably good value, with a swimming pool and complimentary continental breakfast. Still on the mainland, the **Brevard Hotel** ((407) 636-1411, at 112 Riverside Drive, Cocoa, is a quiet place overlooking the Indian River but within walking distance of the bustle of Cocoa Village. Another good budget choice is the **Ocean Suite Hotel** ((407) 784-4343, at 5500 Ocean Beach Boulevard, Cocoa Beach, next to the Canaveral Pier.

WHERE TO EAT

Expensive

The elegant **Black Tulip** ((407) 631-1133, at 207 Brevard Avenue, is probably the most fashionable restaurant in Cocoa Village. The starters are particularly delicious, and include crab cakes served on Kaiser rolls and artichoke hearts in mustard sauce. The beef, poultry, and seafood entrees are less interesting, but still very edible. **Bernard's Surf** ((305) 783-2401, at Two South Route A1A in Cocoa Beach, has a big reputation and even bigger menu, on which you will find such culinary curiosities as bear meat and chocolate-covered ants. Their crab and lobster are deservedly celebrated locally, but my favorite dish was the freshwater salmon, batter-dipped and fried and served with toasted almonds.

Moderate

The **Dixie Crossroads** ((407) 268-5000, at 1475 Garden Street, Titusville, is a large, family-oriented restaurant specializing in — what else? — seafood. Hint: try the smoked mullet. For a meal before or after your visit to the Space Center you could drop in at the **Kountry Kitchen** ((407) 459-3457, 1115 North Courtenay Parkway, Merritt Island, which serves up hearty bacon-and-egg breakfasts and mountainous dinners; or at **Victor's Family Restaurant** ((407) 459-1656, 320 North Courtenay Parkway, which — surprisingly — has a selection of tasty Greek dishes.

Inexpensive

At **Desperadoes** ((407) 784-3363, 30 North Route A1A, Cocoa Beach, chef Manuel Mer-

cado rustles up some of the most exquisite *chimichangas, tamales* and *tostadas* on the Atlantic Coast, which you can wash down with Mexican beer or — heresy! — with wine. You can sit in the sun at the **Pasta Garden** ((407) 639-8343, 220 Brevard Avenue, Cocoa Village, Cocoa, and enjoy fairly straightforward Italian food and seafood. The **Peking Garden** ((407) 459-2999, at 155 East Route 520, Merritt Island, serves quite respectable Chinese food. But if your priority is quieting down the kids, let me recommend the **Village Ice Cream and Sandwich Shop**

((407) 632-2311, at 120-B Harrison Street in Cocoa Village.

HOW TO GET THERE

The Melbourne International Airport ((407) 723-6627, about 30 miles (48 km), south of Cape Canaveral, is regularly served by a large number of national airlines. Hertz ((407) 723-3414; and Avis ((407) 723-7755, both have offices at the airport.

The three north-south routes to the Space Coast are the same three as for the entire eastern Florida coast: I-95, Route 1, and Route A1A.

Relaxing in the shadow of the Rocket Garden.

DAYTONA

Daytona and Ormond Beach, a few miles to the north, emerged from the great Florida Sun Rush at the end of the nineteenth century as two of the resorts most favored by prosperous northerners. The wide expanse of hard-packed, white beach between the two resorts must surely be the only beach in the world which owes its fame to being driven upon. It all began at the end of the nineteenth century when two motoring enthusiasts named R.E. Olds and Alexander Winton — watched by their friend Henry Ford from his rocking chair on the verandah of the Ormond Hotel — raced their cars down Ormond beach in what has become known as America's first drag race.

BACKGROUND

By extending his Florida East Coast Railroad to the area in the late 1880s, Henry Flagler laid the tracks which property developers and winter-weary northerners were soon to follow. Flagler enlarged his own hotel empire by buying and renovating a venerable hostelry in Ormond Beach, the Ormond Hotel. Also in Ormond Beach, John D. Rockefeller established a winter residence, The Casements, where he spent much of his later life.

The resorts continued to develop and to attract the rich in increasing numbers. Organized racing began in 1904 with an event called the Winter Speed Carnival, which drew speed merchants and their society financiers from all over the world to the Daytona and Ormond beaches. In 1928 Malcolm Campbell, a slightly dotty and speed-obsessed English millionaire, arrived at Daytona with a car powered by an aircraft engine. He waited for the surf to create a sufficiently flat beach, then accelerated across it at a record speed of 207 mph (333 kph). He subsequently raised this record to 276 mph (444 kph) on the beach at Daytona.

They no longer race cars on the beach, but Daytona's love affair with machines and speed lives on with stock-car racing

and speedways. The speed limit on the beach these days is 10 mph (16 kph) and the fastest thing you'll see is a surfer riding the waves.

GENERAL INFORMATION

The Daytona Beach Chamber of Commerce ((904) 255-0415, is at 126 East Orange Avenue, P.O. Box 2775, Daytona Beach, FL 32015. Its staff can give you information on accommodation or attractions. For a complimentary copy of the *Daytona Beach Resort Area Visitors Guide*, call TOLL-FREE (800) 535-2828. The Ormond Beach Chamber of Commerce ((904) 677-3454, is at 165 West Granada Street, P.O. Box 874, Ormond Beach, FL 32074.

Other useful telephone numbers (all in area code 904):

Daytona International Airport	255-8441
Volusia County Medical Association	258-1611
Dental service	734-1355

WHAT TO SEE AND DO

Sights

First, **the beach**. It's big (23 miles or 37 km long, 500 ft or 152 m wide) and it's a highway (but remember, no faster than 10 mph or 16 kph).

You can drive onto the sand at Ormond Beach, and you can go as far south as Ponce de León Inlet. Stick to the main track, avoid the water, and heed the warning signs about soft, unsafe areas of the beach. You can park anywhere you like on the beach.

For those who drive in the fast lane Daytona is something of a Mecca. From January onwards there are the qualifying rounds for the **Daytona Grand National Stock Car Race** held in mid-February. The track gives way to a **Motorcycle Classic** in the first week of March, and the speedway (car racing) culminates at the end of June with the **Paul Revere 255** and the **Fire-cracker 400**. All the action is at the **Daytona International Speedway**, Volusia Avenue, near the airport off Route 92, three miles (five kilometers) west of Daytona, which took

Daytona Beach, where the speed limit is now a stately 10 mph (16 kph).

over from the beach in 1959 as the venue for the races. Tickets for the races start at $15 and rise to $65. For further information contact the Daytona International Speedway, P.O. Drawer S, Daytona, FL 32015. Daytona USA is a new interactive motorsports attraction at the Speedway, where you can design your own car, take part in a racing team pit stop and learn more about the history of racing in the Daytona Beach area.

The **Museum of Arts and Sciences** ((904) 255-0285, at 1040 Museum Way, Daytona Beach, houses one of the world's finest

If you want to get some idea of how the Timucuan Indians used to live, visit the **Tomoka State Park** ((904) 676-4050, just north of Ormond Beach on North Beach Street, off Route 40. A museum there has exhibits showing the history of the ancient Timucuan village of Nocoroco. The *Dixie Queen II* riverboat will take you in comfort along the Halifax River (which is the name given to the section of the Intracoastal Waterway which flows between mainland Daytona and the barrier islands). Sunset and moonlight cruises, with dinner, are

collections of Cuban art and sculpture. The main attraction of the science collection is a Pleistocene mammal which weighed in at five tons and was a good few yards taller than most of the unfortunate creatures it encountered. In neighboring Ormond Beach you can visit John D. Rockefeller's former winter house, **The Casements** ((904) 676-3216, at 25 Riverside Drive. The house, which was built opposite a hotel which hadn't treated the great man with the proper respect, is now a cultural center exhibiting Hungarian and Italian artifacts and American art; admission is free and the center is open Monday to Thursday 9 AM to 9 PM, Friday 9 AM to 5 PM and Saturday 9 AM to 12 PM.

especially popular. The *Dixie Queen II* ((904) 255-1997, leaves from 841 Ballough Road, Daytona Beach.

Sports

Daytona has a dozen **golf courses** within a couple of miles of the beach. Some Daytona hotels have discount green fees for their guests and will happily arrange tee-off times for you as well. Three courses are particularly recommended: Tomoka Oaks Country Club ((904) 677-7117, Route 1 and Nova Road, Ormond Beach; Indigo Lakes ((904) 254-3607, Route 92 at I-95, Daytona Beach; and Daytona Golf and Country Club ((904) 250-3119, 600 Wilder Boulevard, Daytona Beach.

There are eight public **tennis courts**; the city's recreation department ((904) 253-9222, will direct you to the one nearest you.

For those wild about **water sports**, pontoon boats and jet skis can be rented from the Dixie Queen Marina ((904) 255-1997, 841 Ballough Road, and surfboards from Daytona Beach Surf Shops ((904) 253-3366, 520 Seabreeze Boulevard.

Shopping

Seabreeze Boulevard is where you will find the best choice of shops in Daytona Beach.

((904) 255-5059, at 640 North Grandview Avenue, Daytona Beach, reverberates to the live sounds of southern rock and country bands, while for those who prefer their music middle-of-the-road as well as the middle of the dance floor there is the **Club Mocambo** ((904) 258-9413, at 637 North Route A1A, Daytona Beach. The collegiate crowd tends to congregate at **P.J.'s** ((904) 258-5222, 400 Broadway, Daytona Beach, where there is always cheap beer to go with the rock music during happy hour (6 to 7 PM).

There is, for example, an enormous range of sports and swimwear at the Bikini Company ((904) 253-1120, at N° 504, and much for the chiclets at Touché ((904) 252-2365, just down the street at N° 310.

Nightlife

The **Clarendon Plaza Hotel** ((904) 255-4471, at 600 North Route A1A, Daytona Beach, has three night clubs. There is the rock-video music of Penrod's; there are live bands and early-hours disco at the Plantation Club and the 701 offers recorded rock music throughout the night. Earlier in the evening you can do your warm-up exercises at the **Oyster Pub** ((904) 255-6348, 555 Seabreeze Avenue, Daytona Beach. **Finky's**

WHERE TO STAY

Luxury

The **Daytona Beach Hilton** ((904) 767-7350 TOLL-FREE (800) 445-8667, at 2637 South Route A1A, Daytona Beach Shores, has 215 spacious rooms, the larger among them having private balconies overlooking the sea. There's a games room for children, and a swimming pool, and two restaurants, one of which is on the roof of the hotel offering panoramic views of the city and the sea. Five miles (eight kilometers) out of Daytona is the **Indigo Lakes Resort** ((904) 258-6333

OPPOSITE: The pier at Daytona Beach.
ABOVE: A snake-like bridge lights the way to Daytona Beach.

TOLL-FREE (800) 223-4161, at 2620 West International Speedway Boulevard, Daytona Beach. The idyllic grounds contain a championship golf course, 10 tennis courts, and a health institute and spa. The resort's restaurant is so good, with so many sinfully tempting dishes, you will need these sport and health facilities.

Mid-range
Perry's Ocean Edge ℭ (904) 255-0581, 2209 South Route A1A, Daytona Beach Shores, has oceanfront rooms and enclosed garden

some rooms, each with its own balcony, and a beachfront location — and is still moderately priced.

Inexpensive
A new and increasingly popular hotel is the **Captain's Quarter Inn** ℭ (904) 767-3119, at 3711 South Route A1A, Daytona Beach, which has earned its reputation for being especially welcoming. Another friendly welcome awaits guests at the **Del Aire Motel** ℭ (904) 252-2563, 744 North Route A1A, Daytona Beach, right next to the beach.

rooms in addition to ones overlooking the solarium swimming pool, whirlpool, and solar-heated spa. Along this main road you will find quite a selection of medium-sized hotels with well-appointed rooms and swimming pools, all very conveniently located for the beach. Among the nicest: the **Treasure Island** ℭ (904) 255-8371 TOLL-FREE (800) 874-7420; the **Daytona Sands** ℭ (904) 767-2551; and the **Sun Viking Lodge** ℭ (904) 252-6252 TOLL-FREE (800) 874-4469.

The **St. Regis Hotel** ℭ (904) 242-8743, at 509 Seabreeze Boulevard, Daytona Beach, overlooks a green lawn instead of a sandy beach, and is wonderfully quiet. The **Nautilus Inn** ℭ (904) 254-8600, at 1515 South Route A1A, Daytona Beach, has very hand-

Cheaper than these and closer to the speedway is the **Econo Lodge** ℭ (904) 255-3661, at 2250 Volusia Avenue, Daytona Beach.

WHERE TO EAT

Expensive
The **St. Regis Hotel Restaurant** ℭ (904) 252-8743, at 509 Seabreeze Boulevard, Daytona Beach, has one of the most elegant dining rooms in Daytona to go with its classic French cuisine. **La Crêpe en Haut** ℭ (904) 673-1999, at 142 East Granada Boulevard in Ormond Beach, on the upper floor of a courtyard mall next door to the Birthplace of Speed Museum, is renowned for its crêpes and sweetbreads but also has some superb

steaks. Fresh fish is what draws people to **The Chart House** ((904) 255-9022, 645 South Beach Street, Daytona Beach. The same, but Italian-accented, goes for the **King's Cellar** ((904) 255-3014, at 1258 North Route A1A, Daytona Beach.

Moderate

It can be unsettling to walk into a restaurant and see *Isten Hozott* ("God welcomes you") written above the entrance, but God has clearly smiled on Marie and Hugo Tischler, who have splendidly recreated the menu

of Ponce de León Inlet, where you will find the **Inlet Harbor** ((904) 767-4502, an extremely agreeable restaurant overlooking the harbor.

Inexpensive

Also to be found in Ponce de León Inlet, at Timmon's Fishing Camp, is **Down the Hatch** ((904) 761-4831, which has its own fleet of boats bringing in seafood from the ocean. In the Outlet Mall in South Daytona Beach is **Duff's Smörgasbord** ((904) 788-0828, which is a simple, unfussy eat-as-

and ambiance of Marie's old Budapest restaurant at the **Hungarian Village** ((904) 253-5712, 424 South Ridgewood, Route 1, Daytona Beach. Four miles (six and a half kilometers) west of Route A1A on Route 92, **Gene's Steak House** ((904) 255-2059, offers seven different kinds of prime steak cooked over hickory coals. At **Aunt Catfish's** ((904) 767-4768, 4009 Halifax Drive, Daytona Beach, you can have your catfish cooked in any of a number of ways: garlicky, Cajun-style, fried, or blackened. Aunt Jim Galbreath also has a specialty called "Florida Cracker"— a concoction of chicken, crab fritters, catfish fingerlings, shrimp, and coleslaw. Seven miles (11 km) south of Daytona on Route A1A is the small village

much-as-you-like (for under $6) place. Cheaper still is the **Piccadilly Cafeteria** ((904) 258-5373, in the Volusia Mall at 1700 Volusia Avenue, Daytona Beach.

HOW TO GET THERE

Daytona International Airport is served by a number of national airlines. An alternative is to fly into Orlando Airport, which is better served than Daytona, and then take the Daytona-Orlando Transit Service (DOTS) to the coast.

OPPOSITE: Bronze cannon detail at the Castillo de San Marcos in St. Augustine. ABOVE: The fort, begun in 1672, was completed in 1756.

ST. AUGUSTINE

The juxtaposition of old and new is one of the most striking features of St. Augustine. Some of the nation's oldest buildings and churches stand next to modern shopping malls, bars, and restaurants. The city also presents a pleasing blend of grand houses with walled courtyards, balconies overhanging winding lanes, and wide tree-lined avenues. Much of the old city is built of *coquina* — a material consisting of seashells

Menéndez de Avilés. He named the colony after San Augustin, having first sighted the coast on August 28, the saint's feast day. The town was intended to be Spain's principal military base along Florida's northeast coast. Nine wooden fortresses were built, all of which succumbed to hostile forces (one of them being a British squadron led by Sir Francis Drake) or to the elements, before construction of the Castillo de San Marcos commenced in 1672. The final touches were put to the castle in 1756.

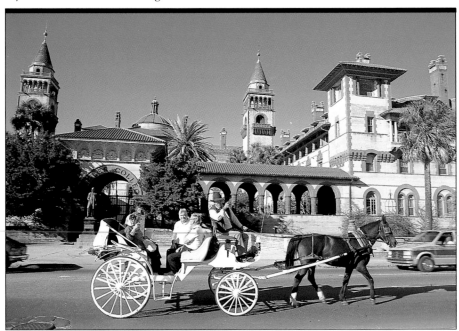

embedded in a lime mortar — which adds to its distinctive appearance. Near the Old City Gate is the massive fortress, Castillo de San Marcos, built over a period of 70 years by the Spanish, which often served as a refuge for the townspeople during a siege. Nowadays the only invaders who lay siege to the city are the hordes of tourists who have come to appreciate the charms of this lovely city.

BACKGROUND

St. Augustine was founded on September 8, 1565 — 42 years before the British established Jamestown in Virginia — by the Spanish admiral and ex-smuggler Pedro

During the eighteenth century the city was controlled in turn by the English, French, and Spanish (all of whom left their architectural marks on the place). It endured many sieges before being ceded — along with the rest of Florida — to the United States by Spain in 1821. After the Civil War the city began to flourish as a commercial seaport for the nearby plantations, and the arrival of Henry Flagler's railway in the early 1880s brought trainloads of rich tourists from the north into town. Flagler built the luxurious Ponce de León and Alcazar hotels to accommodate them, and used the city as the base from which to push his railway-and-hotel empire south along the length of Florida's east coast.

GENERAL INFORMATION

The St. Augustine Chamber of Commerce ((904) 829-6477, at One Riberia Street, St. Augustine, FL 32084, will furnish you with maps and brochures listing all the city's attractions. Even more detailed information is available from the St. Augustine Visitor Information Center ((904) 824-3334, located at 10 Castillo Drive, St. Augustine, FL 32084. For details on guided tours of the city, call **Spanish Heritage Tours** ((904) 829-3726.

WHAT TO SEE AND DO

Sights

St. Augustine is dense with sightseeing attractions, especially in the labyrinthine streets of the old town. A tour in a horse-drawn carriage is a pleasant way of seeing the city: **Colee's Carriages** leave from One Castillo Drive, charging $6 for adults and $3 for children aged five to 11. Alternatively, you can take one of the **Sightseeing Trains** ((904) 829-6545, from 170 San Marco Avenue, for a narrated tour which allows you to disembark at any point along the route and rejoin a later train. The trains run every 15 minutes and tickets are $9 for adults and $4 for children aged six to 12.

You could conduct your own tour on foot by passing through the **Old City Gate**, near the Visitor Information Center on Castillo Drive, to the **Castillo de San Marcos**, a Spanish castle which remained unconquered throughout its military history. Admission is $2, for which you receive a guided tour through exhibits that re-create the castle's history; the view from the ramparts is in itself worth the price of admission. Opening times are 8:45 AM to 4:45 PM daily.

Opposite the castle and centered around St. George's Street, is the **San Augustin Antiguo**, a quarter of the city where the houses and environment of an eighteenth-century Spanish colonial town have been re-created. The crafts and activities of the time are demonstrated by costumed artisans. The quarter is home to some of the oldest buildings in America, including the **oldest wooden schoolhouse** situated at 14 St. George Street, which dates from 1778 and is the oldest wooden building in the city. The conditions of an eighteenth-century classroom have been re-created inside the schoolhouse.

Dating from 1723, the **Oldest House** at 14 Francis Street is, well, the oldest house in the United States. The Spanish, French, and British refurbishments that have taken place over the centuries can be seen room by room in both the decor and the furnish-

ings. Next door to the house is the **Webb Museum**, which contains exhibits from all periods in the city's colonial history. Admission to both house and museum is $5 for adults and free for children under 12; they are both open from 9 AM to 5 PM daily.

The miniscule **St. Photios Chapel** on St. George Street has a stunning altar surrounded by frescoes and Greek icons; there is also a display outlining the history of Greeks in America. The **Basilica Cathedral** of St. Augustine on Treasury Street can be toured daily, and has the oldest parish

OPPOSITE: Seeing the sights of St. Augustine in a horse-drawn carriage. ABOVE: The Bridge of Lions, St. Augustine leads visitors to some of the oldest buildings in the nation.

records in the country. Ponce de León once searched for the legendary waters in this area, but you should have less trouble finding the **Fountain of Youth Discovery Park** at 155 Magnolia Avenue, which has a planetarium, space globe, a re-created Indian village, and a fountain — all for $4.50 adults and $3 children, and it's open from 9 AM to 5 PM daily. Or you can marvel at the thousands of fascinating and thought-provoking exhibits at **Ripley's Believe It or Not** ((904) 824-1606, at 19 San Marco Avenue. Admission $7.50.

One of Florida's best collections of antiques, decorative arts and crafts, and musical instruments can be seen at the **Lightner Museum** ((904) 824-2874, in the City Hall complex at King Street and Cordova Street; and if you can handle another dose of antiquity, the **Oldest Store Museum** ((904) 829-9729, at Four Artillery Lane, is home to thousands of gloriously useless items of the kind which people have always bought from stores and then thrown in the attic, where they are found years later by great-grandchildren and donated to museums.

At the **St. Augustine Alligator and Crocodile Farm** ((904) 824-3337, South Route A1A, you can see one of the state's most serious gangs of unhurried, unworried reptiles. A little further south down Route A1A you will find **Marineland of Florida** ((904) 471-1111, at 9507 Ocean Shore Boulevard, where you can watch dolphins show off, and see men of questionable sanity swimming around with hungry sharks and hand-feeding them. Admission is $12 for adults, $9.60 for children aged two to 11; it's open 9 AM to 5 PM daily.

Shopping

The **Fiesta Mall** at One King Street has insinuated itself very successfully into its old Spanish surroundings despite being home to the trendiest boutiques in town. The traditionally produced crafts in **San Augustin Antiguo** are all for sale, and City Gate Crafts at Nº 1 St. George Street has a range of tapestries, leather goods, and silver as finely crafted as anything in the old town. The best antiques around can be found at the **Lightner Antique Mall**, King and Granada streets, behind the Lightner Museum. The mall is in the (now drained) swimming pool of Henry Flagler's old Alcazar Hotel and has stalls selling, for example, lovely linen and china at very reasonable prices.

Nightlife

Spanish food followed by Spanish music and dancing is to be found at **El Caballero** ((904) 824-2096, in the Fiesta Mall. The English influence can be seen at the **White**

Lion ((904) 829-2388, St. George and Cuna streets, where the ale flows copiously during the "Lion's Roar Happy Hour". The **Conch House Marina Lounge** ((904) 829-8646, is a quieter place by the riverfront at 57 Comares Avenue, where the notes of a single guitar fill the air.

For those who would prefer to dance, the discs spin into the early hours at **Sister Sally's** ((904) 471-2555, in the Holiday Inn at 1060 South Route A1A, and until 1 AM at **Mario & Chickies** ((904) 824-2952, at 180 Anastasia Boulevard.

OPPOSITE: The interior of St. Augustine's oldest house, dating from 1723. ABOVE: The Spanish façade of St. Augustine. OVERLEAF: St. Augustine's Bridge of Lions at night.

Sports

The best **golf course** in the area is the Ponce de León Shores ((904) 829-5314, on Route 1 North, where a round costs $25 and golf cart rental $10. The city's recreation department ((904) 829-8807, can tell you all about the 20 public **tennis courts** in the city. **Surfers** can rent a surf board from Surf Station ((904) 471-9011, at 1020 Anastasia Boulevard; while Velasurf ((904) 471-6228, at 3639 South Route A1A, rents sailboards.

WHERE TO STAY

Luxury

The **Casa de Solano** ((904) 824-3555, at 21 Aviles Street, overlooks Matanzas Bay and has rooms furnished with local antiques; complimentary chocolates and a decanter of sherry are in every room also. The **Westcott House** ((904) 824-4301, at 146 Avenida Menéndez, is an elegant Victorian building dating from the 1880s, and its eight guest rooms have exquisite European and Oriental furnishings along with a complimentary bottle of wine for each new arrival. The **Conch House Marina Resort** ((904) 829-8646 TOLL-FREE (800) 432-6256, at 57 Comares Avenue, is a hotel with its own fishing pier. It has suites with kitchen and dining facilities, two restaurants, outside beach bars, and a cocktail lounge built on pilings near the shore.

Mid-range

In the heart of the old town the **Victorian Inn** ((904) 824-5214, at 11 Cadiz Street, has been transformed from a derelict boarding house into a quaint hotel, tastefully furnished and decorated. The **Casa de la Paz** ((904) 829-2915, at 22 Avenida Menéndez, is a Mediterranean-style hotel with a stucco exterior and walled courtyard. It also has — a nice touch, this — a cozy and well-stocked library. One of the few hotels in St. Augustine with its own swimming pool is the **Kenwood Inn** ((904) 824-2116, at 38 Marine Street, which also has a lovely patio shaded by a large pecan tree. Care and imagination have gone into the interior design, so that the rooms are decorated according to different "themes" — English, maritime, Spanish, honeymoon, and so

forth. Also in the old town, with 10 comfortable, high-ceilinged rooms, plus a small pond in the middle of an attractive courtyard, is the **St. Francis Inn** ((904) 824-6068, at 279 St. George Street.

Inexpensive

The bullfight paintings might be a little off-putting, but otherwise the rooms at the **Monsoon Motor Lodge** ((904) 829-2277, 32 Avenida Menéndez, are quite comfortable, and some come with a kitchen. There is less to trouble one's aesthetic sensibility

at the **Park Inn** ((904) 824-4352, 116 San Marco Avenue, apart from the view of the parking lot, but here again you get good value for your money.

WHERE TO EAT

Expensive

The **Columbia** ((904) 824-3341, located at 98 St. George Street, offers delicious Spanish cuisine, including an especially tasty *paella Valenciana*, accompanied by Spanish guitar music. The German-Swiss Sinatsch family have a wildly eclectic but lovingly prepared array of dishes on their menu at **Le Pavillon** ((904) 824-6202, 45 San Marco Avenue. The **Raintree** ((904) 824-7211, at

102 San Marco Avenue, is best known locally for its vast stock of beers and wines, but it also deserves mention for cooking the most basic food very well indeed.

Moderate

Scarlett O'Hara's ((904) 824-6535, located at 70 Hypolita Street, has an imaginative variety of soups, salads, seafoods, and sandwiches to choose from. Conch chowder is the house specialty at **Captain Jim's Conch Hut** ((904) 829-8646, by the ocean at 57 Comares Avenue. For uncomplicated English-style

How to Get There

The nearest airport is Jacksonville International Airport. The principal road from the west is Route 207.

JACKSONVILLE

Embracing 840 sq miles (2,177 sq km) on either side of the mouth of the St. Johns River, Jacksonville is the state's largest city (and one of the largest, in area, in America).

cooking, go to **Monk's Vineyard** ((904) 824-5888, at 56 St. George Street. For typically satisfying American food, try the **Gypsy Cab Company** ((904) 824-8244, at 828 Route A1A, Anastasia Island.

Inexpensive

The **Café Alcazar** ((904) 824-2618, located at 25 Granada Street, only serves lunch but it has an unusual and fun menu, including "croissandwiches". Fried shrimp lovers should head for **O'Steens** ((904) 829-6974, at 205 Anastasia Boulevard, while those looking for good burgers, fried chicken, or Mexican food will be happy to find themselves at **Panama Hattie's** ((904) 471-2255, on Route A1A South, near the beach.

The Atlantic Coast

It is also Florida's financial center. Amelia Island, with its 13 miles (21 km) of beach, and Fernandina Beach lie just to the north of Jacksonville, providing a quiet retreat from the city.

BACKGROUND

A French garrison was established at Fort Caroline, by the mouth of the St. Johns River, in 1564, but in the following year it fell to a Spanish force from St. Augustine. Like St. Augustine, Jacksonville was controlled by different European powers for

ABOVE AND OPPOSITE: Eventide and endless tide.

the next two and a half centuries, until Andrew Jackson marched into the city in 1821 as the first American territorial governor of Florida — hence the name Jacksonville. The city assumed prominence during the Civil War as a strategic port, and later for the export of the citrus produce of the hinterland. The arrival of the Florida East Coast Railroad in 1883 ensured that the city became the principal industrial and shipping center of Florida.

GENERAL INFORMATION

The Jacksonville Chamber of Commerce ((904) 366-6000, is at Three Independent Drive, Jacksonville, FL 32202. The Amelia Island-Fernandina Beach Chamber of Commerce ((904) 277-0717, is at 102 Center Street, Fernandina Beach, FL 32034.

Other useful telephone numbers (all in area code 904):

Jacksonville International Airport	741-2000
Yellow Cabs	354-5511
Duval County Medical Society	335-6561
Dental Information and Referral Service	356-6642

WHAT TO SEE AND DO

Sights

Jacksonville has some of the finest art museums in Florida, including the **Jacksonville Art Museum** ((904) 398-8336, at 4160 Boulevard Center Drive, which houses an exceptional collection of Oriental porcelain and pre-Columbian artifacts. The world's largest collection of Meissen porcelain can be seen at the **Cummer Gallery of Art and Gardens** ((904) 356-6857, 829 Riverside Avenue, which also houses a fine collection of European and Japanese art; in addition, the Italian-style gardens are a delight. The **Amelia Island Museum** ((904) 261-7378, at 233 South Third Street, Fernandina Beach, charts the complex military, political, and cultural history of the area, while the **Jacksonville Museum of Science and History** ((904) 396-7062, at 1025 Gulf Life Drive, will take you even further back in time.

A replica of the fort established by the French in 1564 can be seen at the **Fort Caroline National Memorial** ((904) 641-7111, 12713 Fort Caroline Road, daily from 9 AM to 5 PM, free of charge. To complete your historical overview visit the **Kingsley Plantation** ((904) 251-3537, on Fort George Island, County Road 105 off Route A1A, where Zephaniah Kingsley ran a worldwide slave trade and lived with his African princess wife. Open daily 9 AM to 5 PM. Admission is free.

For the children, the **Jacksonville Zoo** ((904) 757-4463, at 8605 Zoo Road, half a mile (800 m) east of Heckscher Drive, mostly dispenses with cages, employing moats to separate watcher and watched, and features elephant rides. Admission is $4 for adults and $3 for children. For a less elephantine trot, you can hire a horse, for $18 to $25 an hour, from **Sea Horse Stable** ((904) 261-4878, on Route A1A South, Amelia Island, and go galloping along the beach. After the ride, you should go for a stroll among the new-Gothic and Victorian architecture of Fernandina Beach, Amelia Island's main village.

Back in Jacksonville you can relax along the **Riverwalk** on the south bank of the river, then cross the Main Street Bridge to reach **Jacksonville Landing** at Two Independent Drive to soak up the street life of musicians, buskers, shops, bars, and cafés.

Sports

Golfers will be challenged by the links at the Dunes Golf Club ((904) 641-8444, 11751 McCormick Road, Jacksonville, or the Jacksonville Beach Golf Club ((904) 249-8600, Penman Road, Jacksonville Beach. On Amelia Island the City of Fernandina Golf Course ((904) 261-7804, at 2800 Bill Melton Road, Fernandina Beach, welcomes visiting players.

Tennis players should ring the city's recreation department ((904) 633-2540, for information about the various municipal courts in Jacksonville.

You can hire a sailboat or receive **sailing instruction** at Amelia Island Charters ((904) 261-7086, 116 Center Street, Fernandina Beach, while surfboards and sailboards can be hired from Aloha Wind 'n' Surf ((904) 241-4886, at 407 Route A1A, Atlantic Beach.

Shopping

There are over 100 medium-sized shops, catering to almost every taste, at the recently developed **Jacksonville Landing** ((904) 353-1188, Two Independent Drive, on the north bank of the St. Johns River. It is a festival marketplace on two levels, with a number of cafés and restaurants in which to retreat from the hurly-burly. On Amelia Island, Fernandina Beach's **Center Street** is the main artery of the shopping district.

Nightlife

Regular jazz combos perform in the snazzy surroundings of **Juliette's** ((904) 355-6644, in the Omini Hotel at 245 Water Street. At **57 Heaven** ((904) 721-5757, 8136 Atlantic Boulevard, Atlantic Beach, you can boogie to dance music from the Fifties and Sixties. A younger crowd strut their stuff to mod-rock, heavy metal, and reggae at **Metropolis** ((904) 355-6410, 43 West Monroe Street, while others prefer the live rock music at **Einstein-A-GoGo** ((904) 249-4646, 327 North First Street.

On Amelia Island, serious drinking goes on until early hours of the morning at what is reputed to be Florida's oldest bar, the **Palace Saloon** ((904) 261-9068, 115 Center Street.

WHERE TO STAY

Luxury

The **Omini Hotel** ((904) 355-6664 TOLL-FREE (800) 228-2121, at 245 Water Street, is probably the fanciest in town, with superb service to match its sumptuous accommodation. Every room has a view across the beach at **Adeeb's Sea Turtle Inn** ((904) 279-7402 TOLL-FREE (800) 831-6600, One Ocean Boulevard, Jacksonville Beach. The hotel has a well-equipped games room and an excellent restaurant.

On Amelia Island is the residential resort complex, **Amelia Island Plantation** ((904) 261-6161 TOLL-FREE (800) 342-6841, on Route A1A. Accommodation ranges from rooms in the hotel itself to villas scattered across the compound (some with private pools). There are shops and bars on the Plantation and the leisure facilities include 20 tennis courts, a golf course, a beach, fishing lagoons, Jacuzzis, and a gym. If you would like a room with a 360-degree view, you can have one at **The Lighthouse** ((904) 261-5878, 748 Route A1A, Fernandina Beach. If you have the money you can rent all four floors and have the lighthouse to yourself — with service, of course.

Mid-range

Overlooking Riverwalk and the river is the **Jacksonville Hotel** ((904) 398-8800, 565 South Main Street, which has rooms with private balconies and is well positioned for both the town and the beach. **Seaside Studios** ((904) 241-7000, at 222 14th Avenue North in Jacksonville Beach, has efficiency suites and a congenial central courtyard with a grill and loungers under small palm trees.

The inviting **Bailey House** ((904) 261-5390, can be found at 28 South Seventh Street in Fernandina Beach, where its Victorian gables, porches, and towers greet the eye. The interior tastefully maintains an Old World feel, with antiques and lace curtains gracing spacious rooms. The **Seaside Inn** ((904) 261-0954, at 1998 South Fletcher Avenue, Fernandina Beach, has rather more character than its name suggests. Ceiling fans cool the air, baskets of fruit await new guests in their rooms, and complimentary afternoon tea is served on the verandah.

WHERE TO EAT

Expensive

Brett's ((904) 261-2660, at 501 South Eighth Street, Fernandina Beach, offers a continental menu almost as lavish as the restaurant's surroundings. Chef Tim Felver of the **Florida Café** ((904) 737-2244, 8101 Phillips Highway, Jacksonville, specializes in Californian cuisine; especially recommended are his mesquite-grilled meat, quail, and Alaskan salmon dishes. The **Olive Tree** ((904) 249-1300, at 1249 Penman Road, Jacksonville, serves up some exceptional Spanish and Italian dishes, and the **Wine Cellar** ((904) 398-8989, at 1314 Prudential Drive, Jacksonville, is worth a visit for its game alone.

Moderate

If you like deep-fried chicken gizzards with sautéed peppers and onions you will be kept happy at the all-American **Homestead** ((904) 249-5240, 1721 Beach Boulevard, Jacksonville Beach, where you can find other, less demanding dishes as well. Steak-lovers are advised to try the **1878 Steak House** ((904) 261-4049, at 12 North Second Street in Fernandina Beach. Those who prefer an Iberian ambiance should go to **Salud!** ((904) 241-7877, at 207 Atlantic Boulevard, Atlantic Beach, which has delicious gazpacho, conch fritters, and deep-fried crab wontons. **Crawdaddy's** ((904) 396-3546, at 1643 Prudential Drive, Jacksonville, includes alligator and traditional Cajun food on its menu.

Inexpensive

You will get very generous portions of Oriental pork, beef, and chicken at **Chiang's Mongolian Bar-B-Q** ((904) 241-3075, 1504 North Route A1A, Jacksonville Beach. **The Slightly Off Center Bakery and Deli** ((904) 277-2100, at South Second Street on Amelia Island, is a convivial eatery offering sandwiches, hamburgers, and Cajun food. A good place for cheap Italian food is **Patti's** ((904) 753-1662, at 7300 Beach Boulevard, Jacksonville Beach, while sushi-lovers should make a bee line for **Ieyasu of Tokyo** ((904) 353-0163, at 23 West Duval, Jacksonville.

HOW TO GET THERE

Many national and international airlines fly in to Jacksonville International Airport. Airport limousines charge $10 to downtown Jacksonville. The principal north-south roads are still I-95 and Routes 1 and A1A, while the main highway from the west is I-10.

The mighty Castillo de San Marcos was never conquered.

Central Florida

EVIDENCE that Florida was once covered by the sea runs from north of Ocala south to Sebring, above Spring Lake, in the form of a limestone ridge which was once a prehistoric coral reef. This ridge is the backbone of the Florida peninsula and rises to about 330 ft (100 m) above sea level. Many of the hillsides along the ridge are lined with citrus groves, while the plains to either side form the state's vegetable garden. In the north, in the hills of Ocala, grass and corrals signify that this is horse country: while in the south, around the old cowboy town of Kissimmee, are the sandy scrublands of cattle country.

The agricultural plains are fed by the pellucid waters of thousands of springs, rivers, and lakes. The waters of Ocklawaha River, which runs through the Ocala National Forest, and the chain of lakes created by it are particularly pristine, thus making fishing and boating even more enjoyable than usual. The Ocala National Forest, the largest sandy pine forest in the world, is understandably very popular with riders, campers, and seasonal hunters.

Oh yes, there's also Walt Disney World.

BACKGROUND

Early settlers, known as "crackers" (derived from the crack of the cattle whips they used to drive cattle), were tough and industrious people who worked a living from the land, and herded the same breed of cattle which the Spanish had introduced to the region in the sixteenth century. The citrus and cattle industries established by the crackers became the foundation of the region's economy, ensuring that Orlando grew to become one of the state's most important commercial centers. The farmers and ranchers of the region lived alongside the warlike Seminole Indians. A band of them massacred 139 United States soldiers on December 28, 1835, igniting the bloody and bitter Second Seminole War. It is generally accepted that Orlando derives its name from one Orlando Reeves, a soldier who was killed fighting the Seminoles.

The coming of the steamboat encouraged tourism and greatly boosted the economy of central Florida, while the arrival of the railroads in the 1880s added further impetus to the area's development. So far, so good — and so quietly. Then, in 1971, something happened. Walt Disney World opened, 20 miles (32 km) south of Orlando at Lake Buena Vista, and suddenly central Florida was the most popular vacation destination in the world.

WALT DISNEY WORLD

The Disney people chose the Orlando area as the site for their eastern United States theme park because of the availability of vast quantities of flat land at reasonable (read: cheap) prices, good transportation facilities, and a year-round sunny climate. Eventually, after much surreptitious wheeling and dealing, Disney's agents slowly, slowly acquired 28,000 acres (11,336 hectares) — that's 42 sq miles (67 sq km), an area twice the size of Manhattan — because Disney wanted enough space to build a wholly self-contained and self-servicing complex which wouldn't attract the sort of ugly metropolitan collar that chokes Disneyland in California. Disney himself died in 1966, three years before work started on the site. The first visitor walked through the completed park's gates in the summer of 1971; by 1985 another 250 million had walked through, making it easily the greatest tourist attraction in the world.

A month-long celebration greeted the opening, in 1982, of Epcot Center, a futuristic showcase extension to the park. "Epcot" stands for Experimental Prototype Community of Tomorrow, and was Walt Disney's own brainchild: he envisioned a self-governing community existing alongside the theme parks. It has worked out pretty much as Mr. Disney planned it: the Walt Disney World Vacation Kingdom (to give it its full name) is known in the Florida statute books as the Reedy Creek Improvement District, which is the legal governing body of the entire Disney complex, with powers to enforce building codes, construct roads, and supervise the election of mayors to the district's two towns, Bay Lake and Lake Buena Vista.

OPPOSITE: The Magic Kingdom gives a surrealistic quality to the Disney World skyline.

A third theme park, Disney MGM Studios, shows, naturally, all the glamor, technical wizardry and artistry associated with the silver screen.

The facilities and services of this Utopian kingdom are indeed highly advanced: the first fully electronic telephone system in the world, a land transport system based on an elevated, noiseless, and computerized monorail, supported by — Mr. Ripley would have loved this — a fleet of 400 ships, from steamboats to submarines, making it the fifth largest navy in the world.

then take you to the **Ticket and Transportation Center** (TTC), where you buy tickets for entry to the parks.

Ticket Prices

The term "ticket" means that you get a single day's admission to either the Magic Kingdom, the Epcot Center or MGM Studios (one only); "passports" admit you to all attractions and grant you unlimited use of the internal transportation system. The prices — one-day ticket: $40.81 adults, $32.86 children; four-day passport: $136.74

GENERAL INFORMATION

For all enquiries about Disney World contact Walt Disney World ((407) 828-3481, Box 10000, Lake Buena Vista, FL 32830. They will be happy to send you a copy of the *Walt Disney World Vacation Guide.*

Try to arrive at Disney World before 9 AM as the place becomes packed very quickly. A $5 parking fee is paid at the entrance, after which you follow the signs either to the **Magic Kingdom**, **Epcot Center** or **MGM Studios**. Be sure to remember the name of your lot and line number. Trams

adults, $109.18 children; five-day passport: $207.76 adults, $166.42 children.

Each day upon entry your passport is stamped; the remaining days can be used at any time in the future. All tickets and passports can be bought from the Ticket and Transportation Center; registered guests can buy theirs from on-site hotels. A Disney World kiosk sells tickets and passports in the main terminal at Orlando International Airport or you can order them before you travel from Admissions, Walt Disney World, at the address above. Tickets take about five weeks to arrive. All prices are subject to variation but can be confirmed by Walt Disney World Information if you call ((407) 824-4321.

The Disney World elevated monorail speeds past Space Mountain ABOVE to Epcot Center and Spaceship Earth OPPOSITE.

Opening Hours

Disney World opens at 9 AM all year round (although they often let you in early). To avoid the worst crowds, visit the Magic Kingdom and MGM Studios in the afternoon — or, better still, in the evening — and Epcot in the morning, working your way back to the entrance gates from the more distant attractions. In the summer months the Magic Kingdom closes at midnight, Epcot Center and MGM Studios at 11 PM (earlier in the winter). Monday, Tuesday, and Wednesday are the busiest days; Friday and Sunday the quietest. I don't know why. Late afternoon and evening are the best times of the day for getting on rides and getting served. Peak times are Christmas through New Year and all the major holidays. Late August is the summer's quietest period.

Transportation

The transport is both varied and efficient. The monorail operates daily from 7:30 AM to 11 PM from the Transportation and Ticket Center (TTC), whence all other modes of transport depart to the various attractions. All buses are color-coded according to their destination. If you prefer to travel around by water, ferries and launches also leave from the TTC. For those staying in an on-site hotel, or for holders of a joint Magic Kingdom-Epcot Center passport, all transport is free.

Tips

It's almost impossible to see everything in the Magic Kingdom and Epcot Center in the same day. Both are huge and several miles apart. To relax, allow three days between the two, and five days if you want to take in the outlying attractions of the complex, which include River Country, Blizzard Beach, Typhoon Lagoon, Pleasure Island, Discovery Island, the Shopping Village, and Hotel Plaza. Get a map from City Hall in the Magic Kingdom or from Earth Station in Epcot Center and plan some sort of route: it will help you to get more in. A good way to avoid the worst queues at the rides in the Magic Kingdom is to go during the daily parade of Disney characters which begins at 3 PM and lasts half an hour.

Useful telephone numbers (all in area code 407):

Guest relations	824-4500
Accommodation reservations	824-8000
Dining and Recreation Information	824-3737
Tours of Magic Kingdom and Epcot Center	827-8233
Disney MGM Studios	824-4521
Magic Kingdom Lost and Found	824-4521
Epcot Center Lost and Found	827-8236
Shopping Village Information	823-3058
KinderCare Child Care	827-5444

For more comprehensive information, including many helpful hints, get a copy of Sehlinger and Finley's *The Unofficial Guide to Walt Disney World and Epcot*, published by Prentice-Hall.

WHAT TO SEE AND DO

Magic Kingdom

A monorail or ferry boat takes you from the TTC to the gates of the Magic Kingdom in a few minutes. You then walk through the gates into the **Town Square** which contains the City Hall, the information center and the lost-and-found office, and a railway station from which you can take a 15-minute train journey around the 98 acres (39 hectares) of the park's rides and attractions. The Town Square is a lively place with stalls, Dixieland bands, and Disney characters to welcome you.

Main Street, USA stretches away from the Town Square. It is a thoroughfare lined with arcades, ice cream parlors, cinemas, shops, cafés and restaurants with turn-of-

Railroad, a hair-raising runaway-train ride through a mine, and the *Country Bear Jamboree*, featuring singing, cavorting, audio-animatronic bears. For relative peace try *Tom Sawyer Island*, which can be reached by taking a raft.

The fourth *Land* is **Liberty Square**, which has as its themes Colonial and American history. Adults and older children will enjoy the *Hall of Presidents*, with animated figures of the nation's past leaders delivering famous speeches. There is a 15-minute movie charting the history of the American

the-century façades. The Disney characters parade down the street to the Town Square every day at 3 PM, and from 9 PM to 11 PM there's the *IllumiNations Parade* of giant floats.

At the end of Main Street you cross a bridge over a moat and come to the 18-story Cinderella's Castle. The castle is at the heart of the Magic Kingdom; from here you can take any of the routes which lead to the various *Lands* — Main Street is the first such *Land*.

Adventureland

Adventureland is one of the most crowded in the kingdom. The top attractions are the *Pirates of the Caribbean*, which, among other buccaneering experiences, takes you through a cannon battle; the *Swiss Family Robinson Treehouse*, which is a labyrinthine concrete structure offering great views of the park; and the *Jungle Cruise*, which manages to go down the Nile and up the Amazon in one 10-minute journey.

Frontierland takes you back to the Old West of the Gold Rush days. The main attractions are the *Big Thunder Mountain*

Constitution. Slightly more attention-getting is the popular *Haunted House* and the riverboat that takes you past scenes depicting the Old West.

Fantasyland is the farthest removed from the "real world" that the Magic Kingdom has to offer, and is easily the most popular with children. The attractions include a replica of Captain Nemo's submarine from *20,000 Leagues Under the Sea*, a trek through a forest to meet *Snow White and the Seven Dwarfs* and *Cinderella's Golden Carousel*. All of Disney's fairy-tale and cartoon characters will be encountered on the rides or streets of Fantasyland. Another attraction in this part of the park is *It's a Small World*, a voyage aboard a small boat

ABOVE TO OPPOSITE BOTTOM: The Moroccan, English, French and Chinese pavilions at Epcot Center.

across a dreamworld of dolls representing the global village in songs.

The last *Land* is **Tomorrowland**, where the roller-coaster ride — simulating space travel — at *Space Mountain* is heart-stopping (children under three cannot go on it and those under seven must be accompanied by an adult). The *Grand Prix Raceway* is popular with children who can get excited by a top speed of seven miles per hour (11 kph).

From Tomorrowland you can take the route to Cinderella's Castle and Main Street back to the entrance gate. From there it's a three-mile (five-kilometer) monorail ride to Epcot Center.

Epcot Center

The *Experimental Prototype Community of Tomorrow* (Epcot) is an educationally-oriented complex, about twice the size of the Magic Kingdom, with two distinct areas — *Future World* and *World Showcase* — sepa-

rated by a lagoon. It is best to explore World Showcase in the morning and Future World later in the day to get ahead of the crowds. You enter Epcot Center beneath *Spaceship Earth* (a 17-story spherical structure 180 ft or 55 m at its highest point) where you can pick up a guide to both areas at *Earth Station*.

Future World starts at Spaceship Earth, and World Showcase can be reached by taking the sidewalk which skirts the lagoon.

World Showcase is a collection of pavilions, each based on a replica of one of the host nation's landmarks or typical buildings (the Eiffel Tower, a Japanese pagoda, an English pub, that sort of thing). Displays, films, and exhibits portray the art, culture, and general way of life of the country in question. There are daily displays of that country's crafts in front of each pavilion, as well as live folk music and dance, while inside there are stalls selling these crafts and other artifacts. Examples of the national cuisine are also served up, so be sure to visit the French, Mexican and Japanese pavilions.

The centerpiece of the World Showcase is the host pavilion, the **American Adventure**, which is based around a Colonial-style house and features a show in which audio-animatronic characters re-enact scenes from American history. The show's hosts are Mark Twain and Benjamin Franklin. The other pavilions fan out from American Adventure. The countries you can "visit" on your international tour are Mexico, China (with a brilliant reproduction of Beijing's Temple of Heaven), Germany, Italy (featuring a reproduction of St. Mark's

Square in Venice), Japan, France, the United Kingdom (featuring the Rose and Crown pub with Guiness ale), Canada, Morocco, and Norway. Soon to come, at this writing, are pavilions from Spain, Israel, and Equatorial Africa.

Future World

Walk back around the lagoon to the Future World starting point in *Spaceship Earth*. Future World features an educational and entertaining tour through the technological and scientific advances of man, exploring such subjects as transportation, communications, energy, and computers. In Spaceship Earth you are guided through displays and exhibits which show the history of man's attempt to communicate his ideas and make himself understood, from the time of the first cave paintings to the latest satellite technology.

Children will enjoy the educational computer games at **Innoventions**, where you can also gain an insight into the complex computer system which helps maintain the smooth functioning of the entire Disney World complex and amazing scientific developments from around the world. The **Universe of Energy** dramatizes the formation of fossil fuels in prehistoric times with simulated earthquakes and volcanic eruptions; there are also audio-animatronic dinosaurs stalking around the display. **Horizons** is a journey through time in the opposite direction: solar-powered theater cars take you on a ride into the twenty-first century, where you will find farms run by robots, cities under the ocean, and zero-gravity baseball in space.

Journey into the Imagination features *Henry, I Shrunk the Audience*, in a fascinating thrilling ride. Characters called Dreamfinder and Figment then escort you through exhibits which try to show how art, literature, and films originate in one idea which expands and is modified to become the completed work. The least imaginatively named attraction at Future World is *The Land*, which will have greater appeal for adults than for children. The land covers six

acres (2.5 hectares) and offers walking tours through displays of the latest methods of food production, including one showing how food might one day be grown in outer space. Produce from The Land can be tasted at the Good Turn Restaurant. One of the most spectacular attractions is **The Living Seas**, which features an underwater restaurant and "sea-cab" service in a six-million-gallon (23-million liter) aquarium that is five fathoms deep and inhabited by hundreds of different kinds of sea life, including dolphins and barracudas.

The Disney MGM Studios

In the center of the park, inside a replica of the famous Grauman's Chinese Theater of Hollywood, **The Great Movie Ride** takes

---

The Swan Hotel runs a free ferry service to Disney World.

you on a 20-minute train journey through Hollywood's history and brings you face to face with the big stars in audio-animatronics form.

In the **Backstage Studio Tour**, a 30-minute shuttle ride takes you behind the scenes of a working motion picture and television studio to see the costumes, props and backlot; and discover how the movies create floods, earthquakes and gigantic fires during a terrifying excursion through Catastrophe Canyon.

Magic of Disney Animation depicts Disney artists at work on animated features and reveals television production techniques used in such movies as *Honey, I Shrunk the Kids*. **Jim Henson's Muppet Vision 3-D** introduces the *Muppet Show*

characters. Don't miss the stunts and special effects of the Indiana Jones Stunt Spectacular. **Star Tours** is a ride through space recreating effects in *Star Wars*. The **Twilight Zone Tower** of Terror is a heart-throbbing 13-story "drop" in a hotel elevator which opens its doors revealing the park below, then the doors shut, just when the elevator drops straight down. Latest attractions include Disney's *The Hunchback of Notre Dame: A Musical Adventure,* and *Ace Ventura Detective Live in Action.*

Children particularly enjoy the newly-built playground based on the movie *Honey, I Shrunk the Kids*, which has grass 30 ft (nine meters) high, giant ants and spider webs.

The studio is next to Epcot Center off Buena Vista Drive.

OTHER THINGS TO SEE IN DISNEY WORLD

Blizzard Beach Water Park is a ski resort with runs down 90 ft (27 m) Mt. Gushmore into a tropical lagoon. It is situated next to Disney's new All-Star Resorts.

River Country ((407) 824-3737, a popular spot in summer, at the Fort Wilderness Campground Resort by Bay Lake off Vista Boulevard, is an aquatic park with water slides, white-water rapids, waterfalls, and swing ropes around a huge pool. Admis-

sion is $14.85 per day for adults and $11.66 per day for children aged three to nine.

Discovery Island is in Bay Lake and can be reached by boat from either the Magic Kingdom or River Country. It is a sanctuary for exotic flora, over 60 species of birds (such as the bald eagle and the stunning scarlet ibis), and small animals. Tickets can be bought from the TTC, River Country, or on the island itself and are $10.07 for adults and $5.57 for children aged three to nine. The island's walkways and foot bridges offer a retreat from the rest of Disney World.

Shopping

If you have any money left, you might like to visit the Walt Disney World Village at Lake Buena Vista (go west on Epcot Center Drive, then north on I-4). The village has a shopping complex with the latest fashions from around the world, electronic goods, and quality gifts. The prices, however, are high; you would be better off shopping in Orlando.

Nightlife

There is a good selection of nightlife in Disney World itself and in the nearby town of Kissimmee, five miles (eight kilometers) to the east on Route 192.

The Polynesian Revue and **Mickey's Tropical Revue** ((407) 824-8000, in the Polynesian Village Resort, Disney World, are shows with South Pacific themes featuring hula dancing which are held outdoors with barbecue dinner included. The **Giraffe Lounge** ((407) 828-2828, in the Hotel Royal Plaza, has live dance music every evening. In the Australian surroundings of the **Laughing Kookaburra Good Time Bar** ((407) 827-2727, in the Buena Vista Palace, you will have a choice of over 100 beers; and for the best in German beers there is the **Biergarten** at the World Showcase in Epcot Center.

In Kissimmee, **Murphy's Vine Street Emporium Dance Palace** ((407) 396-6500, at 4763 West Route 192, has a dance floor as endless as its name and the sounds of a live dance band until the early hours.

WHERE TO STAY

Walt Disney World and environs has a truly vast selection of hotels to chose from. The first decision you will have to make is whether to stay inside or outside the grounds of Disney World. The main advantages of being in the grounds are that you are close to all the things you want to see, with free use of the quick and efficient internal transportation. Moreover, on-site guests receive a guest identification card which allows them to charge anything at Disney World (except in the Magic Kingdom) to their hotel room.

Your second decision will be whether to stay in one of the hotels owned by Disney World, most of which overlook Bay Lake next to the Magic Kingdom, or to stay in one of the independently owned hotels within the grounds at Lake Buena Vista in the Walt Disney World Village. These hotels are further away from the main attractions, but most run a shuttle service to and from the theme parks. Some of the hotels in the village have self-catering facilities and there is a supermarket in the shopping complex nearby.

To make reservations for any on-site hotels contact the **Walt Disney Central Reservation Office** ((407) 824-8000, P.O. Box 10100, Lake Buena Vista, FL 32830, as far in

The **Polynesian Village** has 644 rooms and tries to re-create the atmosphere of a South Pacific island, with a miniature "rain forest" in the lobby consisting of palm trees and sundry exotic plants. The accommodation is in 11 three-story "longhouses". Most of the rooms have balconies and some overlook the Magic Kingdom. The hotel has its own beach and marina where you can rent canoes and boats for sailing, fishing, and water-skiing on the lake. The 1,053-room **Contemporary Hotel** has the monorail running straight through its lobby. This 15-

advance of your stay as possible. All-inclusive vacation packages, with admission tickets, automobile rental, and hotel reservations inside or outside the Disney World grounds, can be arranged through **the Walt Disney Travel Company** ((407) 828-3232, 1675 Buena Vista Drive, Lake Buena Vista, FL 32830.

All on-site hotels, whether Disney-owned or not, range from the expensive to the very very expensive.

On-Site Hotels owned by Walt Disney World

All of the hotels mentioned below should be contacted through the Central Reservation Office mentioned above.

story, ultra-modern hotel is constructed mainly of glass. The facilities include two swimming pools, a health club and sauna, and a fifteenth-floor lounge with dancing and entertainment every night. The hotel is next to Bay Lake. Many of the hotels are based on themes such as music or sports.

The **Resort Villas** are in the Walt Disney World Village alongside the independently-run hotels. The villas enjoy all the extensive sporting facilities, shopping, and nightlife which the village has to offer. There are several villas to choose from. **Vacation Villas** offers 139 one-bedroom efficiency units

OPPOSITE: The Floridian Hotel at Disney World.
ABOVE: Surely you joust: the Middle Ages live in Kissimmee, at the Medieval Times Restaurant.

which can accommodate up to four people, and 87 two-bedroom units, each accommodating up to six people and having kitchen facilities. Vacation Villas also has two swimming pools. **Two-Bedroom Villas** has 64 two-bedroom efficiency units, accommodating up to six people, in a delightful cedar structure next to the Lake Buena Vista golf course.

Among the other Disney hotels near Epcot Center and MGM Studios are the sumptuous **Walt Disney World Dolphin** and **Swan**, the **Grand Floridian Beach Resort**, the **Disney Inn by Bay Lake**, **Club-Suite Villas** in the World Village, the **All-Star Sports Resort** and the **All-Star Music Resort**. The increasingly popular **Tree-houses**, tucked away in quiet woods between the World Village and Bay Lake, will appeal to those who want to escape the crowds while remaining within striking distance of the theme parks. It is now possible to be married in any of the Walt Disney attractions, and there are even secluded honeymoon cottages.

Independent Hotels in Walt Disney World Village

The **Buena Vista Palace** ((407) 827-2727 TOLL-FREE (800) 327-2990, at 1900 Lake Buena Vista Drive, Lake Buena Vista, is a 27-story, 841-room hotel which cost $93 million to build. Many of its modern, spacious rooms overlook Epcot Center. The facilities include swimming pools, tennis courts, a games room, and several bars and restaurants, including Arthur's 27, a splendid top-floor eatery offering great views of Disney World. The **Hilton Hotel** ((407) 827-4000 TOLL-FREE (800) 445-8667, at 1751 Hotel Plaza Boulevard, Lake Buena Vista, has the latest in electronic technology, including lights that turn themselves on and off as you enter or leave the room, and all sorts of devices that control the central heating, the air conditioning, and the television.

At the Colonial-style **Grosvenor Resort** ((407) 828-4444 TOLL-FREE (800) 624-4109, 1850 Hotel Plaza Boulevard, Lake Buena Vista, all the rooms are handsomely decorated and each has its own VCR (you can rent movies from the hotel). There are two swimming pools, basketball and volleyball courts, and a children's playground. Other luxury hotels include the **Hotel Royal Plaza** ((407) 828-2828 TOLL-FREE (800) 248-2424, at 1905 Hotel Plaza Boulevard; and the **Pickett Suite Resort** ((407) 934-1000 TOLL-FREE (800) 742-5388, at 2305 Hotel Plaza Boulevard.

As an inexpensive alternative to these hotels, you can stay at the **Fort Wilderness Campground Resort** ((407) 824-8000, which is next to Bay Lake in the Disney World grounds. You can rent efficiency trailers that accommodate four to six people, or bring your own trailer, or simply pitch a tent. There are two "trading posts" in the campground, and the recreational facilities include canoeing, riding, and Disney film shows.

Hotels Outside Disney World

There are two areas close by Disney World where you can find a wide selection of mid-range and inexpensive hotels: the Maingate area, east off I-4 just above Disney World's northern entrance, and the Route 192 Corridor area east of Disney World running to Kissimmee. A selection is as follows :

MID-RANGE

In the Maingate area: **Days Inn Orlando Lakeside** ((407) 351-1900 TOLL-FREE (800) 777-3297, 7335 Sandlake Road, Orlando; and the following four, all situated on International Drive, Orlando: № 6515, the **Holiday Inn** International ((407) 351-3500; № 7400, the **Hilton Inn Florida Center** ((407) 351-4600 TOLL-FREE (800) 327-1363; № 8001, **Orlando Marriott Inn** ((407) 351-2420 TOLL-FREE (800) 228-9290; and, the **Sheraton World** ((407) 352-1100 TOLL-FREE (800) 325-3535, № 10100.

In the *Route 192 Corridor* area: the **Colonial Motor Lodge** ((407) 847-6121, 1815 West Wine Street, Kissimmee; the **Radisson Inn Maingate** ((407) 396-1400 TOLL-FREE (800) 333-3333, 7501 West Spacecoast Parkway, Kissimmee; the **Spacecoast Motel** ((407) 933-5732 TOLL-FREE (800) 654-8342, 4125 Spacecoast Parkway, Kissimmee; the **Gemini Motel** ((407) 396-2151, 4624 Route 192, Kissimmee; and the **Hawaiian Village Inn** ((407) 396-1212, 4559 Route 192, Kissimmee.

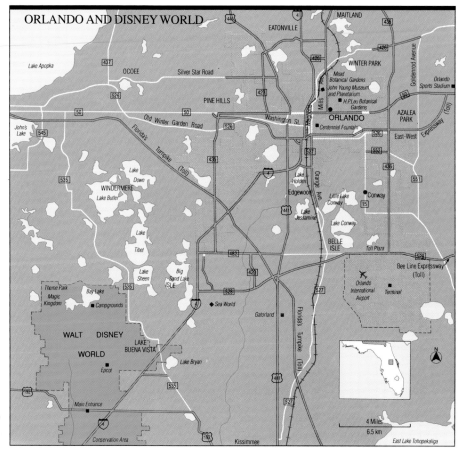

ORLANDO AND DISNEY WORLD

INEXPENSIVE

In the Maingate area: the **Knight's Inn Orlando Maingate West** ((407) 396-4200, 7475 West Irlo Bronson Highway; the **Quality Inn Plaza** ((407) 345-8585 TOLL-FREE (800) 228-5151, 9000 International Drive, Orlando; and the **Comfort Inn** ((407) 855-6060 TOLL-FREE (800) 327-9742, 8421 South Orange Blossom Trail, Orlando.

In the Route 192 Corridor area: the **Golden Link Motel** ((407) 396-0555, 4914 Route 192, Kissimmee; the **Casa Rosa Inn** ((407) 396-2020, 4600 Route 192, Kissimmee; and the **Lakeside Cedar Inn** ((407) 396-1376, 4960 Route 192, Kissimmee.

WHERE TO EAT

Pavilions in Epcot Center's World Showcase have restaurants with a menu of the host nation's cuisine. The restaurants also have special children's menu at reduced prices.

World Showcase Restaurants

Three eminent French chefs — Paul Bocuse, Roger Verge, and Gaston Lenôtre — have put together a classic menu at **Les Chefs de France** in the French Pavilion. The **San Angel Inn** is a romantic, candlelit restaurant in the Mexican pavilion, where the atmosphere is enhanced by the sounds of Mexican guitar and song. The cuisine here is actually much closer to Tex-Mex than to Mexican; the specialties you should certainly try are the Baja lobster with peppers marinated in white wine and the red snapper with onions. **Alfredo's** inside the Italian pavilion is extremely popular, thanks to its wide selection of traditional pastas, but no thanks to its selection of Italian singing waiters. Also recommended is the ploughman's lunch at the English pavilion's **Rose and Crown Pub,** or the couscous and pork bastilas of the **Marrakesh** in the Moroccan pavilion.

Making a Reservation at World Showcase Restaurants

Guests at any on-site hotel can make reservations by phoning ((407) 824-4000 a day or two in advance. Take your guest identification card with you when you go to the restaurant.

Visitors to Disney World who are not staying in one of the on-site hotels cannot make telephone reservations, and can only book a table on the day of the meal. **World-key Information screens** are the quickest way to make a reservation. They can be found at Earth Station in Future World's Spaceship Earth; there are more in a kiosk by the lagoon as you emerge from Future World. Of course you can also book in person at the restaurant of your choice, but you should do it early in the morning. All the World Showcase restaurants are moderately priced.

Walt Disney World Village Restaurants

The **American Vineyards** ((407) 827-4000, in the Hilton at 1751 Hotel Plaza Boulevard, specializes in wine-based sauces that lend an exceptional flavor to their beef and veal. The menu also includes an extensive selection of seafood cooked with Cajun seasonings and papaya butter. Regarded as one of Florida's premier restaurants, **Arthur's 27** ((407) 827-3450, can be found at the top of the Buena Vista Palace Hotel, 1900 Lake Buena Vista Drive. In the same hotel is a more family-oriented restaurant, **The Outback** ((407) 827-3430, which, as you might expect, specializes in Australian-style barbecued lamb and beef, and lots of beer. **Planet Hollywood** ((407) 827-7827, 1506 East Buena Vista Drive, part owned by Arnold Schwarzenegger, Sylvester Stallone and other stars, serves fun food.

HOW TO GET THERE

No problem. Many international airlines and over 30 national airlines serve Orlando International Airport, including Delta TOLL-FREE (800) 827-7786, which offers package tours to Disney World. An airport limousine service TOLL-FREE (800) 423-5566, goes to Disney World every half-hour, and costs $11 (the limos can carry up to 11 people). If you want to go from the airport to the door of your hotel, inside or outside the grounds of Disney World, you will have to pay about $30.

For those traveling in their own car, I-4 passes by the entrance to Disney World. From the northwest, you approach via Florida's Turnpike (a toll road) and join I-4 at Junction 75. You should also take the turnpike if you are coming from the Gold Coast. The I-4 approaches Disney World from the west and northeast (Tampa and Daytona). If you are traveling from the south, take Route 27 as far as Junction 54, where you join I-4.

GREATER ORLANDO

The Greater Orlando area, with a population approaching one million, is one of the most rapidly expanding metropolises in America. The growth of the city, and its transformation into a business and tourist center, is largely due, of course, to the proximity of Walt Disney World. The city, however, does have its own character and attractions distinct from those of Disney World.

BACKGROUND

United States soldiers were the first non-native inhabitants of the area when Fort Gatlin was established in 1838 as a military outpost to keep the local Seminole Indians in check. By 1875 the Seminoles had been subdued, increasing numbers of settlers were coming into the region, and the slowly growing community around the fort had been named Orlando. The city's early economy was based on citrus produce and cattle raising, despite the exceptionally cold weather during 1884 and 1885 which wiped out many of the citrus groves in the area. The local farmers, ever resourceful, turned to cereals and vegetables as replacement crops.

In the 1880s railroads reached central Florida, bringing tourists who were attracted by the waters and springs of the region. Orlando was a favorite base for these visitors, whose custom further boosted the city's economy. In those days Orlando could offer only a handful of hotels for visitors to choose from, but the city has steadily grown and prospered over the years and there are now some 60,000 hotel rooms in the Greater Orlando area.

GENERAL INFORMATION

The Greater Orlando Tourist Information Center ((407) 351-0412, is at 8445 International Drive, Orlando, FL 32819, where you can pick up a complimentary copy of the guidebook, *Discover Orlando*. The Orlando-Orange County Convention and Visitors Bureau ((407) 363-5800, is at 7208 Sand Lake Road, Suite 300, Orlando, FL 32819. For news of upcoming local events get the *Orlando Sentinel/Central Florida Guide*.

Other useful telephone numbers (all in area code 407):

Orlando International Airport 825-2001
Yellow Cabs 423-4455
Town and Country Cabs 828-3035
Orange County Medical Society 898-3338
Emergency Dental Care 425-1616

WHAT TO SEE AND DO

Sights

Route 192 west of Disney World is known locally as the "Tourist Trail", along which you will find **Old Town** ((407) 396-4888, at 5770 West Route 192, Kissimmee, home to a variety of Old World-style shops and restaurants, as well as the **Museum of Woodcarving** ((407) 396-4422, which contains over 400 beautifully carved works by Joseph T. Barta. At the **Jungleland Zoo** ((407) 396-1012, 4580 West Route 192, Kissimmee, visitors can see more than 100 species of endangered wildlife. Admission is $9.95 for adults and $6.95 for children. There are more "'gators" and 'gator wrestling just up the road at **Gatorland** ((407) 855-5496, on South Orange Blossom Trail, Kissimmee. Admission is $11.95 for adults and $8.95 for children.

Splendid China ((407) 396-7111, the area's latest attraction on US 192, west of I-4, is home to over 60 replicas (full scale or miniature) of China's best known scenic, historic and cultural sites. It also has shows, shops and restaurants.

Further north, before you get to downtown Orlando, there are more attractions grouped around International Drive. The most popular of these is **Sea World** ((407) 351-3600, at 7007 Sea World Drive, which considers itself the world's premier marine life theme park. It features shows with killer whales, dolphins, and sea lions, plus a nerve-testing ride along a tunnel made of *very* (read: completely sharkproof) thick acrylic which passes through a shark-infested tank. Wild Arctic, the park's latest attraction, is a thrill ride through exhibits

featuring animals of the frozen north. There are also gardens and restaurants in the park, which is open from 9 AM to 7 PM daily; admission is $39.95 for adults and $32.80 for children aged three to 11.

Other attractions in this area include the **Mystery Fun House** ((407) 351-3355, at 5767 Major Boulevard, which is full of haunting effects, mirrors, and a moving floor; **Wet 'n' Wild** ((407) 351-1800, at 6200 International Drive, is a 25-acre (10-hectare) waterpark with wave machines and huge water slides; at **Fun 'n' Wheels** ((407) 351-5651, at 6739 Sand Lake Road at Interna-

ABOVE: A killer whale rises to the occasion at Orlando's Sea World. OVERLEAF: The silent beauty of Lake Kissimmee State Park.

tional Drive, where you can race go-carts or settle some scores in bumper cars; and **Church Street Station** ((407) 422-2434, at 129 West Church Street, a nighttime entertainment complex with Dixieland, folk music, bluegrass, discos and restaurants.

In downtown Orlando you will find, among other attractions, the beautiful grounds of **Lake Eola Park** off of Orange Avenue, which retains the serene atmosphere of old Orlando. Watch out for the spectacular **Centennial Fountain**, especially at night, when water and light combine to dazzling effect. Another interesting collection can be seen at the **Cartoon Museum** ((407) 273-0141, 4300 South Semoran Boulevard, which features rare super-hero comic books from the earliest days of cartoon art. Just north of the downtown area is the **Orlando Science Center** ((407) 896-7151, at 810 East Rollins Street, which has a practical approach to teaching science: a computer will analyze your risk of a heart attack, and another machine will convert your bodily energy into electricity.

Universal Studios Florida ((407) 363-8000, 1000 Universal Studios Plaza (off Kirkman Road), is the largest motion picture and television facility outside Hollywood. It is a theme park offering more than 40 rides, shows and realistic backlot sets where famous scenes in cinematic history are recreated for visitors. Latest attractions include *Back to the Future*, and *Terminator 2*, the world's first 3-D virtual reality adventure. Admission is $39.22 for adults, $31.80 for children aged three to nine. Parking is $5. Open at 9 AM daily.

Orlando offers several ways of escaping the theme parks and the crowds, including **Scenic Boat Tours** ((407) 644-4056, which leave from 312 East Morse Boulevard in Winter Park, North Orlando, on a one-hour tour of the area's canals and lakes past some lovely countryside. Alternatively, you can go up and away with **Balloon Flights of Florida** ((407) 422-2434, at 129 West Church Street, Orlando.

Sports

Baseball fans might want to make the 40-mile (64-km) journey southwest, on I-4 and then Route 557, to Winter Haven to watch the

Boston Red Sox in spring training at the Chain of Lakes Park ((813) 293-2138, Cypress Gardens Boulevard. In Orlando, the Minnesota Twins train from mid-February to the end of March at Tinker Field ((407) 849-6346, on the corner of Tampa Avenue and Church Street. From April to September the minor-league Orlando Twins play at the same stadium.

Walt Disney World has three championship **golf courses** in its grounds, all of which are included in the PGA tour package. Green fees are $55. Call ((407) 828-3741 for details. The Cypress Creek Country Club at 5353 Vineyard Road in Orlando charges about $30 a round, including a cart. Golfpac ((407) 660-8559, Box 484, Maitland (north of Orlando), prearranges rounds for visitors at numerous courses around Orlando.

Tennis players should head for Oak Street Park ((407) 847-2388, Palm and Oak streets, Orlando, or the Orange Lake Country Club Resort ((407) 239-0000, at 8505 Route 192, Kissimmee.

Water sports enthusiasts can rent canoes, airboats, or motorboats from U-Drive Airboat Rentals ((407) 847-3672, at 4266 West Vine Street, Kissimmee, or receive lessons in jet-skiing, parasailing, windsurfing, or water-skiing on one of Orlando's lakes by contacting Splash-N-Ski ((407) 352-1494, at 10000 Turkey Lake Road, Orlando.

Shopping

The fashion-conscious tend to make tracks to the upmarket **Park Avenue** in Winter Park, North Orlando, which is lined with stylish boutiques and antique shops. The **Florida Mall** at 8001 South Orange Blossom Trail, near International Drive, Orlando, offers a wide selection of merchandise in over 160 shops. Nearby, at 8445 International Drive, you will find the brick streets and Mediterranean-style shopfronts of the **Mercado Shopping Village**, where over 50 shops specialize in arts, crafts, jewelry, and Oriental curios. Buskers, street entertainers, and some very decent restaurants add to the flavor of this charming shopping complex.

Nightlife

The **Mardi Gras** ((407) 351-5151, in the Mercado Shopping Village, offers one of the best dinner shows in town. The food has a Deep Southern accent, and a New Orleans jazz band plays during dinner. Caribbean and Latin American music, as well as Dixieland, follow dinner, allowing you to dance away the calories. With any luck, you will be able to catch golden oldsters from Fats Domino and Bo Diddley at Little Darlin's **Rock 'n' Roll Palace** ((407) 396-6499, in the old town, 5770 West Route 192, Kissimmee, which has live music from the Fifties and Sixties seven nights a week.

The most vibrant night spot in downtown Orlando is probably the complex of **Church Street Station** ((407) 422-2434, at 129 West Church Street, which offers a great variety of entertainment, including Dixieland bands, cancan dancers and vaudeville acts at **Rosie O'Grady's**, the live country-western bands of the **Cheyenne Saloon**, which also has a traditional American restaurant; and the live folk and bluegrass music at **Apple Annie's Courtyard**. Church Street Station is also home to one of the trendiest discos in town, **Phileas Phogg's Balloon Works**, where you can dance until 2 AM.

WHERE TO STAY

The hotels along the "Route 192 Corridor" and those around International Drive are all within half an hour's drive of Orlando. For more information about the city's seemingly endless list of hotels contact the Greater Orlando Tourist Information Center or the Orlando/Orange County Convention and Visitors Bureau. Here is a small selection of the hotels in the area:

Luxury
The **Park Plaza Hotel** ((407) 647-1072, is in Orlando's exclusive Winter Park suburb at 307 Park Avenue. It is an particularly welcoming hotel with a genuine southern feel and 29 handsome rooms which all open out onto flower-bedecked balconies looking out over stylish Park Avenue. At the **Colonial Plaza Inn** ((407) 896-9858, 2801 East Colonial Drive, Orlando, there are four suites each with their own small swimming pools, but all the hotel's guests can enjoy the Jacuzzi facilities. Victorian antiques contrib-

ute tastefully to the interior of the **Norment-Parry Inn** ((407) 648-5188, at 211 North Lucerne Circle East, Orlando, which is in a choice position with sweeping views over Lake Lucerne.

In downtown Orlando the **Harley Hotel** ((407) 841-3220 TOLL-FREE (800) 321-2323, at 151 East Washington Street, is in a beautiful spot next to Lake Eola Park. The Harley has a gorgeous swimming pool and an elegant restaurant with a lovely view over the park.

Mid-range
The friendly, family-run **Langford Hotel** ((407) 644-3400, in Winter Park at 300 East New England Avenue, is one of the best values in town considering the extensive facilities, which include a courtyard swimming pool, a Jacuzzi and sauna, and the Empire Room restaurant with its excellent food and live musical entertainment. The **Fugate House** ((407) 423-8382, a small and *gemütlich* hotel, can be found in Orlando's Lake Cherokee district, tucked away at 545 Margaret Court, Orlando, and is particularly recommended for its friendly service. **Howard Johnson's** ((407) 841-8600, at 2014 West Colonial Drive in midtown Orlando, offers the usual reliable service and quality of any Howard Johnson's but in this case is distinguished for the mouth-watering Southern-style food up at its restaurant, Aunt Polly's.

Inexpensive
Good budget bets in Orlando include the **Econo Lodge Orlando Central** ((407) 293-7221, 3300 West Colonial Drive; the **Howard Vernon Motel** ((407) 422-7162, at 600 West Colonial Drive; and **TraveLodge Downtown Orlando** ((407) 423-1671, at 409 Magnolia Avenue.

WHERE TO EAT

Expensive
For the most romantic ambiance, and some of the best seafood to be found, go to **Park Plaza Gardens** ((407) 645-2475, at 319 Park Avenue South, Orlando, where in absolutely delightful surroundings you can enjoy such specialties as flounder meunière

and shrimp in curry sauce. There is another elegant garden setting at the **Ran-Getsu** ((407) 354-0044, 8400 International Drive, Orlando, a Japanese restaurant that includes on its menu such innovations as Florida rolls — sushi rice, avocado, cucumber, and crab — as well as the more traditional fare. **Christini's** ((407) 345-8770, at the intersection of Sand Lake Road and Dr. Phillips Boulevard in the Marketplace Shopping Center, Orlando, is a highly-regarded Italian restaurant which has invented its own *zuppa di pesce alla Mediterrania* — lobster, shrimp, clams, and mussels in a light red sauce. Another restaurant worth visiting is **Royal Orleans** ((407) 352-8200, in the Mercado Shopping Village at 8445 International Drive, Orlando, which specializes in Cajun food, with Creole variations.

Moderate

For traditional French cuisine your best bet is the **Coq au Vin** ((407) 851-6980, at 4800 South Orange Avenue, Orlando, where Louis and Magdalena Perotte have created an excellent menu and a charming atmosphere. You would also do well to try the chateaubriand and the fish in wine sauce at **La Belle Verrière** ((407) 645-3377, 142 Park Avenue South, Orlando. The tandoori cooking of northern India can be enjoyed at the elaborately decorated **Darbar** ((407) 345-8128, 7600 Dr. Phillips Boulevard, Orlando. Despite its name, **La Cantina** ((407) 894-4491, at 4721 East Colonial Drive, Orlando, is a splendidly straight forward American restaurant, which means, among other things, that it serves wonderful steaks.

Inexpensive

It's friendly and informal, it serves six-ounce (18 ml) martinis and tasty fresh seafood, and it's called **Gary's Duck Inn** ((407) 843-0270. It can be found at 3974 South Orange Blossom Trail, Orlando. The **Greek Place** ((407) 352-6930, in the Mercado Shopping Village, 8445 International Drive, Orlando, is a *good* Greek place. The quaint **British Tearoom** ((407) 677-0121, at 1917 Alona Avenue, Winter Park, offers such typical (yawn) English fare as ale pie, Cornish pastries, and cheese on toast, all washed down by tea. **Skeeter's**

((407) 298-7973, by contrast, is a rough-and-ready place where you can tuck into hash browns, waffles, pancakes, hot dogs, and fried eggs, all washed down with beer. This very popular local diner is at 1212 Lee Road, Orlando.

OTHER ATTRACTIONS IN CENTRAL FLORIDA

SOUTH OF ORLANDO

Take Route 540 for Winter Haven, and the Florida Cypress Gardens ((813) 324-2111, a 223-acre (89-hectare) park with beautifully-tended botanical gardens, a zoological park, and a miniature railway. You can also see the Great American Ski Show, which fea-

OPPOSITE: An orange juice cannery in central Florida.

tures water-skiing, powerboat racing, and water-ski jumping. The gardens are open daily from 9 AM to 6 PM, and admission is $29.50 for adults and $19.50 for children aged three to 11.

For somewhat more natural surroundings, head further south down Route 27 until you reach **Bok Tower Gardens (** (813) 676-1408, just before the town of Lake Wales. A Gothic tower 200 ft (61 m) high, blessed with a 57-bell carillon, is surrounded by 123 acres (49 hectares) of tranquil gardens and nature trails. Classical music recitals are performed in the gardens on selected summer evenings. The gardens are open daily from 8 AM to 5 PM, and admission is free for children up to age 11, and $4 for everyone else.

If you prefer something wilder you should head east out of Lake Wales to the **Lake Kissimmee State Park** at 14248 Camp Mack Road, Lake Wales, which has excellent fishing, hiking trails, and also features rodeos. There are campsites in the park for those wishing to stay overnight.

Some useful addresses and telephone numbers for tourist information south of Orlando:

The Kissimmee/St. Cloud Convention and Visitors Bureau ((813) 696-1112, P.O. Box 422007, Kissimmee, FL 32742.
The Haines City Chamber of Commerce ((813) 422-3751, P.O. Box 986, Haines City, FL 33844.
The Lake Wales Area Chamber of Commerce ((813) 676-3445, 340 West Central Avenue, Lake Wales, FL 33859.

NORTH OF ORLANDO

About 20 miles (32 km) northeast of Orlando on I-4 is the town of Sanford, where you have the choice of two excursions up the St. Johns River. **Captain Hoy's Riverboat Fleet (** (407) 330-1612, specializes in daytime narrated tours which point out the abundant wildlife of the river; the boats leave from Sanford Boat Works, Route 415, Sanford. Catamarans depart for evening cruises, which include cocktails, dinner, and dancing, from **River Romance (** (407) 321-5091, at 433 North Palmetto Avenue, Sanford; tickets start at $25. Just north out of Sanford on I-4 in Lake Monroe, you will

come to the **Central Florida Zoological Park** ((407) 323-4450, which houses over 400 exotic animals and has picnic areas set in the woods.

Fifty miles (80 km) northwest of Orlando on Route 441 is the town of Ocala, well known for its Victorian architecture but even better known as the state's racehorse center and home to some of the nation's best thoroughbreds. Some of the horse farms in the hills surrounding Ocala welcome visitors, including **Grosse Point Stud Farm** ((904) 237-3348, at 8998 West Fort King Street, and **Bonnie Heath Farm (** (904) 237-2121, at 5400 Southwest College Road. If you go to Ocala you can see a varied and interesting collection at the **Appleton Museum of Art (** (904) 236-5056, 4333 East Silver Springs Boulevard, which includes Persian, Oriental, Peruvian, Andean and Mexican artifacts.

To the east of Ocala is the **Ocala National Forest,** (see YOUR CHOICE, BACKPACKING) over 300,000 acres (120,000 hectares) of unspoiled woodland, springs, rivers, and lakes, through which there is a scenic drive known as the Backwoods Trail. The recreational activities include canoeing, hiking, hunting, fishing, and tubing (a revived craze among collegians, involving floating downstream on an inner tube). Maps of the forest, and information on campgrounds and picnic sites, and everything else, can be obtained from the USDA Forest Service ((904) 625-2520, 227 North Bronough Street, Suite 4061, Tallahassee, FL 32301. The forest is home to the state's oldest attraction, **Silver Springs (** (904) 236-2121, which dates from 1890 as a leisure park. The limestone artesian springs are the largest in the world, beautifully clear and teeming with fish life, as the glass-bottom tour boats will demonstrate. The springs are off I-75 on Route 40, east of Ocala, and are open from 9 AM to 5:30 PM daily (extended in the summer); admission is $27.95 for adults and $18.95 for children.

For further information, contact the Ocala/Marion County Chamber of Commerce ((904) 629-8051, P.O. Box 1210, Ocala, FL 32678.

The Bok Tower at Lake Wales.

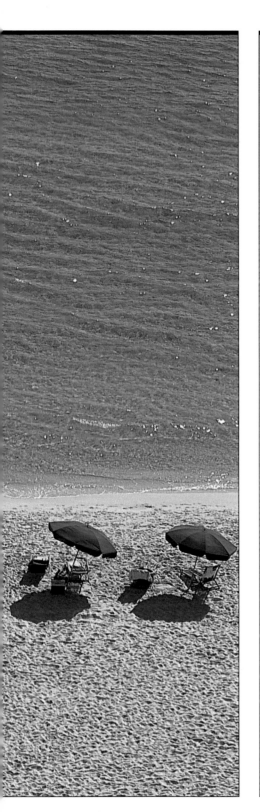

The
Panhandle

FIRST-TIME visitors to Florida's Panhandle are invariably surprised by the diversity of its attractions. There is the state's sophisticated capital city, Tallahassee, and there are all the small towns that have not yet Gone with the Wind; there are the rich resort spots such as Fort Walton Beach and Destin, and the quaint old fishing villages on the marshy coastline between the mouths of the Suwannee and St. Marks rivers. There are crystalline streams flowing through pine and oak forests southwest of Tallahassee, and there are miles of deserted white sand beaches married to the azure Gulf waters west of Panama City. The Panhandle has all this to offer, plus inhabitants who are as welcoming and hospitable as any others in Florida.

After the Civil War the east and west coasts of Florida were transformed by commercial enterprises and by tourism, but the Panhandle remained relatively undeveloped, which could help to explain why the region has so successfully retained its distinctive characteristics. The only substantial commercial activity in the region after the Civil War was in the ports, which thrived on the business of sending out wood and forest products to the peninsula's developing east and west coast cities. But for the most part the Panhandle was and remained until the middle of this century, a region of sharecroppers and tenant farmers working a meager living from the land. As many of these people had come from Alabama and Georgia, they gave the Panhandle a Deep South character not found in other parts of Florida.

Many people only see the Panhandle from the inside of a car, as they hurry to the warmer climate and more loudly trumpeted attractions further south. But it would be well worth your while to get off the beaten Interstate tracks and take the time to explore this often overlooked but thoroughly charming region of the state.

TALLAHASSEE

Like the entire region, Tallahassee is an interesting blend: it is the capital city of Florida, it is the most important commercial city in the Panhandle, it is home to two universities, Florida State and Florida A&M, and it has an historic district dating from the early nineteenth century.

BACKGROUND

When Spain ceded Florida to the United States in 1821 the territory's two most important cities were Pensacola and St. Augustine. In 1823, the legislature of the territory, recognizing the need for one capital, proposed that it be established midway between Pensacola and St. Augustine. Thereupon two delegates set out, one from each city; they met in the foothills of the Appalachians and named the site Tallahassee (an Indian word meaning "old town").

From the 1830s, Tallahassee was the distribution center for cotton grown in Florida and the Deep South, and its commercial prominence in the region was secured when the state's first railway was built from the town to the coast at St. Marks. During the Civil War the town was fiercely Confederate, and the defeat of Union troops at the nearby battle of Olustee ensured that Tallahassee remained the only town east of the Mississippi not to be taken by the Union. Since then the state's center of gravity has moved steadily southward towards Miami, but Tallahassee still remains the home of Florida's government.

GENERAL INFORMATION

The Tallahassee Area Convention and Visitors Bureau ((904) 413-9200, is at 200 West College Avenue, P.O. Box 1639, Tallahassee, FL 32302.

Other useful telephone numbers (both in area code 904):

Tallahassee Regional Airport	574-7800
Capital Medical Society	877-9018

WHAT TO SEE AND DO

Sights
The modern **Florida Capitol** and the **Old Capitol** ((904) 488-6167 (which dates from 1845) stand next to each other at Apalachee

Between palm and flag: lining up the putt.

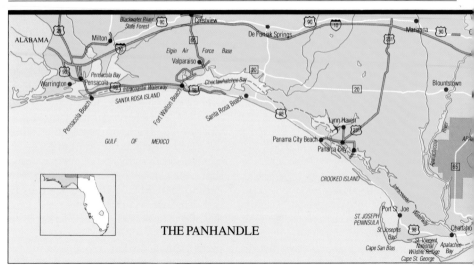

THE PANHANDLE

and South Monroe Streets. You can tour the new Capitol on weekdays from 8:30 AM to 4:30 PM; there is a wonderful view of the city from the Capitol's dome. The Old Capitol is now home to exhibits tracing Florida's political history and is open daily to visitors. The oldest commercial building in the state is the **Old Union Bank** ((904) 487-1902, at South Carolina Street and Apalachee Parkway, which houses a display of old state currency. For a look at the city's antebellum houses and buildings stroll around the historic district along Park and Calhoun streets.

Four blocks west of the Old Union Bank can be found the **Museum of Florida History** ((904) 488-1484, in the R.A. Gray building, 500 South Bronough Street, home to a collection of historic artifacts and relics portraying the state's past; admission is free. The **Tallahassee Museum of History and Natural Science** ((904) 575-8243, at 3945 Museum Drive, is a 52-acre (21-hectare) park which includes an 1880s farm with demonstrations of blacksmithing, sheep-shearing, and weaving. The hours are 9 AM to 5 PM Tuesday to Saturday, and 12:30 PM to 4:30 PM on Sunday; admission is $5 for adults and $3 for children.

The **University Gallery and Museum** ((904) 644-2098, on the Florida State University campus, in the Fine Arts Building at Copeland and Call streets, features American, Japanese, and Dutch painting, and the **LeMoyne Art Foundation** ((904) 222-8800,

at 125 North Gadsden, has displays of local art, sculpture, and photography.

Just to the north of the city, off Route 27 at 1313 Crowder Road, are the **Lake Jackson Indian Mounds** ((904) 562-0042, where excavations have discovered evidence of an Indian ceremonial site dating from 1100 AD. There are also picnic areas and a nature trail on the site, which is open from 8 AM to dusk every day.

If you would like an overview of the city and surrounding area, take a balloon ride from **Aeronauts & Balloons** ((904) 893-1282, at 1355 Market Street, Tallahassee. If you take the ride you will see that the **Apalachicola National Forest** comes right up to the city's southwest limit. Tallahassee is a good base from which to explore the forest and enjoy its unparalleled fishing, hiking, canoeing, swimming, and picnic facilities — on which you can get more information from the city's Visitor's Bureau ((904) 643-2282.

Ten miles (16 km) south of Tallahassee, at One Springs Drive, Wakulla Springs, off Route 267, is the **Edward Ball Wakulla Springs State Park** ((904) 222-7279, where you can swim in the clear springs, take a riverboat tour, or walk through the lovely grounds.

Sports

You can play **golf** at the Seminole Golf Course ((904) 644-2582, 2550 Pottsdamer Road. You can also play a nine-hole course

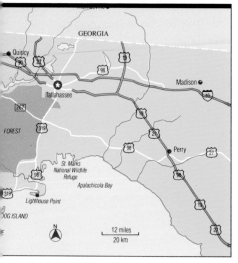

at the Jake Gaither Community Center and Golf Course ((904) 222-7259, on Bragg Drive. The center also has **basketball** and **tennis** courts. The city's recreation department ((904) 222-7259, can provide further information on the city's tennis facilities. **Canoeists** ((904) 576-5335, should contact the Canoe Shop at 111-B Orange Avenue, which rents boats and will direct you to all of the local rivers.

Shopping

The **Market Square** at Thomasville and Timberlaine Roads is the place for gift shops and stalls selling local produce. The **Outdoors Shop** ((904) 368-4180, at 3251 Thomasville Road, has everything for the hiker, camper, angler, and hunter, as well as a comprehensive selection of sportswear. The staff can also give you a lot of helpful information about the area. Overall, Thomasville Road probably has the best selection of shops in Tallahassee.

Nightlife

The **Moon** ((904) 222-6666, at 1105 Lafayette Street, is a disco with live music some evenings, while **Studebaker's** ((904) 656-2191, at 1103 Apalachee Parkway, is a disco serving up popular music from the Fifties and Sixties. If you want to join the student crowd, go along to the **Flamingo Café Lounge** ((904) 224-3534, at 525 West Tennessee Street, where live bands play into the early hours most nights.

WHERE TO STAY

Luxury

What sort of place is it that serves complimentary breakfast with the morning newspaper in rooms with four-poster beds and antique furniture, and has a free limousine service to any point within five miles (eight kilometers) of the hotel, and allows free local calls, and serves complimentary cocktails in the evening? It's the place where the Governor of Florida stays when he's in town, and it's called the **Governor's Inn** ((904) 681-6855, and can be found next to the Old Capitol at 209 South Adams Street. The **Radisson Hotel** ((904) 224-6000, is in a good downtown position at 415 North Monroe Street, and has very handsome rooms to go with its elegant lounge and restaurant. Also in the downtown area is the **Tallahassee Sheraton** ((904) 224-5000, at 101 South Adams Street, which has 246 attractive and spacious rooms, as well as 25 plush suites.

Mid-range

The **Leisure Inn** ((904) 877-4437, at 202 Apalachee Parkway, off Route 27, is a reasonably-priced hotel with a tasteful sunken parlor where you can enjoy your complimentary continental breakfast. Every room has a view over the city and surrounding countryside at the **Holiday Inn University Center** ((904) 222-8000, 316 West Tennessee Street. The Camelot dining room has copious seafood and salad buffets each night, after which you can relax in the rooftop Viking Lounge. The **Capital Inn Parkway** ((904) 877-3141, a mile (1.6 km) from the downtown area at 1302 Apalachee Parkway, off Route 27, is surrounded by lawns and has a swimming pool.

Inexpensive

With free in-room movies and a children's playground among its amenities, the **Days Inn South** ((904) 877-6121, at 3100 Apalachee Parkway, off Route 27, is very good value. There are a number of pleasant hotels on North Monroe Street including: N° 2726, the American Inn ((904) 386-5000; N° 2735, Cabot Lodge North ((904) 386-7500; and

Nº 2681, the Econo Lodge North ((904) 424-4777.

If you would rather stay in the country-side around Tallahassee, contact the Convention and Visitors Bureau ((904) 681-9200, at 100 North Duval Street, P.O. Box 1639, which will be happy to send you the *Tallahassee Area Fishing Camps and Lodges Guide.*

WHERE TO EAT

Expensive
At **Andrew's Second Act** ((904) 222-2759,

Apalachicola oysters are a house specialty. If you want to choose from a menu that has a good selection of both Chinese and Japanese dishes you should try **Ms. Lucy's Bamboo Gardens** ((904) 878-3366, located at 2814 Apalachee Parkway, where you will be greeted by Lucy Ho, a charming and graceful Chinese lady. **Anthony's** ((904) 224-1477, at Betton Place, is an intimate restaurant serving traditional Italian cuisine. If you are in the mood for fondue you should head for the **Melting Pot** ((904) 386-7440, at 1832 North Monroe Street, which

102 West Jefferson Street, do try the exceptional *tournedos St. Laurent* — lean tenderloin coated with garlic, scallion, and parsley butter, and served with asparagus. The fanciest restaurant in town is **The Golden Pheasant** ((904) 222-0241, at 109 East College Avenue, which features a continental atmosphere to go with its French haute cuisine. Hint: Have the pheasant baked in pastry.

Moderate
American cuisine gets a makeover with a Greek accent at **Brothers Three** ((904) 386-4193, 2696 North Monroe Street. Their

Tallahassee: The Governor's Inn LEFT and State Capitol RIGHT.

has delicious cheese, meat, seafood, and chocolate fondues.

Inexpensive
Restaurants with names like **Julie's Place** ((904) 368-7181, are normally friendly, and Julie's is no exception. Her place — which has very good nachos, pizzas, and quiches — is in the La Quinta Motor Inn, 2905 North Monroe Street. Another popular and cheap eatery is the **Adams Street Café** ((904) 222-3444, at 228 South Adams Street. An especially down-home atmosphere can be found at 4175 Apalachee Parkway, where the Violante couple run **Mom and Dad's** ((904) 877-4518, a very nice little Italian restaurant.

HOW TO GET THERE

The Tallahassee Regional Airport is served by a number of national airlines. Tallahassee Taxis and Yellow Cabs both operate from the airport, where you can also find the offices of the major car rental firms.

Approaching Tallahassee by car from the east or west, drivers should take I-10. Routes 27 and 319 enter the city from the north, and you should take Route 319 if you are traveling from the south.

PANAMA CITY

The city lies on that stretch of coast often jokingly called the "Redneck Riviera", and is one of the Panhandle's most popular resorts, having a lively nightlife, an amusement park with arcades and rides overlooking one of the finest white sand beaches anywhere, and good facilities for water sports. Quieter (even deserted) stretches of beach can be found to the east and west of Panama City, and two state parks — St. Andrews and Dead Lakes — are within striking distance of the city. In short, there are attractions to suit all tastes and age groups, which is why Panama City is a particular favorite with tourists traveling *en famille*.

GENERAL INFORMATION

The Panama City Beach Convention and Visitors Bureau ((904) 233-5070, is at P.O. Box 9473, Panama City Beach, FL 32417. It can provide you with all the information you may need about the area.

Other useful telephone numbers (all in area code 904):

Bay Walk-In Clinic	234-8442
Beach Taxi	234-5202
Tallahassee Regional Airport	574-7800
The Panama City-Bay County International Airport	763-6751

WHAT TO SEE AND DO

Sights

The **Miracle Strip Amusement Park** ((904) 234-5810, at 12000 West Highway 98-A, Panama City Beach, the biggest on the city's Gulf-front road, has arcades, roller-coasters, carousels, and dozens of other rides. Admission is $18 for adults and $16 for children under 11. You can see performing porpoises and sea lions at **Gulf World** ((904) 234-5271, 15421 West Highway 98-A, Panama City Beach, from 9 AM to 7 PM daily in the summer; admission $14.88 for adults and $8.88 for children aged five to 12. If you would like to take a boat trip to the wonderfully scenic Shell Island off the coast of Panama City, you should go to **Captain Anderson's Marina** ((904) 234-5940, at 5550 North Lagoon Drive, Panama City Beach, whence excursions leave for the island at 9 AM and 1 PM daily. Tickets are $9 for adults and $5 for children.

There are two interesting museums in the city. The **Museum of Man and the Sea** ((904) 235-4101, located at 17314 Hutchinson Road, has exhibits of early diving equipment, treasures from Spanish shipwrecks, and great moments in man's exploration of the ocean. The **Junior Museum of Bay County** ((904) 769-6128, offers exhibits showing how Indians and early settlers worked and lived; it's located at 1731 Jenkins Avenue.

The **St. Andrews State Recreation Area** ((904) 233-5140, located at 4415 Thomas Drive, southwest of the city at the end of Route 392, includes wetlands, pinewoods, dunes, and beaches, as well as numerous sites for camping. The **Dead Lakes State Recreation Area** ((904) 639-2702, about 30 miles (48 km) east of Panama City on Route 22, near the village of Wewahitchka has some lovely nature trails and wonderful fishing spots.

Sports

Golf enthusiasts can take on the challenge of the par-70 Signal Hill Golf Course ((904) 234-5051, at 9615 Thomas Drive, Panama City Beach, or try out the attractive course at the Creek Golf and Country Club ((904) 871-2623, off Route 22 East, Panama City.

Golf and **tennis** players are catered to at the Holiday Golf and Tennis Club ((904) 234-1800, 100 Fairway Boulevard, Panama City Beach. The recreation department ((904) 763-6641, will provide you information about the city's 19 public tennis courts.

Panama City Beach offers a variety of water sports: The Hydrospace Dive Shop ((904) 234-9463, at 3605 Thomas Drive, runs **diving trips** offshore in waters up to 98 ft (30 m) deep, and will also take you **snorkeling**. Trained divers from the **Panama City Dive Center** ((904) 235-3390, at 4823 Thomas Drive, can take you diving in some of the freshwater springs in the area. **Surfers** can rent a board from Lawrence Rentals ((904) 234-2432, at 15000 West Highway 98; and Jet Winds ((904)

235-0338, at 12705 West Highway 98-A, rents **jet skis** for $35 an hour, and **sailboats** for $25 an hour.

Shopping

For swimwear and everything else for the beach, try the variety of shops in **Field's Plaza** at 12700 West Highway 98-A, Panama City Beach, open from 9 AM to 9 PM.

The **Galleria**, located at 2303 Winona Drive, Panama City, is the place for gift and specialty shops. For local crafts and souvenirs check out the **Olde Towne Mini Mall** at 441 Grace Avenue, Panama City.

Nightlife
There's a Caribbean flavor to the live music and the cocktails at **Pineapple Willie's** ((904) 235-8928, 9900 Beach Boulevard, Panama City Beach, one of the liveliest night spots in town. **Spinnaker III** ((904) 234-7882, is set among the dunes at 8813 Thomas Drive, Panama City Beach; the music and dance goes on until 4 AM, but it's open from 11 AM to give you plenty of time to get warmed up.

Spring Break at Panama City.

At 5550 North Lagoon Drive, Panama City Beach, you can board a boat and enjoy **Captain Anderson's Dinner Cruise** ((904) 234-5940, and have a meal followed by music and dancing. Alternatively, you could board the **Southern Elegance** ((904) 785-3006, which leaves from 5505 West Highway 98, Panama City Beach; dinner, live music, and film shows are included in the price, and there is also a casino on board.

The place for live country music is the **Ocean Opry** ((904) 234-5464, at 8400 West Highway 98-A, a large venue with more than a whiff of Nashville about it.

WHERE TO STAY

Luxury
The **Edgewater Beach Resort** ((904) 235-4977 TOLL-FREE (800) 874-8686, at 11212 Fort Beach Road, Panama City Beach, is one of the best hotels in the Panhandle. The efficiency apartments have everything from marble sinks to washing machines, and overlook either the ocean or the beautifully landscaped grounds. The amenities include a swimming lagoon with waterfalls and a bar, nine tennis courts, a beachside clubhouse, and a nine-hole golf course. Matching the Edgewater for luxury is the **Marriott's Bay Point Resort** ((904) 234-3307 TOLL-FREE (800) 874-7105, at 100 Delwood Beach Road, Bay Point, Panama City Beach, which has a 200-room hotel and efficiency villas in its 1,000-acre (400-hectare) grounds, which also include two golf courses, over 30 lakes and ponds, a forest, restaurants and shops. The resort's boat takes patrons across St. Andrews Bay to the beaches of Shell Island.

Mid-range
The **Sugar Sands Hotel** ((904) 234-8802, at 20709 West Highway 98-A, is in a splendid situation right on the beach, and offers comfortable rooms and suites, with a cook-it-yourself barbecue next to the hotel's swimming pool. All the rooms face the ocean and have private balconies at the **Rendezvous Inn** ((904) 234-8841, at 17281 West Highway 98-A, Panama City Beach. The **Flamingo Motel** ((904) 234-2232, at 15524 West High-

way 98, Panama City Beach, has a delightful courtyard where palmettos and tropical plants surround a swimming pool. The rooms are cozy, and some have kitchenettes. Small and intimate, **Cobb's Gulfview Inn** ((904) 234-6051, at 21722 West Highway 98-A, Sunnyside Beach, has five charming rooms and serves a delicious full breakfast.

Inexpensive
There is a reasonable choice of cheaper places to stay in Panama City Beach, including the **Bikini Beach Motel** ((904) 234-3392, at 11001 West Highway 98; and at 8601 Surf Drive, there is the **Silver Sands Motel** ((904) 234-2201. In Panama City you can expect good deals at **Howard's Motor Lodge** ((904) 763-4998, 4911 West Highway

The town of Seaside quietly, handsomely confronts the Gulf.

The Panhandle

98; and **La Brisa Motor Inn** ((904) 871-2345 on East Highway 98 at N⁰ 5711.

WHERE TO EAT

Expensive

The beamed ceiling, stone walls and fireplace make for a genuinely English ambiance at the **Boar's Head** ((904) 234-6628, 17290 West Highway 98-A, Panama City Beach, where prime rib of beef with Yorkshire pudding adds an English accent to an excellent continental menu which also has very tasty Greek dishes. **Sylvia's** ((904) 234-0184, at 9850 South Thomas Drive, Panama City Beach, has a most attractive multilevel design and a resident pianist whose sounds reach all levels. Try the lobster meat *en*

croute in sherry and mushroom sauce.

Moderate

The food is Italian-American at **Caporelli's** ((904) 763-2245, 8713 Front Beach Road, Panama City Beach, as is the promenading violinist who adds a sweetly romantic touch. At the **Harbour House** ((904) 785-9053, 3001-A West 10th Street, Panama City, the luncheon buffet of salads, cold cuts, and vegetables is a big hit, as is every charcoal-broiled steak served in the evening.

Continental cuisine with a French bias is on the menu at the café-like **Greenhouse** ((904) 763-2245, 443 Grace Avenue, Panama City; while **Claudio's** ((904) 769-8722, at 1013 Beck Avenue, Panama City, specializes in spicy Italian fare.

Inexpensive

There is a distinctly Louisianan flavor to the interior and to the menu of the **Cajun Inn** ((904) 235-9987, at 477 Beckrich Drive, Panama City Beach. Don't miss the Bayou Teche jambalaya with a side order of Cajun-spiced potatoes. Good Mexican food is available at **Los Antojitos** ((904) 769-7081, 4809 Front Beach Road, Panama City Beach, which serves memorable margaritas. Bargain crêpes, quiches, and pastas are the stars at **The Cheese Barn** ((904) 769-3892, 425 Grace Avenue, Panama City. For seafood go to the **Gulf Cafeteria** ((904) 234-6457, 12628 Front Beach Road, Panama City Beach.

HOW TO GET THERE

Several national airlines serve the Panama City-Bay County Regional Airport, notably ASA, Northwest and USAir. Arriving by car, Route 98 enters the city from the east and west, and Route 231 from the north.

PENSACOLA

Florida's western-most city has a population of over a quarter of a million people, who live mainly on the hillsides which climb away from the downtown area next to the bay. The downtown area contains the historic district, whose heart is the Seville Quarter, where most of the museums, antebellum houses, and restaurants are to be found.

BACKGROUND

A Spanish explorer called Tristan de Luna established a colony at Pensacola in 1559. Two years later, however, ferocious tropical storms destroyed much of his fleet and the colonists were forced to abandon the settlement. The Spanish did not return to Pensacola until the 1690s, when they formed a military garrison at the bay. They co-existed peacefully with the French —their main rivals in the region — but were forced to abandon Pensacola again in 1821 due to American military strength rather than the weather. There is still a military connection in the city, however, as the Pensacola Naval Air Station became the United States Navy's first flight training center in 1914.

GENERAL INFORMATION

The **Pensacola Area Chamber of Commerce Visitor Information Center** ((904) 434-1234, is at 1401 East Gregory Street, Pensacola, FL 32501.

Other useful telephone numbers (all in area code 904):

Pensacola Regional Airport	435-1746
Blue and White Cab	438-1497
Escambia County Health Department	438-8571

WHAT TO SEE AND DO

Sights

In the downtown historic district, around Seville Square, you will learn all about the city's and the region's past — Indian, European, and American — at the **Pensacola Historical Museum** ((904) 433-1559, in the Old Christ Church at 405 South Adams Street; and at the **West Florida Museum of History** ((904) 444-8905, 200 East Zaragoza Street. Where Zaragoza Street meets Tarragona Street you will find the **Historic Pensacola Village**, a quarter full of old restored houses and stores.

The Zoo and Botanical Gardens ((904) 9832-2229, off Route 98, 10 miles (16 km) east of Pensacola at 5801 Gulf Breeze Parkway, Gulf Breeze, is home to more than 700 animals, including Colossus, a lowland gorilla who at 600 lb (1,320 kg) is believed to be the largest in captivity in the world. Elephant rides and a children's petting zoo are other features. Admission is $9.75 for adults and $5.75 for children aged three to 11; the zoo is open daily from 9 AM to 5 PM in the summer.

Aviation enthusiasts will not want to miss the **National Museum of Naval Aviation (** (904) 452-3604, which has over 50 air-

Route 1 off Route 90 at Holt, which offers excellent canoeing.

Sports
You can play **golf** at the Santa Rosa Shores Country Club **(** (904) 456-2761, on Pensacola Beach; the Carriage Hills Golf Course **(** (904) 944-5497, at 2355 West Michigan Avenue, Pensacola; or the Green Meadow Par-3 **(** (904) 944-5483, at 2500 West Michigan Avenue, Pensacola.

There are 18 **tennis courts** at the Scott Tennis Center **(** (904) 432-2939, Cordova

craft on display, including the NC-4 (the first to cross the Atlantic in 1919), jet fighters, and the Skylab command module. Take Route 98 west out of town to Navy Boulevard and enter the Naval Air Station. The famed air-display team, the Blue Angels, frequently perform at the Air Station.

Southwest of Pensacola, you will find the **Big Lagoon State Recreation Area (** (904) 492-1595, at 12301 Gulf Beach Highway, where you can swim, boat, fish, camp, and hike. The **Gulf Island National Seashore (** (904) 934-2604, is over the water, off Route 399; the Spanish fort **San Carlos de Barrancas**, open to the public, is on the seashore. To the northeast of Pensacola is the **Blackwater River State Park (** (904) 623-2363,

Park; and the Pensacola Racquet Club **(** (904) 434-2434, at 3450 Wimbledon Drive, has 10 courts.

Scuba diving and **snorkeling** excursions off the coast of Pensacola can be arranged through the Southern Breeze Dive Shop **(** (904) 492-3492, at 10121 Sinton Drive, Pensacola; or Aquatic Orientations **(** (904) 9832-1944, at 31 Hoffman Drive, Gulf Breeze. **Surf** and **sail boards** can be hired from the Key Sailing Center **(** (904) 932-5520, at 289 Pensacola Beach Road; and **sailboats** can be

OPPOSITE: A balcony in the Seville Quarter of Pensacola. ABOVE: Vintage wheels LEFT enter a vintage part of town. Sand traps and sea views RIGHT on a Panhandle golf course. OVERLEAF: Bass fishing on the Suwannee River.

hired from Break Away ((904) 438-1711, in Harbor Village.

Shopping

In **Seville Square** and the streets that lead into it there are numerous shops selling craft items and artwork, antiques, jewelry, and gifts; there are similar items on offer at the charming **Quayside Thieves Market**, 712 South Palafox Street, Pensacola. For designer boutiques, try the **Harbourtown Shopping Village**, a modern mall at 913 Gulf Breeze Parkway, Gulf Breeze.

lobby of the **Pensacola Grand Hotel** ((904) 433-3336, at 200 East Gregory Street, Pensacola. The hotel has penthouse suites with Jacuzzis and bars, and rooms on the upper floors have terrific views over the city. There is an international flavor to the **New World Landing** ((904) 432-4111 TOLL-FREE (800) 258-1103, at 600 South Palafox Street, Pensacola, where the 16 tasteful rooms have either American, French, Spanish, or English furnishings and decor. The hotel's restaurant also has a splendid continental menu. On Pensacola Beach the best hotel is **The Dunes**

Nightlife

Live bands play every night at **Flounder's Ale House** ((904) 932-2003, 800 Quietwater Beach, Pensacola. Lively bars include the **Seville Inn** ((904) 433-8331, at 223 East Garden Street; the **Red Garter Saloon** ((904) 433-9229, on South Palafox Street in Pensacola; and, liveliest of all, **McQuire's Irish Pub** ((904) 433-6789, at 600 East Gregory Street, Pensacola, which has live Irish music and good food to go with the beer.

WHERE TO STAY

Luxury

Pensacola's old railway station concourse has been restored and converted into the

((904) 932-3526, at 333 Fort Pickens Road, where children stay free. Most of the rooms here overlook the Gulf, and there are indoor and outdoor swimming pools.

Mid-range

The accommodation at the **Residence Inn** ((904) 479-1000 TOLL-FREE (800) 331-3131, 7230 Plantation Road, Pensacola, surrounds a courtyard which has basketball and tennis courts, a Jacuzzi and a swimming pool. The hotel serves a complimentary continental breakfast, and has a cocktail party for guests on weekends. If you reserve in advance, the **Days Inn** ((904) 238-4922 TOLL-FREE (800) 874-0710, will send a car to pick you up at the airport. The hotel is near the historic district downtown at 710 North Palafox Street, Pensacola. There are cottages and rooms with kitchenettes to choose from at the **Sandpiper Inn (** (904) 932-2516, which is next to the ocean on Pensacola Beach at 23 Via de Luna.

Inexpensive

There are 120 small but comfortable rooms at **Motel 6 (** (904) 477-7522, 5829 Pensacola Boulevard, Pensacola, and you will receive a similarly good deal at **Days Inn (** (904) 477-9000, 6911 Pensacola Boulevard. The **Gulf Aire Motel (** (904) 932-2319, at 21 Via de Luna, Pensacola Beach, has rooms with kitchens, and is close to the beach; and **Two Tom's Bed and Breakfast (** (904) 939-2382, has six pleasant rooms looking out on some lovely scenery close to Navarre Beach, east on Route 98 at Navarre.

WHERE TO EAT

Expensive

There is nowhere in town that you will find better French food than at **Jamie's (** (904) 434-2911, 424 East Zaragoza Street, Pensacola, in a cozy Victorian-style cottage. The elegant **Jubilee (** (904) 934-3108, restaurant at 400 Quietwater Beach Road, has a large skylight to accentuate the decor and a menu which includes the most delicious sweetbreads and sautéed chicken breasts with crayfish. The **Driftwood (** (904) 433-4559, at 27 West Garden Street, successfully mixes an American atmosphere with a continental cuisine.

Moderate

There is much to recommend at the **Angus Steak Ranch (** (904) 432-0539, 1101 Scenic Highway, Pensacola, where chef Spero Athanasios hasn't limited himself to steaks; try his snapper casserole with oysters, shrimps, and scallops, accompanied by a Greek salad. The Scotto family welcomes you at **Scotto's Ristorante Italiano (** (904) 434-1932, 300 South Alcaniz Street, Pensacola. The homemade desserts are the highlights here. The Oysters Rockefeller steal the show at the **Dainty Del (** (904) 438-1241, 286 North Palafox Street, a friendly seafood restaurant popular with the local cognoscenti. For Creole cuisine, try **Beignet's**

(904) 434-7225, at 312 East Government Street, which also has live jazz on Sundays.

Inexpensive

In 1948, Arkie Ma Hopkins established **Hopkins' Boarding House (** (904) 438-3979, and her son Ed continues to serve your basic fried chicken, beef stew, and black-eyed peas at 900 North Spring Street, Pensacola. The freshest and, for the quality, the cheapest seafood in Pensacola is at **Captain Joe Patti's (** (904) 434-3193, 610 South C Street. Simple but satisfying fare is available at **E.J.'s Food**

Company ((904) 432-5886, 232 East Main Street, while filling but tasty breakfasts and lunches are at the **Coffee Cup (** (904) 432-7060, 520 East Cervantes.

HOW TO GET THERE

The Pensacola Regional Airport is served by several national airlines, and taxis and car rental firms operate from the airport.

If you are traveling by car, the principal east-west route into and out of Pensacola is I-10. From Panama City you would take Route 98, and from the north Route 29.

OPPOSITE AND ABOVE: The Panhandle coastline at Destin shows off its many shades of blue.

The
Gulf
Coast

FLORIDA'S Gulf Coast, which extends almost 200 miles (320 km) from Cedar Key in the north down to Marco Island in the south, is punctuated by offshore sandbars and numerous inlets, islands, lagoons, bayous, and estuaries. Ideal conditions, in other words, for the coast's first commercial enterprise: piracy. Pirates such as Black Caesar, José Gaspar and others operated along this coast during the eighteenth century, using their knowledge of the labyrinthine coastline to spring attacks and avoid capture. Their activities played a large part in discouraging European settlement of the Gulf Coast; in any case, the Spanish, French, and English were more concerned with consolidating themselves on Florida's east coast and protecting its important sea routes.

The pirates and the regions' indigenous Timucuan, Calusas, and Seminole Indian tribes remained relatively undisturbed until 1824, when United States Army bases were established at Tampa and Fort Myers for the purpose of subduing the Seminoles. The bases attracted civilian settlers, two towns were born, and then more settlements began to appear all along the coast once the army had defeated the Seminoles and gained complete control of the region. Many fishing villages emerged, some of which survive to this day between Naples and Marco Island, where the inhabitants live much as their forebears did.

From the 1880s onward the Gulf Coast's story is similar to that of the east coast. Developers suddenly realized that what Flagler was doing from Jacksonville to Miami could certainly be done from Tampa down to Naples — i.e., entice rich northerners with prospects of good transportation, luxury hotels, and year-round sunshine. The last condition being guaranteed, Henry Plant got to work on the first two, bringing a railway to Tampa by 1884 and completing the Tampa Bay Hotel by 1891 and the Bellview Hotel in Clearwater by the end of the century. In Sarasota, further south, John Ringling, founder of the Ringling Brothers, Barnum and Bailey Circus, built hotels and an art museum (sometimes using circus elephants on the job), as well as his own winter home, which was modeled on the Doges Palace in Venice.

The tourists took the bait and the Gulf Coast has flourished ever since, to the extent that between Venice and Tampa, towns are now gradually merging as their suburbs sprawl and overlap. To the south, the beaches of the Charlotte Harbor area and the coastline and offshore islands below Naples are largely protected areas or wildlife reserves. In these areas the laws on development are very strict, but the rest of the Gulf Coast continues to be developed, with Fort Myers being one of the fastest growing cities in the country.

TAMPA

Tampa is Florida's third largest city with a population of 300,000, including the Hispanics of Ybor City, a western district, and a large number of Greeks who first arrived at the turn of the century to dive for sponges off the coast at Tarpon City, which became the largest sponge center in the world during the 1930s. Tampa is also the seventh largest port in the country, and the most important commercial and industrial city in western Florida. Unfortunately, because of the volume of traffic in and out of the port (ships carrying 51 million tons of cargo annually), and the industrial waste, Tampa Bay is seriously polluted and unfit for swimming. On the coast to the north of the city and around St. Petersburg there are beaches washed by clear seas.

BACKGROUND

In its early days in the first half of the nineteenth century, Tampa (an Indian word meaning "sticks of fire") was a small community of fishermen and farmers clustered around Fort Brooke. The city's growth accelerated dramatically in 1885 when Vincente Martínez Ybor, due to labor problems in Key West and the prospect of lower taxes in Tampa, moved his cigar factory to the city. This brought with it a wave of immigrant workers who settled in the area now known as Ybor City, whose clubs, restaurants, shops, and culture remain overwhelmingly Cuban-Hispanic.

East meets West in downtown Tampa.

The Gulf Coast

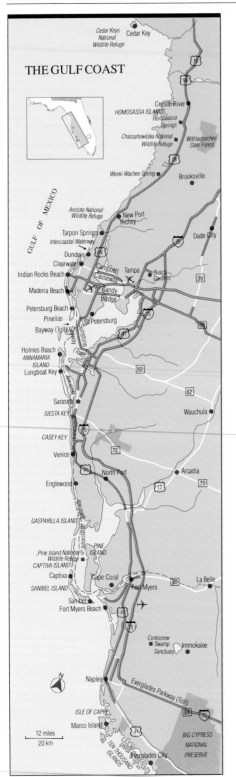

THE GULF COAST

The arrival in 1898 of one man and his army of 30,000 gave Tampa its next big boost — both to the city's economy and to its status as one of Florida's most important cities. Theodore Roosevelt set up his headquarters in the Tampa Bay Hotel, and his force of "Rough Riders" trained in its grounds before going on to Cuba to fight in the Spanish-American War. The hotel now houses the University of Tampa administration offices and a museum.

GENERAL INFORMATION

The Tampa/Hillsborough Convention and Visitors Association ((813) 223-2752, is at 111 Madison Street, Suite 1010, Tampa, FL 33602; and the Greater Tampa Chamber of Commerce ((813) 228-7777, is at 801 East Kennedy Boulevard, Tampa, FL 33601. For information on the area's hotels contact Tampa/St. Petersburg Reservations Center ((813) 596-9944.

Two newspapers, the *Tampa Tribune* and the *Tampa Times*, and a magazine, *Tampa Bay*, are full of information on local attractions and upcoming events.

Other useful telephone numbers (all in area code 813):

Tampa International Airport	870-8700
Yellow Cabs	253-0121
Emergency clinic	877-8450

WHAT TO SEE AND DO

Sights
Busch Gardens — The Dark Continent
((813) 987-5082, at 3000 Busch Boulevard, is home to over 3,000 predominantly African animals, birds, and reptiles, is one of the most highly rated zoos in the world — and the second most popular tourist attraction in the state after Disney World. The park has different areas, each with a particular theme. For example, the *Serengeti Plain* has free-roaming zebras, giraffes, rhinos, lions, and cheetahs, among other "plains" animals, all of which you can view from a monorail; the *African Queen* is a jungle cruise on which you can see all kinds of wildlife in the water and on the riverbanks; *Eagle Canyon*, a vast structure, which allows you a rare opportunity to watch American bald eagles and the mag-

nificent golden eagles, and the *Myombe Reserve* where you can have face-to-face encounters with gorillas. There is also an amusement area with some of the world's most challenging roller-coaster rides, stalls, shops, and restaurants. The park is open from 9:30 AM to 6 PM daily, admission $35.95 for adults and $29.95 for children aged two and over.

Near Busch Gardens at 4545 Bougainvillea Avenue, is **Adventure Island (** (813) 987-5000, a water theme park for all the family. The fun includes wave pools, beaches, water slides, inner-tube runs, swimming pools, stalls, and shops. In the peak holiday season between May 26 and August 19 the park is open from 9 AM to 8 PM daily. Admission is $19.95 for adults and $17.95 for children. For an insight into the old way of life of the state's most famous Indian tribe visit the **Seminole Culture Center (** (813) 623-3549, at 5221 North Orient Road, which has a reconstruction of a Seminole village, a museum with various artifacts, and shops selling Seminole crafts. There is also a poisonous snake show and the ever-popular alligator wrestling.

The city is home to a couple of interesting collections, one of contemporary American art and one of exhibits of art from ancient Rome, Greece, and Egypt, at the **Tampa Museum of Art (** (813) 223-8130, 601 Doyle Carlton Drive. Exhibits which chart the history of the city and portray its culture are on display at the **Henry Plant Museum (** (813) 254-1891, which is in the old Tampa Bay Hotel at 401 West Kennedy Boulevard. For lots of fresh air and views of Davis Island in Tampa Bay, stroll along the longest continuous sidewalk in the world — six and a half miles (10.5 km) alongside Bayshore Boulevard. At one point you won't be able to miss the 300-ton pirate ship **José Gasparilla**, named after a legendary buccaneer of the Gulf Coast, which is docked on the bayshore and fully rigged out as it would have looked in the eighteenth century. The ship is open to the public.

The heart of Ybor City, in Tampa's old Cuban and Hispanic quarter, is **Ybor Square** at Eighth Avenue and 13th Street, where there is a selection of arts and crafts shops, boutiques, and some very good restaurants.

At **Tampa Rico Cigars** in the square you can watch cigars being rolled by hand, and then you can sample them. The **Ybor City State Museum** at 1818 East Ninth Avenue will show you how this district originated and how it has changed over the years; in the museum, you will also find the **Ybor City Visitor's Center (** (813) 248-3712.

The best beaches near Tampa are **Clearwater Beach**, an island 15 miles (24 km) west of Clearwater across the Memorial Causeway; **Dunedin Beach**, north of Clearwater, near the charming neo-Scottish village of

Dunedin (from which you can take ferries to the beautiful Caladesi or Honeymoon islands); and **Sand Key Beaches**, just south of Clearwater off Gulf Boulevard.

Sports

Baseball fans will be interested to know that three major-league teams converge on the Tampa area for spring training and exhibition games during February and March: the Philadelphia Phillies can be seen at the Jack Russell Stadium in Clearwater, the Toronto Blue Jays at Grant Field in Dunedin, and the Cincinnati Reds in Tampa itself at Al Lopez Field. Call **(** (904) 488-0990 for

ABOVE: Boats stacked in Dunedin.

The Gulf Coast

information on all the teams' training schedules and games.

You can see NFL **football** from August to December at Tampa Stadium ((813) 461-2700, 4201 North Dale Mabry Highway, which is the home of the Tampa Bay Buccaneers. It is also where the Tampa Bay Rowdies **soccer** team plays from April to August.

Two municipal **golf** courses which offer lessons and a lounge/snack bar among their facilities are Rocky Point ((813) 884-5141, at 4151 Dana Shores Road; and Rogers Park ((813) 234-1911, at 7910 North 30th Street. There are also several private clubs around the city which welcome non-members. There are numerous **tennis courts** in Tampa, including 11 courts at Riverfront Park ((813) 253-6038, 900 North Boulevard, and good facilities at the City of Tampa Courts ((813) 253-3782, 15 Columbia Drive. For details on all golf courses and tennis courts, call the city's recreation department ((813) 238-6451.

Shopping

The city has several large shopping malls, but you can find the best range of shops — including three major department stores — at the **Tampa Bay Center** at Himes and Buffalo Avenues near the football stadium. Luxury shops and exclusive boutiques jostle for space at the **Harbour Island Market**, 601 South Harbour Island Boulevard. You can rummage through antiques in over 20 shops in the **Interbay Antique Row District** along MacDill and El Prado Avenues, and you are bound to find something authentically Cuban to take home with you in the gift shops of **Ybor Square** at Eighth Avenue and 13th Street.

Nightlife

There is a good choice of live music in Tampa, including **MacDinton's Tavern** ((813) 254-1661, at 405 South Howard Avenue, which features rhythm and blues and rock bands; **Parker's Lighthouse** ((813) 229-3474, which offers live rock and jazz bands in the Harbour Island Market (see SHOPPING, above); and **Dallas Bull** ((813) 985-6877, at

A windsurfer's sail echoes the geometric shape of the Sunshine Skyway Bridge, over Tampa Bay.

8222 Route 301, which specializes in country and western music. Another popular live venue which serves up jazz, reggae, rhythm and blues, and new wave music is the **Skipper's Smokehouse** ((813) 971-0666, at 910 Skipper Road.

Stingers ((813) 968-1515, at 11921 North Dale Mabry Highway, is one of the city's liveliest night clubs, where women can get free drinks Thursday to Sunday from 8 PM to 11 PM. Another popular night spot is **Killians Backbeat Lounge** ((813) 884-8965, 4235 West Waters, which features live bands from Wednesday to Sunday, and a disco the rest of the week. It also shows games on a large-screen television during the football season.

WHERE TO STAY

Luxury

One of the few Tampa hotels with its own beachfront is the **Radisson Bay Harbor Inn** ((813) 281-8900 TOLL-FREE (800) 333-3333, at 7700 Courtney Campbell Causeway, on the eastern shore of Tampa Bay, which most of the rooms' balconies overlook. Free sailing and windsurfing lessons are among the amenities. Another first-class place to stay around Tampa Bay is the **Wyndham Harbour Island Hotel** ((813) 229-5000, at 725 South Harbour Island Boulevard, nicely designed and furnished, with an attentive and friendly staff. Fifteen miles (24 km) north of Tampa, off Route 54 (exit 58) at 100 Saddlebrook Way, Wesley Chapel, is the award-winning **Saddlebrook Golf and Tennis Resort** ((813) 973-1111, which is regularly ranked among the top 50 resorts in the world. Their extensive sports facilities in the scenic wooded grounds include a golf course designed by Arnold Palmer, 17 tennis courts, and an Olympic-size swimming pool.

Downtown Tampa offers the ultra-modern **Sheraton Grand Hotel** ((813) 286-4400, located at 4860 West Kennedy Boulevard, which has a highly-regarded restaurant, J. Fitzgerald's. Another sleek downtown hotel is the **Hyatt Regency** ((813) 225-1234 TOLL-FREE (800) 228-9000, at Two Tampa City Center, where there are suites with Jacuzzis and kitchenettes, and complimen-

tary continental breakfasts served in the stylish Regency Club.

Mid-range

The **Holiday Inn Busch Gardens** ((813) 971-4710, at 2701 East Fowler Avenue, is especially welcoming to families and has a swimming pool, sauna, health club, in-room movies, and a free shuttle service to Busch Gardens. Also near the African theme park and zoo is the **Howard Johnson's Busch Gardens Main Gate** ((813) 988-9191, at 4139 East Busch Boulevard, where the decor and furnishings are determinedly exotic, with lush color schemes and plenty of tropical plants and bamboo chairs.

You can take a free shuttle to local shopping malls and golf courses from the **Days Inn** ((813) 884-2000, at 7627 Courtney Campbell Causeway, on Rocky Point Island, which has tennis courts and a swimming pool, and a lounge featuring evening discos. In the heart of the downtown area, on the riverfront, is the **Holiday Inn Ashley Plaza Hotel** ((813) 223-1351, at 111 West Fortune Street, whose modern and attractive rooms are very reasonably priced, considering the enviable location of the hotel.

Inexpensive

The **Expressway Inn** ((813) 837-1971, at 3696 Gandy Boulevard, has simple but well-furnished rooms and a swimming pool. The same facilities can be found at the **Tahitian Inn** ((813) 877-6721, 601 South Dale Mabry Highway. Conveniently placed for Busch Gardens, at bargain prices, is the **Garden View Motel** ((813) 933-3958, at 2500 East Busch Boulevard.

WHERE TO EAT

Expensive

The Sheraton Grand Hotel at 4860 West Kennedy Boulevard, is home to one of Tampa's finest restaurants, **J. Fitzgerald's** ((813) 873-4400, which serves exquisitely-prepared continental dishes. At the **Monte Carlo** ((813) 879-6245, 3940 West Cypress Street, the chef, Romeo Berranini, specializes in seafood, and particularly in new ways to serve lobster. At **Bern's Steak House** ((813)

251-2421, 1208 South Howard Avenue, there are 38 different cuts of beef to choose from and nearly 7,000 different wines. The **Lauro Ristorante** ((813) 884-4366, at 4010 West Waters Avenue, is regarded as one of the best Italian restaurants in west Florida; and the pick of the Hispanic restaurants in Ybor City is the **Columbia** ((813) 248-4961, at 21st Street and Broadway, which features on its menu traditional Spanish dishes such as paella, pork salteado, and delicious bean soups all served in a romantic setting with tableside serenades by Spanish troubadours.

as curried crab meat and cheese in wonton pockets, go to the closeby **Jasmine Thai** ((813) 968-1501, at 13248 North Dale Mabry Highway.

Inexpensive

Attractively priced steaks, seafood, and hamburgers are on offer at **Club Key West** ((813) 832-4115, 4115 South MacDill Avenue; while **Coyotes** ((813) 831-9759, another friendly eatery, specializes in ribs at 4426 Gandy Boulevard. If you want a jolly bohemian atmosphere in which to enjoy a masterpiece

Moderate

One of Florida's best-liked seafood restaurants, **The Colonnade** ((813) 839-7558, can be found at 3401 South Bayshore Boulevard, overlooking Tampa Bay. At **Selena's** ((813) 251-2116, 1623 Snow Avenue, you can choose from Creole or Sicilian food, and from some subtle combinations of the two. The **Café Pepe** ((813) 253-6501, is a very lively and popular Spanish-Cuban restaurant at 2006 West Kennedy Boulevard, serving up spicy food in a cosmopolitan atmosphere. For expertly prepared sushi, sashimi, and teriyaki in a beautifully simple restaurant, try the **Kaoribana** ((813) 968-3801, at 13180 North Dale Mabry Highway; and for equally masterful Thai cuisine, such

like *capelli di l'Angelo* — smoked salmon and caviar, tossed with spinach and pasta in a vodka and cream sauce — at unbelievable poor-student prices, go along to the **Bella Trattoria** ((813) 254-3355, at 1413 South Howard Avenue. In Ybor City there are many cheap Cuban restaurants. I like **La Tropicana** at 1822 East Seventh Avenue.

How to Get There

Tampa International Airport is served by a large number of national and international airlines, and there are half a dozen car rental companies with offices at the airport.

Tall masts and skyscrapers jut into the evening sky at Tampa Bay.

Motorists approaching Tampa from the Panhandle should take Route 19. From the northeast or the south you want I-75; from the east take either I-4 (from Orlando) or Route 60 (from Lake Wales).

ST. PETERSBURG

For many years the popular image of St. Petersburg was of a sleepy retirement town for the elderly who began to arrive in large numbers after the American Medical Association declared the area's environ-

ment and sea air to be good for the constitution. In recent years, however, St. Petersburg Beach and other beaches to the north have been developed, giving the area a younger, sprightlier image. Tourists — not just retirees — now come to the city in ever greater numbers, lured by the wonderful beaches and pristine waters of the "Suncoast" between St. Petersburg and Clearwater. The city itself has a developing downtown area and some delightful parks and gardens.

GENERAL INFORMATION

The St. Petersburg and Clearwater Convention and Visitor Bureau ((813) 582-7892, is

at the St. Petersburg Thunder Dome, One Stadium Avenue, St. Petersburg, FL 33701. St. Petersburg/Clearwater Convention and Visitors Bureau ((813) 582-7892, is at One Stadium Drive, Suite A, St. Petersburg, FL 33705. For information about the resorts and beaches north of St. Petersburg, contact the Pinellas County Tourist Development Council ((813) 530-6132, located at Newport Square, 4625 East Bay Drive, Suite 109, Clearwater, FL 34624.

WHAT TO SEE AND DO

Sights

The city's cultural renaissance is happening down on the cosmopolitan bayfront, where in the **Salvador Dali Museum** ((813) 823-3767, at 1000 Third Street South, you can see the largest collection in the world of the Spanish surrealist's works, including oils, watercolors, drawings, and graphics. Admission is $8 for adults and $4 for students; the museum is open from 10 AM to 5 PM Tuesday to Saturday, from noon to 5 PM on Sunday. Many excellent paintings by the French Impressionists are on exhibit at the **Museum of Fine Arts** ((813) 896-2667, at 225 Beach Drive, alongside oriental and American art, and photographic exhibits. The opening hours are the same as those at the Dali museum, and admission is free.

One of the strangest sights on the bayfront is **The Pier** ((813) 821-6164, which has a five-story inverted pyramid structure at the end of it, containing continental stores and restaurants; there is a platform at the top affording great views over the bay, which The Pier juts into from 800 Second Avenue. Among the most beautiful on the Gulf Coast, the **Sunken Gardens** ((813) 896-3187, is a well-ordered tropical jungle with over 50,000 varieties of plants, flowers, and trees, and an exotic bird aviary. The gardens are downtown at 1825 Fourth Street North, and are open from 9 AM to 5:30 PM daily. Admission is $14 for adults and $8 for children. If you would like to go on a day cruise of the bay, with entertainment and food included, go to the Port of St. Petersburg at First Street and Eighth Avenue and board the **SeaEscape** ((813) 432-0900.

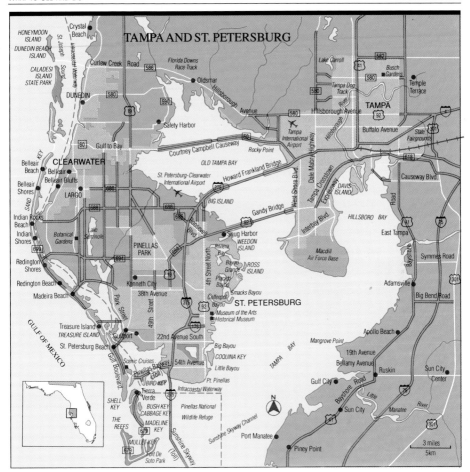

Fort DeSoto Park at 34th Street on Mullet Key is in the mouth of the bay. You can
explore the fort, which was built during the
Spanish-American War, or simply relax on
the island's beaches. If you head north from
Mullet Key on Route 679 and then join Gulf
Boulevard you will reach St. Petersburg
Beach. Gulf Boulevard continues north
along a chain of islands which includes
Madeira Beach, Indian Rocks Beach, Belle-
air Beach, and Clearwater Beach, which
with St. Petersburg Beach comprise the
"Suncoast".

Sports

There are 31 **golf courses** in the St. Petersburg area (Pinellas County), including Mangrove Bay ((813) 893-7797, three miles (five
kilometers) north of the city at 875 62nd
Avenue, which is one of the best known in
the state. Tarpon Springs Golf Club ((813)

937-6906, at 1310 Pinellas Avenue South; and
Pasadena Golf Club ((813) 345-9329, at 6100
Gulfport Boulevard, St. Petersburg, are two
of 15 public courses.

Tennis players should make their way
to the St. Petersburg Tennis Club ((813) 894-
4378, at 650 18th Avenue South, which has
15 courts, or call the city's recreation department ((813) 893-7441, for information on
other courts.

Windsurfers and **surfers** can receive
instruction and rent a board from Windsurfing Florida Suncoast Inc. ((813) 360-
3783, at 6200 Gulf Boulevard, St. Petersburg
Beach. **Sailboats** are for rent at Gulfcoast
Sailboat Charters ((813) 367-4444, 9600 West
Gulf Boulevard, Treasure Island. **Divers**
should get in touch with the Madeira Dive
Shop ((813) 392-8978, at 13613 Gulf Boule-

A young Tarpon Springs woman enjoys the sun.

vard, for information about diving trips, instruction, and rental equipment.

Shopping

The Pier (see SIGHTS, above) at 800 Second Avenue contains exclusive boutiques and expensive gift shops. On Madeira Beach at 12925 East Gulf Boulevard is the **Johns Pass Village and Boardwalk**, which is home to gift shops and sportswear outlets. For the best arts and crafts shops in town head for the **St. Petersburg Arts and Crafts Emporium** at 333 First Street Northeast. Further

Boulevard, Indian Rocks Beach, and **Cadillac Jack's (** (813) 360-2099, at 145 107th Avenue, Treasure Island. Also recommended are **Don's Beach Bar (** (813) 360-5531, at the Bilmar Hotel, 10650 Gulf Boulevard, St. Petersburg Beach; **Studebaker's (** (813) 799-4147, at 2516 Gulf Boulevard, Clearwater, where you can musically re-live the Fifties adolescence you might not have lived; and for a good laugh, the **Coconuts Comedy Club** at Barnacle Bill's **(** (813) 360-4575, in Howard Johnson's, 6110 Gulf Boulevard, St. Petersburg Beach.

north you can find shops selling Greek products in the old fishing village of Tarpon Springs, and Scottish tartan in Dunedin.

Nightlife

The two joints that do the most jumpin' in the downtown area — which is rather supine in the evening — are the **Bayfront Center (** (813) 893-3367, at 400 First Street South, which features live rock and country bands, and the **Alessi Café at The Pier (** (813) 804-4659, 800 Second Avenue, where you can hear live jazz on weeknights and live rock on weekends.

Most of the nightime action, however, happens on the islands, especially at **The Beach Place (** (813) 596-5633, 2405 Gulf

WHERE TO STAY

Luxury

The Heritage ((813) 822-4814, can be found at 234 Third Avenue North, where mahogany bars, oak floors, and antique furnishings lend a turn-of-the-century ambiance; the indoor swimming pool and the Jacuzzis add late-in-the-century appeal.

There are several luxury-class hotels in St. Petersburg Beach, including the exotic **Trade winds (** (813) 367-6461 TOLL-FREE (800) 282-5553, at 5500 Gulf Boulevard, where gondolas or paddleboats, operating on an internal canal system, deliver guests to their rooms. The recreational facilities are outstanding and feature a water sports center on the hotel's own beach, which has equipment for windsurfing, jet-skiing, water biking, and parasailing. Similar amenities are available at the pink Mediterranean-style **Don CeSar Beach Resort** ((813) 360-1881 TOLL-FREE (800) 237-8789, 3400 Gulf Boulevard, home of the celebrated King Charles restaurant, and a hotel long frequented by celebrities ranging from Scott Fitzgerald to Babe Ruth.

Mid-range

In St. Petersburg, the **Edgepark Hotel**

Long Key Beach Resort ((813) 360-1748, 3828 Gulf Boulevard, and the **Dolphin Beach Resort** ((813) 360-7011, boasts 174 spacious rooms and, like the Cadillac Motel, its very own swath of white sandy beach at 4900 Gulf Boulevard.

Inexpensive

For more economical rates in St. Petersburg you should pay a visit to the **Avalon Hotel** ((813) 822-4783, located at 443 North Fourth Avenue, or the **Beach Park Motor Inn** ((813) 898-6325, at 300 Northeast Beach Drive. In

((813) 894-9435, is a quiet and comfortable hostelry at 256 First Street North. A verandah with wicker chairs is provided for postprandial relaxation, and all the rooms are very neatly turned out. The **Bayboro House** ((813) 823-4955, is one of the city's oldest buildings, with conch shells lining the porch, and marble tables and grandfather clocks dotting the interior. The hotel is at 1719 Beach Drive Southeast.

In St. Petersburg Beach, the **Colonial Gateway Resort Inn** ((813) 367-2711 TOLL-FREE (800) 282-5245, at 6300 Gulf Boulevard, has a children's play area with a pool, another pool with a bar for grownups, and 800 ft (244 m) of beach. There are 43 rooms and apartments overlooking the sea at the

St. Petersburg Beach, take a look at the **Carlida Apartments and Motel** ((813) 360-7233, at 610 69th Avenue, which stands out for its good value on this otherwise pricey stretch of the coast.

WHERE TO EAT

Expensive

The **King Charles** ((813) 360-1881, on the fifth floor of the Don CeSar Beach Resort, at 3400 Gulf Boulevard in St. Petersburg

The Don CeSar Beach Resort OPPOSITE in St. Petersburg and the Belleview Biltmore Hotel ABOVE in Clearwater are two shining examples of the luxurious accommodations found along the Gulf Coast.

Beach, offers superb continental cuisine which you can enjoy while looking at the Gulf through the restaurant's French windows. Another treasure is **Peter's Place** ((813) 822-8436, at 208 Beach Drive Northeast, St. Petersburg, which has a delicious Moroccan couscous and a tastefully prepared filet wrapped around garlic-buttered shrimp. Rather more imaginative, however, is the veal Kentucky in bourbon sauce at the restaurant of **Palm Court** ((813) 360-0061, in the Tradewinds Hotel, 5500 Gulf Boulevard, St. Petersburg Beach. If you have a yearning for charcoal-grilled seafood, you can satisfy it at **Girard's** ((813) 576-7076, up the coast at 3580 Ulmerton Road, Clearwater.

Moderate

You can watch the fishing boats docking from the comfort of the **Crab Market** ((813) 360-4656, located at 955 Blind Pass Road in St. Petersburg Beach, which specializes in varieties of tenderly cooked crabmeat. Those who prefer non-shellfish seafood should go to **Ted Peters** ((813) 381-7931, at 1350 Pasadena Avenue South, St. Petersburg, where mullet and mackerel are smoked over red oak. In St. Petersburg there is good Italian food at the inaptly-named **Bahama Bill's** ((813) 821-4931, 320 Fourth Street North.

Inexpensive

There are numerous inexpensive restaurants in St. Petersburg, among the best of which are **China City** ((813) 822-3713, at 1221 Fourth Street North, which serves simple and well-prepared Chinese food; and the very popular **Big Tim's Bar-B-Que** ((813) 327-7388, at 530 34th Street, a local legend for its rib and pork barbecue sandwiches with spicy sauce. You should also try **Carol's Seafood and Steak House** ((813) 522-9907, at 7220 Fourth Street North. And in St. Petersburg Beach the **Pelican Diner** ((813) 363-9873, 7501 Gulf Boulevard, serves up some great home cooking in an old dining car.

The pier at Naples silhouetted by the coppery sunset. Located along the Shell Coast, Naples has 41 miles (66 km) of beaches.

HOW TO GET THERE

The St. Petersburg-Clearwater International Airport, 10 miles (16 km) southeast of Clearwater, is served by a reasonable number of national and international airlines. Probably, though, you will prefer to fly in to Tampa International Airport, on the eastern side of Old Tampa Bay.

Motorists should use the same roads for St. Petersburg as for Tampa. If you are coming from the south you can leave I-75 north of Ellenton and take the Sunshine Skyway over the mouth of Tampa Bay to reach St. Petersburg.

SARASOTA

Known as the "Culture Capital" of Florida, Sarasota offers theater, classical music, opera, and a number of much-respected art galleries. Over the years increasing numbers of artists, musicians, and writers have settled in Sarasota, attracted by the city's reputation for being hospitable to the arts. So if you are looking for culture to go with your sand, sea, and sun, this is the place for you.

BACKGROUND

Sarasota began to make itself noticed in 1927 when John Ringling of circus fame established a winter residence for his family — and his circus — in the city. An avid art collector, with a special passion for Italian Renaissance and Baroque works, he built a museum to house his acquisitions. He also invested heavily in civic improvements for his adopted city, building hotels and island causeways and generally subsidizing the arts. The theaters and art galleries which proliferate in the city today testify to Ringling's enthusiastic patronage.

GENERAL INFORMATION

The Sarasota Convention and Visitors Center ((941) 957-1877, is at 655 North Tamiami Trail, Sarasota, FL 34236. The Sarasota Chamber of Commerce ((941) 955-8187, is at 1551 Second Street, Sarasota, FL 33577.

Other useful telephone numbers (all in area code 941):

Sarasota-Bradenton Airport	355-5200
Airport Taxi	365-1360
Yellow Cabs	955-3341
Sarasota County Health clinic	365-2020

WHAT TO SEE AND DO

Sights

Three miles (five kilometers) north of downtown Sarasota, at 5401 Bayshore Road off Route 41, you'll find the 68 landscaped acres

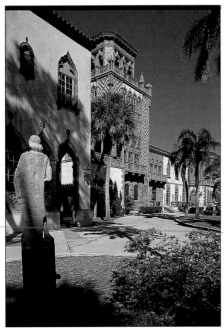

(27 hectares) of the **Ringling estate**, now open to the public. You can tour the 32-room mansion — modeled on the Doges Palace in Venice and built at a cost of $1.5 million at a time when $1.5 million was serious money — which served as Ringling's winter residence, **Ca'd'Zan** (venetian patois meaning "House of John"). Also on the estate, the **Ringling Museum of Art** ((941) 359-5700, is home to one of the nation's premier collections of Italian Renaissance and Baroque art, as well as a valuable series of paintings and cartoons by Rubens and works by Rembrandt and El Greco.

Next to the art museum is the rococo-style **Asolo Theater** ((941) 355-8000, which Ringling brought in pieces from an Italian

castle in Asolo to his estate, where he had it reassembled. You can also see all kinds of circus memorabilia from the great days of the Big Top at the **Circus Galleries**. The Ringling estate is open from 10 AM to 5:30 PM. Admission (which covers the house and the museums) is $8.50 for adults and $4 for children aged six to 12.

There are some rare and beautiful plants in the attractive **Mary Selby Botanical Gardens** ((941) 366-5730, at 800 South Palm Avenue off Route 41, which has an international reputation for its collection of orchids. There are another 15 acres (six hectares) of tropical growth at the **Sarasota Jungle Gardens** ((941) 355-5305, 3701 Bayshore Road, which features jungle animals, and daily bird and reptile shows.

At the **Mote Marine Science Center** ((941) 388-4441, 1600 City Island Park, swimmers will be keen to learn about the 27 species of shark inhabit the Gulf of Mexico. There is little you can't learn here about the Gulf and its creatures, and the center's aquarium contains specimens such as "Nibbles" the affectionately named nurse shark. If you prefer classic cars to deadly nurses go to **Bellm's Cars and Music of Yesterday** ((941) 355-6228, at 5500 North Tamiami Trail, where there is a collection of 200 lovely old cars, along with antique bicycles and old musical contraptions such as the hurdy-gurdy and the nickelodeon.

For beaches, I would recommend **South Lido** on the southern tip of Lido Key, which has 100 acres (40 hectares) of beach and leisure facilities; or **Siesta Beach** on Siesta Key, which has 40 acres (16 hectares) of beach and superb sports facilities.

Two rural attractions are near Sarasota: the **Oscar Sherer Recreation Area**, about 10 miles (16 km) south on Route 41, which has campsites, nature trails, and fishing; and the **Myakka River State Park**, 15 miles (24 km) east at 13207 Route 72, where you can go on airboat tours of the 29,000-acre (11,600 hectares) wildlife sanctuary, or rent canoes and stay in log cabins.

Sports

Baseball fans should know that the Chicago White Sox and the Pittsburgh Pirates hold their spring training and play their exhibition games here — the White Sox at Payne Park off Route 301, and the Pirates at McKecknie Field, 17th Avenue West and Ninth Street in nearby Bradenton.

There is a good choice of **golf courses** in Sarasota, including the Sarasota Golf Club ((941) 371-2431, at 7280 Leeswynn Drive, off Route 301, and the Bobby Jones Golf Club ((941) 955-5188, at 1000 Circus Boulevard.

There are free public **tennis courts** at Siesta Beach on Siesta Key; and the Forest Lakes Tennis Club ((941) 922-0660, at 2401 Beneva Road, also has public courts. For more information on golf courses and tennis courts, call the Sarasota recreation department ((941) 365-2200.

For **water sports** go to Don and Mike's Boat and Ski Rental ((941) 366-6659, at Marina Plaza on the waterfront downtown, where you can get surfboards, water skis, jet skis, wave jammers, miniboats, as well as windsurfing and water-skiing instruction. Sailing enthusiasts should go to O'Leary's Sarasota Sailing School ((941) 953-7505, near Marina Jack's restaurant off Route 41 on the bayfront, where you can rent sailboats and receive instruction on how to sail them.

Shopping

One of the best known — and exclusive — shopping complexes on the Gulf Coast, **St. Armand's Circle** has over 100 specialty stores, including expensive gift shops and designer fashion outlets. Take Route 41 south to Route 789, turn right and cross Ringling Causeway to reach the circle of shops. For an equally wide choice at considerably lower prices head for the **Sarasota Square Mall** at 8201 South Tamiami Trail, or **Siesta Village** at 5000 Ocean Boulevard on Siesta Key.

Nightlife

The **Asolo Performing Arts Center** ((941) 359-5700, in the Ringling estate at 5401 Bayshore Road, is home to a professional troupe who perform a well-balanced repertoire during a season that runs from December to August. On Monday evenings the Ringling Fine Arts Film Series shows classic and foreign films in the center. A small pro-

fessional company presents contemporary drama, comedies, and musicals at the **Florida Studio Theater** ((941) 366-9796, 1241 North Palm Avenue; and the **Players of Sarasota** ((941) 365-2494, enact comedies, thrillers, and musicals in a community theater at Route 41 and Ninth Street.

The **Florida Symphonic Band** ((941) 955-6660, is comprised of 50 musicians who perform a classical concert each month at the Van Wezel Hall, 709 North Tamiami Trail, and from February to March you can hear internationally known artists, sup-

ported by young in-house apprentice singers, at the **Sarasota Opera** ((941) 953-7030, in a charming old theater at the corner of First and Pineapple Streets.

For rawer entertainment, drop into the **Beach Club** ((941) 349-6311, at 5151 Ocean Boulevard on Siesta Key, which has live music; or try **Club Paradise** ((941) 366-3830, another bustling night club featuring rock music, at 1927 Ringling Boulevard in Sarasota. You can down a few no-nonsense pints with the locals at **The Pub** ((941) 383-2391, at 760 Broadway, Longboat Key; and there's more hard drinking to be done in the

OPPOSITE AND ABOVE: Exterior and interior views of John Ringling's winter residence, Ca'd'Zan in Sarasota.

delightfully seedy **Hemingway's** ((941) 388-3948, at 325 Ringling Boulevard in Sarasota.

WHERE TO STAY

Luxury

The **Hyatt Sarasota** ((941) 233-1234 TOLL-FREE (800) 228-9000, is downtown next to a marina at 1000 Boulevard of the Arts. The hotel's restaurant, Peppercorn's, is much acclaimed, and its other amenities include a sauna, health club, and sailboats. Offering an excellent selection of water sports, the **Harley Sandcastle Hotel** ((941) 388-2181, is on the oceanfront at 1540 Ben Franklin Drive. There is also a playground and games room for children, and two swimming pools, one with a bar. There are 232 beach houses, villas, and apartments set in scenic grounds next to the ocean at the **Colony Beach Resort** ((941) 383-6464 TOLL-FREE (800) 426-5669, 1620 Gulf of Mexico Drive on Longboat Key north of Sarasota. All the accommodations are modern efficiencies with full conveniences, and the resort's sporting and beach facilities are outstanding.

Mid-range

Set in three acres (1.2 hectares) of landscaped grounds, the **Golden Host** at 4675 North Tamiami Trail has stylish rooms with balconies, a palm-ringed swimming pool, and a cocktail lounge with a tropical decor. On South Tamiami Trail at N⁰ 6660, is the modern and very comfortable **Days Inn Sarasota** ((941) 924-4900, which is only a mile (1.6 km) from the beach. Facing the ocean at 459 Beach Road, on Siesta Key is a small, comfortable hotel with friendly service, the **Crescent House** ((941) 346-1786, which serves a complimentary continental breakfast each morning.

Inexpensive

With its own swimming pool and very spacious rooms, the Old Florida-style **Our Hacienda** ((941) 951-1920, is great value at 2803 Browning Street. There are several inexpensive hotels on North Tamiami Trail, among them the **Econo Lodge** ((941) 355-8867, at N⁰ 5340; and the **Hampton Inn** ((941) 351-7734, at N⁰ 5000.

WHERE TO EAT

Expensive

Fresh seafood with crisp salads are served up at **Marina Jack's** ((941) 365-4232, Two Marina Plaza, downtown, which affords a marvelous view over Sarasota Bay. The *Marina Jack II* is a paddle-wheel boat which leaves from Marina Plaza on lunch and dinner cruises. There is a northern Italian bias to the food at **Osteria** ((941) 388-3671, 29 ½ North Boulevard of Presidents, a charming restaurant bedecked with flowers, where the house specialty is their wonderful veal layered with prosciutto. One of the best continental restaurants in the area is the **Café L'Europe** ((941) 388-4415, at 431 Harding Circle on Lido Key, where I would urge you to try the *mignonettes aux poivres* and the red snapper *belle meunière*. For good solid American cuisine try **Michael's on East** ((941) 366-0007, at 1212 East Avenue, Sarasota, where the desserts are sensational.

Moderate

In the nautical surroundings of **Charley's Crab** ((941) 388-3964, at 420 Harding Circle on Lido Key, you can choose from a splendid selection of inventively concocted seafood dishes. The **Indian Cuisine** ((941) 953-5102, at 1522 Main Street in Sarasota, has apart from its eponymous dishes, some interesting Trinidadian fare. Nearby at 1551 Main Street, **Ristorante Bellini** ((941) 365-7380, features northern Italian cooking, which happily includes a *sogliota aurora* — sole in a wine, shrimp, and lemon sauce. For real down-home American cooking try **Poki Joe's Greatest Hits** ((941) 922-5915, at 6614 Superior Avenue, where spinach pie and sausage soup are among the chart toppers.

Inexpensive

Everything on the menu is homemade at the simple, café-like **Der Dutchman** ((941) 955-8007, 3713 Bahia Vista. At **Wildflower** ((941) 349-1758, 5218 Ocean Boulevard, Siesta Key, food for the health-conscious unfairly has to compete with tempting Mexican food. **Walt's Fish Market, Raw Oyster Bar and Restaurant** ((941) 365-1735, is probably all you need to know about

Walt's food at 560 North Washington Boulevard in Sarasota. For hot dogs and barbecued ribs and mountains of fries, head out to Siesta Key and the **Old Salty Dog Pub** ((941) 349-0158, at 5023 Ocean Boulevard.

HOW TO GET THERE

The Sarasota-Bradenton Airport is served by most of the major national airlines; in any case, the larger Tampa and St. Petersburg airports are both convenient for Sarasota.

Sanibel, which have some of the best "shelling beaches" in the world.

Further to the south, the city of Naples has 41 miles (66 km) of beaches and some of the best shopping on the entire Gulf Coast. Continuing down the coast, you come to Marco Island, with its modern Gulf-front condominiums and its carefully preserved fishing villages such as Goodland. At the southern end of the Shell Coast are the Ten Thousand Islands, which are still largely undeveloped and provide a home for a dazzling array of wildlife.

By car, I-75 is the main route in from the north and south (the more picturesque Route 41 also comes in from the south). Routes 64 and 70 enter Sarasota from the east.

THE SHELL COAST

The Shell Coast runs from Captiva Island, near Fort Myers, to the Ten Thousand Islands in the south, near Everglades City. Fort Myers is one of the fastest growing cities in the United States and an important center of commerce, while Fort Myers Beach is a resort community on the offshore island of Estero. There are also luxury resort facilities on the islands of Captiva and

GENERAL INFORMATION

The Fort Myers Chamber of Commerce ((941) 332-3624, is at 1365 Hendry Street, P.O. Box 9289, Fort Myers, FL 33902; and the Fort Myers Beach Chamber of Commerce ((941) 454-7500, is at 17200 San Carlos Boulevard, Fort Myers Beach, FL 33931. The Sanibel-Captiva Chamber of Commerce ((941) 472-1080, is at Causeway Road, Sanibel, FL 33957; and the Naples Chamber of Commerce ((941) 262-6141, is at 3620 Tamiami Trail, Naples, FL 33940.

The Ringling Museum of Art, home of one of the nation's best collections of Italian Renaissance and Baroque works.

WHAT TO SEE AND DO

Sights

Thomas Edison spent his winters in Fort Myers, which means you can go visit **Edison's Winter Home** ((941) 334-7419, at 2350 McGregor Boulevard. In his house is a museum displaying just a selection of the 1,096 (!) inventions which Edison patented, and there are beautiful botanical gardens in the 14-acre (5.5-hectare) grounds which the great man nurtured. The home and gardens

which is home to more than 300 species of birds and 50 species of reptiles. You can walk along nature trails or rent a canoe or boat from the Visitors Center ((941) 472-1100, at One Wildlife Drive. At the southern tip of the island is the historic Sanibel Lighthouse on **Lighthouse Beach**, a popular spot for swimming, soaking up the sun, and shelling.

The best shells on Sanibel Island can be found on **Bowman's Beach**, to the north, which is less crowded than the island's southern beaches.

are open daily, and admission is $10 for adults and $5 for children.

The world's largest collection of shells can be seen at the **Shell Factory** ((941) 995-2141, 2787 North Tamiami Trail, off Route 41 north of Fort Myers, which also has a souvenir shop and a children's theme park.

The **Eden Vineyards** ((941) 728-9463, is just off State Road 80, 10 miles (16 km) east of Fort Myers, and is the southernmost vineyard and winery in the continental United States. It is open for sales, tours and tastings.

On Sanibel Island you can explore and hike through the **J.N. "Ding" Darling National Wildlife Refuge** ((941) 472-1100,

A good way to visit the islands near Fort Myers is to join the **Adventure Sailing Escape Flotilla** whose 16 full-berth yachts sail for a week and spend each afternoon docked at a resort on a different island, including Useppa, Captiva, Sanibel, and Cabbage Key. For more information, contact Royal Palm Tours Inc. ((941) 489-0344, 6296 Corporate Court, Fort Myers.

The main attractions in the Naples area are the **Corkscrew Swamp Sanctuary** ((941) 657-3771, at Sanctuary Road off Route 41 north of Naples, where you can see some of the oldest cypress trees in America as well as rare species of birds; and **Jungle Larry's Zoological Park** ((941) 262-5409, at 1590 Goodlette Road, off Route 41 south of Naples, which has hundreds of exotic animals and a children's petting zoo.

The Marco Island Area Chamber of Commerce ((941) 394-7549, at 1102 North Collier Boulevard, Marco Island, will provide you with information about Marco Island and the Ten Thousand Islands region to the south. One of the best ways to see the islands is on a boat tour which leaves from the Gulf Coast Ranger Station in Everglades City; contact the **Everglades National Park Boat Tours** ((800) 445-7724, in Everglades City, for more details.

Water sports abound on the Shell Coast. In Fort Myers Beach you can rent sailboats, aquacycles, and jet skis from Happy Sailboat Rental ((941) 463-3351, at 1010 Estero Boulevard; Windsurfing of Sanibel ((941) 472-0123, at 1554 Periwinkle Way on Sanibel Island, will fix you up with a sailboard; you can receive instruction in scuba diving from Underwater Explorers ((941) 481-4733, at 12600 McGregor Boulevard; and you can arrange an offshore diving trip and equipment rental from Sealandia Scuba Center ((941) 261-3357, at 625 Eighth Street in Naples.

Sports

There is no shortage of **golf courses** along the Shell Coast, including the Bay Beach Golf Club ((941) 463-2064, located at 7401 Estero Boulevard in Fort Myers Beach; the Beachview Golf Club ((941) 472-2626, at 110 Parkview Drive South on Sanibel Island; and Naples Beach Hotel and Golf Club ((941) 261-2222, at 851 Gulf Shore Boulevard.

There are **tennis courts** at the Bay Beach Racquet Club ((941) 463-4473, at 120 Lenell Street, Fort Myers Beach; The Dunes ((941) 472-3522, at 949 Sand Castle Road on Sanibel Island; and at the Forest Hills Racquet Club ((941) 774-2442, 100 Forest Hills Boulevard, Naples.

The Gulf Coast

Shopping

For the best selection of shops in Fort Myers go to the **Royal Palm Square Shopping Center** located at 1400 Colonial Boulevard.

On Sanibel Island, **Periwinkle Way** is lined with gift shops, shell shops, and a good selections of outlets for sports and swimwear.

The best-quality shops on the Shell Coast, however, are in Naples at the **Old Marine Market Place**, 1200 Fifth Avenue South.

OPPOSITE: Working boats lie at rest, moored at Tarpon Springs. ABOVE: People and pelicans wind up a tranquil evening of fishing on a Sarasota pier.

Nightlife

The Fort Myers area is the best place for living it up after dark on the Shell Coast. In Fort Myers itself there is live music in the open air at **The Beach Club** ((941) 939-2582, 1915 Colonial Boulevard. Live bands play Top 40 hits at **Edison's Electric Lounge** ((941) 482-2900, in the Holiday Inn at 13051 Bell Tower Drive. A lively singles crowd dances to disco at **Norma Jean's** ((941) 275-9997, 4797 Route 41. In Fort Myers Beach, go along Estero Boulevard and you'll find what you're looking for.

Mid-range

The comfortable **Fountain Motel** ((941) 481-0429, at 14621 Mcgregor Boulevard, Fort Myers, has both rooms and apartments; and the **Outrigger Beach Resort** ((941) 463-3131, at 6200 Estero Boulevard, is on the ocean-front in Fort Myers Beach. On Sanibel Island, the **Kon Mai Motel** ((941) 472-1001, is a charming Hawaiian-style resort at 1539 Periwinkle Way. **La Playa** ((941) 597-3123, near Vanderbilt Beach at 9891 Gulf Shore Drive, Naples, is particularly recommended for families.

WHERE TO STAY

Luxury

In Fort Myers, the **Sheraton Harbor Place** ((941) 337-0300, is downtown by the waterfront at 2500 Edwards Drive, with 417 luxurious rooms. In Fort Myers Beach you can find a similar standard at **Seawatch-on-the-Beach** ((941) 481-3636, 6550 Estero Boulevard, which has two-bedroom efficiency suites overlooking the gulf. An excellent hotel on Sanibel Island with superb recreational facilities, the **Sanibel Beach and Tennis Resort** ((941) 472-4151, is located at 1415 Middle Gulf Drive. In Naples there is the deluxe **Ritz-Carlton** ((941) 598-3300, at 280 Vanderbilt Beach Road.

Inexpensive

There are not too many budget deals on the Shell Coast, but three places that I know to be good value for the money are the **Ta Ki Ki Motel** ((941) 334-2135, at 2631 First Street, Fort Myers; the **Beacon Court Motel** ((941) 463-5264, at 1240 Estero Boulevard, Fort Myers Beach; and the **Fairways Motel** ((941) 597-8181, 103 Palm River Boulevard, Naples.

WHERE TO EAT

Expensive

There is some quite exceptional seafood on the menu at **La Tiers** ((941) 337-0300, in the Sheraton Harbor Place Hotel, 2500 Edwards

Drive, in Fort Myers. In Fort Myers Beach, the **Snug Harbor Restaurant and Lounge** ((941) 463-4343, at 645 San Carlos Boulevard, is another restaurant featuring wonderful seafood from local waters. Roast duckling in fruit sauce is the house specialty at **Jean-Paul's French Corner** ((941) 472-1493, 708 Tarpon Bay Road, Sanibel Island. At the **Chef's Garden** ((941) 262-5500, 1300 Third Street South, Naples, there is an interesting choice of Italian, Californian, and Cajun cooking, backed up by an equally eclectic wine list.

Inexpensive

In Fort Myers, **Woody's Bar-B-Q** ((941) 997-1424, at 6701 North Tamiami Trail, is exactly what you might expect — and excellent. In Fort Myers Beach, the **Pelican Restaurant and Inn** ((941) 463-6139, offers good bargains in seafood dishes at 3040 Estero Boulevard. For a cheap sandwich or pizza go to **Island Pizza** ((941) 472-1518, at 1619 Periwinkle Way, on Sanibel Island. Omelettes, fondues, and crêpes are the order of the day at the **Venetian Café** ((941) 261-4050, 4050 Gulf Shore Boulevard, Naples.

Moderate

The seafood is impeccably prepared and presented at **The Prawnbroker** ((941) 489-2226, 6535 McGregor Boulevard, in Fort Myers. Another popular seafood restaurant is the **Mucky Duck** ((941) 463-5519, at 2500 Estero Boulevard, in Fort Myers Beach, where you can enjoy fish-and-chips and bacon-wrapped barbecued shrimp in a quasi-English country-style pub ambiance. For Creole and Cajun food go to the **Thistle Lodge** ((941) 472-9200, at 2255 West Gulf Drive on Sanibel Island. For good, honest just-about-everything in Fort Myers you should head for the **Riverwalk Fish and Ale House** ((941) 263-2734, at 1200 Fifth Avenue South.

HOW TO GET THERE

The Southwest Florida Regional Airport is 10 miles (16 km) southeast of Fort Myers and is served by many national airlines.

The principal north-south roads through the region are I-75 and Route 41. Route 17 approaches the Shell Coast from the northeast, and Everglades Parkway ("Alligator Alley") is the main road from the east into Naples. Route 80 enters Fort Myers from the east.

OPPOSITE AND ABOVE: Two ways of approaching the Gulf.

The
Everglades

EVERGLADES NATIONAL PARK

Most, people imagine a swamp filled with alligators when they think of the Everglades. But the reality is something that more closely resembles a vast midwestern wheatfield: an expanse of sawgrass, interrupted by copses of hardwood and cypress trees, which, at the end of winter before the spring rains, appears totally dry. When the rains do come, and the water levels rise, this grassy plain is transformed into a unique river — over 60 miles (100 km) wide yet only six inches

(15 cm) deep — which flows slowly southward to the Gulf Coast and Florida Bay. The river drops only 13 ft (four meters) over its 100-mile (160-km) length, which gives you some idea of the flatness of the Everglades.

The Indian name for the region is *Pa-hay-okee*, meaning the "grassy waters". An early white surveyor came up with the name River Glades, but later maps changed River to Ever, and the new name stuck. The water sources of the Everglades start with the rivers of central Florida's Kissimmee Valley, which runs into the huge Lake Okeechobee, which in turn feeds the grassy waters. On its

ABOVE: In the Everglades, a pelican thinks things over. OPPOSITE: Alligators flourish in the Florida swamplands.

course southwards, the river passes through a zone where temperate and subtropical climates blend, which is one of the reasons for the great diversity of animal and plant life in the region, which includes such rarities as the manatee and the Florida panther, not to mention half of the 650 species of birds found in North America, as well as 45 kinds of flora that cannot be found anywhere else in the world.

The Everglades are also a source of water for farmlands to the east around the city of Homestead and Florida City, and for the homes of millions of people who live along Florida's southeast coast. The drainage this has involved has had its effect on the ecological balance of the Everglades, with water levels dropping in recent years as demands increase from the thirsty and booming populations of the coast cities.

Everglades National Park consists of 1.4 Million acres (500,000 hectares) of protected land and coastline stretching from Everglades City in the northwest down to the coast near Key Largo in the southeast, all policed by park rangers and carefully tended by conservationists.

BACKGROUND

Calusas, Tequestas, and Mayaimis Indians lived in Pa-hay-okee for two thousand years before white settlers arrived in the latter half of the nineteenth century and set about requisitioning the marshland for agricultural purposes. By 1909, a canal running from Lake Okeechobee to Miami was completed, and numerous dikes and irrigation canals had been installed across the plains, impeding the natural rise and fall of water levels. In the 1920s a series of hurricanes whipped up the waters of Lake Okeechobee, causing floods in the surrounding area which killed 2,000 people. In response, the United States Army Corps of Engineers ringed the lake with the Hoover Dike and constructed a further 1,400 miles (2,254 km) of canals and levees to control and channel the waters of the lake and the Everglades.

All of this drastically upset the ecosystem, which demands that the marshes should be "dry" in winter and crossed by the river in summer. Sometimes, due to

water mismanagement, the cycle was reversed, with devastating results for flora and fauna alike: since 1930 the Everglades have lost about 90 percent of their marsh and wading birds, and without great conservation efforts even the alligator would have disappeared.

A conservationist named Marjorie Stoneman Douglas published a book in 1947 entitled *The Everglades: River of Grass*, which began: "There are no other Everglades in the world." She went on to warn that the region was in danger of being destroyed if action

wasn't taken urgently. The book had an effect. That same year President Truman created Everglades National Park, to the north, and in 1989 a further 107,000 acres (42,800 hectares) of the ecologically crucial Shark River Slough in the northeast were added. There is a water purity project well under way at this writing, and the Army Corps of Engineers have been called back in to undo their well-intentioned but ultimately damaging work.

Meanwhile, and perhaps most importantly, the politicians have realized that the protection of the Everglades is a popular vote-getter. The "grassy waters" may survive after all.

GENERAL INFORMATION

The Greater Homestead-Florida City Chamber of Commerce ((305) 247-2332, is located at 43 North Krome Avenue, Homestead, FL 33030. For full details of accommodation, tours, and activities available in the park, plus literature and maps, contact the Ever-

glades National Park, P.O. Box 279, Homestead, FL 33030. The Everglades City Chamber of Commerce ((813) 695-3941, is located at 32016 East Tamiami Trail, Everglades City, FL 33929. There are three main entrances to the park — at Shark Valley in the northeast, off Route 41; at Everglades City in the northwest on Route 29, off Route 41; and the entrance southwest of Homestead at the main Visitor Center on Route 9336, which is the one I would recommend if you can spend only one day in the park. At this Visitor Center you can see a short film about the wildlife and ecology of the Everglades, and there are free guides and maps explaining the attractions and trails you can find in the park. There are naturalists giving and leading hikes or canoe trips, but you are free to make your own way from the Visitor Center by taking a 38-mile (61-km) park road, the Ingraham Highway, which passes through sawgrass plains, hardwood and cypress copses, and mangrove swamps on its way to the fishing village of Flamingo, 35 miles (56 km) to the southwest.

Along the road there are trails and boardwalks branching off, some of which lead to "hammocks" — raised, tree-clad mounds in the swamps. The first turning on the left will take you to the Royal Palm Visitor Center, which has slide shows and rangers who will direct you along the various nature trails which branch out from the center. The Anhinga and Gumbo Limbo trails are particularly popular boardwalks, from which you can see alligators, egrets, herons, raccoons, opossums, and lizards, among other wildlife. There are several more turnings before you reach Flamingo; the maps and official guides will tell you where they are and what you can expect to see there.

When you arrive in Flamingo, go to the Visitor Center for any information about trails, boat routes, picnic areas, campsites, and special attractions in the area. There is a restaurant, a shop, a motel, and a marina in the village, plus a bayfront observation deck with telescopes with which to view the islands and wildlife offshore.

The best time of year to visit the Everglades is winter — the "dry" season — for two reasons: that is when you will see the greatest concentration of birdlife, and there are far fewer mosquitoes and biting insects, which can be a real problem at other times of the year. (If you do visit in the summer, be sure to take plenty of insect repellent, because there are plenty of repellent insects.) At any times of the year you should be aware of the presence of poisonous plants and snakes (particularly coral snakes, water moccasins, diamondback and pigmy rattlesnakes), all of which the printed guides will clearly identify for you. If you keep to the official trails and follow all written and oral instructions you will have no problems.

If you do decide to head out on your own, be sure to file your planned walking or boating route at the nearest ranger station. The park is vast and there are very few navigational points of reference; reckless amateur explorers have been known to disappear without a trace in the Everglades. What you have to remember is that this is not a theme park or a zoo; this is the real thing: one of the great wild areas in the world.

Finally, *don't* (yes, it has been known to happen) go near or try to touch the alligators, however somnolent they may appear. They have an incredible turn of speed, which could well be your last great surprise if you get too close to one.

WHAT TO SEE AND DO

Sights

The Tamiami Trail (Route 41) runs from Miami to Everglades City along the Gulf Coast, and is a good way to view the park's northern attractions. Twenty-five miles (40 km) west of Miami you will find the **Miccosukee Indian Village** ((305) 223-8380, on the Tamiami Trail, where 600 contemporary Miccosukees live and work. You can watch the Indians at work and buy their handmade ornaments and crafts. Or you can watch alligator wrestling, or take the boardwalks or the airboat rides into the surrounding wilderness. The village is open daily from 9 AM to 5 PM. A mile (1.6 km) down the road from the village is the **Shark Valley** ((305) 221-8455, entrance to the park. You can take a tram ride around a 15-mile (24-km) loop road; the tram stops at an observation tower which affords panoramic views of the surrounding countryside and

such local denizens as alligators, otters, wood storks, and kites. Reservations are advisable for the December–March period. The trams run from 9 AM to 4 PM daily and tickets cost $7.30 for adults and $3.65 for children.

In Everglades City you can take a 12-mile (19-km) boat tour through the offshore Ten Thousand Islands region. The **Everglades National Park Boat Tours** ((941) 695-2591, leave from a dock just under one mile (1.6 km) south of the Gulf Coast Ranger Station on Route 29, off Route 41. If

you are in Chokoloskee Bay at sunset you will be treated to the sight of as many as 20,000 birds returning to the mainland to roost. For more information on the area contact the Everglades National Park Visitor Center ((813) 695-3311, on Route 29 south of Everglades City.

Further south down the coast, the *Bald Eagle* leaves from **Florida Bay Cruises** ((305) 253-2241, at Flamingo Marina, on a 90-minute tour of the islands in Florida Bay, providing close-up views of the islands' fascinating birdlife. The **Back Country Tour** at the same phone number, is a two-hour

OPPOSITE: An osprey keeps a lookout from its lofty vantage point. ABOVE: A boat operator in Everglades National Park.

The Everglades

cruise also out of Flamingo Marina, which explores the tropical estuaries and mangrove swamps of the coast, giving you a chance to see manatees, dolphins, sharks, and a variety of birds, among them the bald eagle. Reservations can be made — and are strongly recommended — in the winter season for all the boat tours.

There is also an inland water route, called the **Wilderness Waterway**, from Flamingo to Everglades City; the route's course is marked with posts along its 99-mile (159-km) length. You can receive more

information about it from the Visitor Center in the village. Outboard motorboats take about six hours to make the trip, and can be rented from Flamingo Marina.

If you want to rent a canoe, go to the **Everglades Canoe Outfitters** ((305) 246-1530, at 39801 Ingraham Highway (the road between Homestead and Flamingo), Homestead. Guided trips are available or you can simply get good advice on planning your own route. **Coopertown Airboat Ride** ((305) 226-6048, operates from Southwest Eighth Street, off Krome Avenue, west of Miami, and offers 30-minute excursions, taking in hardwood hammocks and alligator holes. It's open from 8:30 AM to dusk, and charges $8 for a ride.

For a comprehensive guided tour of the park, including an airboat ride, a visit to the Indian Village, Shark Valley, nature trails, and lunch, contact **Safari Sightseeing Tours** ((305) 226-6923, at 6547 Southwest 116th Place, Miami, FL 33713.

Sports

You can rent a canoe and go on a guided **canoeing trip** from North American Canoe Tours ((941) 695-2746, at Glades Haven, 800 Southeast Copeland Avenue, Everglades City. The daily trips run from November to March; they cost $18 for the first day and $15 for each day thereafter. There are six canoe trails in the Flamingo area, including the southern end of the Wilderness Waterway. Canoes can be rented at the Flamingo Marina, along with skiffs and houseboats.

If you want to go **diving**, contact Pirate's Cove Dive Center ((305) 248-1808, located at 116 North Homestead Boulevard in Homestead. It has equipment for sale or rent as well as diving trips from Homestead Bayfront.

Shopping

The shop at the Flamingo Marina sells the usual gifts and souvenirs, guides to the Everglades, some local crafts, camera film, sun lotion, and the all-important insect repellent. Homestead is the only place in the vicinity of the Everglades with any significant selection of shops. But then you haven't come to the Everglades to shop.

WHERE TO STAY

Some people choose to stay at hotels in the Greater Miami area, but having to struggle through traffic to get to one of the park's entrances seriously reduces one's "quality time". Besides, in Homestead there are several comfortable and moderately-priced hotels, including the **Holiday Inn** ((305) 247-7020, at 990 North Homestead Boulevard, which has 139 rooms and a swimming pool; and the **Greenstone Motel** ((305) 247-8334, at 304 North Krome Avenue. In Florida City there are two similarly attractive hotels: the **Park Royal Inn** ((305) 247-3200, at 100 Route 1, and the **Knights Inn** ((305) 245-2800, at 401 Route 1, which also has efficiency suites.

In Everglades City, there are tasteful rooms and efficiency villas at the **Captain's Table Resort** ((941) 695-4211, 102 Broadway Street. Probably the best-known hotel in the Everglades, the **Flamingo Lodge Marina and Outdoor Resort** ((305) 253-2241, in Flamingo, has 121 rooms and 17 cottages with kitchenettes, a very friendly staff, rooms overlooking Florida Bay, and of course a marina. Advance reservations are strongly advised during the winter season. Like the Captain's Table, the Flamingo Lodge is moderately priced.

WHERE TO EAT

The Tamiami Trail (Route 41) between Miami and Shark Valley and the area from Homestead to Florida City offer the best possibilities of eating well in or near the Everglades.

The **Miccosukee Restaurant** ((305) 223-8388, has such native specialties as pumpkin bread, Indian taco, breaded catfish, and frogs' legs. The restaurant is by the Shark Valley entrance to the park on Route 41 and is very

Campsites in the Everglades are basic (which is to say they have no electricity). You must provide your own food, water (and, again, insect repellent). Note: the park rangers come down hard on litter bugs. Information about the campsites, and permits to stay in them, are available from the ranger stations in Flamingo and Everglades City, or from any of the Visitor Centers located at the entrances to the park and inside the park grounds. There are almost 300 campsites in the Flamingo area alone. During the winter a stay is limited to 14 days. The charge (a permit is required for registration purposes and to control the numbers of campers) is $7 per day in winter and free in summer.

reasonably priced. By contrast, the expensive **Le Kir** ((305) 247-6414, located at 1532 Northeast Eighth Street, Homestead, has a distinctly Gallic menu, on which I would recommend the medallions of veal. **El Toro Taco** ((305) 245-5576, in Homestead at One South Krome Avenue, has superb Mexican food at superbly low prices. For Southern-style bargains try **Potlikker's** ((305) 248-0835, at 591 Washington Avenue in Homestead, where the chicken pie and pot roast are both worth having. In Florida City, **Captain Bob's** ((305) 247-8988, at 326 Southeast First Avenue, specializes in reasonably-priced, Greek-influenced seafood.

OPPOSITE: Visitors focus on the local fauna.
ABOVE: A squadron of black skimmers.

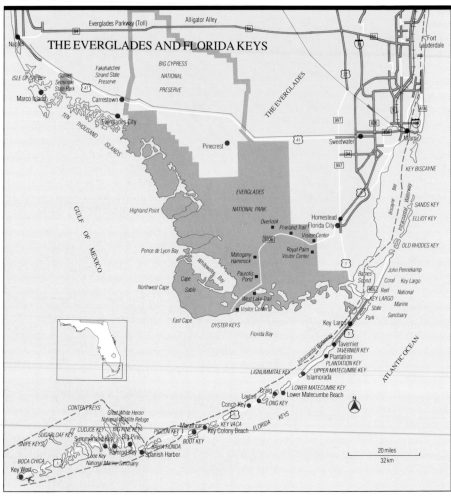

In Everglades City you must try out the **Rod and Gun Club** ((941) 695-2101, located at 200 Riverside Drive, which serves delicious steaks, poultry, and seafood on its porch where you can watch boats drift by as you eat. On the second floor of the Visitor Center in Flamingo, the **Flamingo Restaurant** ((941) 695-3101, has wonderful views over Florida Bay and an eclectic menu featuring Cuban pork loin roasted with garlic and lime, teriyaki chicken, and fried marlin.

HOW TO GET THERE

Most visitors to the Everglades fly in to Miami International Airport. The Airporter ((305) 876-7077, operates a regular shuttle service to Homestead; one can also, of course, rent a car at the airport. An alternative is to fly into Naples Municipal Airport north of Everglades City.

Traveling by car from the north down the east coast, you will take either Route 1 or Route 997 (Krome Avenue) to reach the Homestead-Florida City area. From there you continue on until you reach Route 9336, where you turn right: this will take you to the main Visitor Center and, eventually, to Flamingo. Route 41 — also known as the Tamiami Trail — runs from Miami to the Shark Valley entrance, and then on to Everglades City. Route 41 is also the principal highway down the Gulf Coast to the Everglades.

OPPOSITE: Anhinga nest in the Everglades.

The Florida Keys

THE SEQUENCE of coral and limestone islands known as the Florida Keys, running in a southwesterly curve from Biscayne Bay almost 124 miles (200 km) out to Key West, appears on a map like a long sea wall, battered and breached, but still preventing the waters of the Atlantic from washing over southern Florida's marshlands.

In fact, the Keys have their own sunken defensive wall in the form of a live coral reef (the only one in America) which lies off their eastern coasts. This protective reef means that there is little surf and surprisingly few beaches on the Keys' eastern shores.

The name "key" is derived from the Spanish word *cayo*, meaning "little island." The islands have been known as the Keys since the early 1800s. The name first given to them by the sixteenth-century explorer Ponce de León, was *Los Martires*, and throughout the seventeenth and eighteenth centuries the coves and inlets of Los Martires were ideal home ports for such infamous pirates as Blackbeard and Lafitte, who regularly plundered treasure-laden Spanish ships traveling to and from South America.

By the early nineteenth century piracy had died out and the islands were renamed the Florida Keys. The first American community on the islands was at Key West, which became a major salvaging town with its deep-water port and continued to boom throughout the nineteenth century, while the rest of the Keys remained virtually undeveloped and largely uninhabited — except for a few Indian tribes and a handful of small salvaging villages in the Middle and Upper Keys.

It was in 1905 that the Keys attracted the attention of Henry Flagler, who decided to extend his Florida East Coast Railroad to Key West. He envisioned the railway carrying wealthy sportsmen to lavish resorts, as well as export cargo to Key West. The rail line was completed in 1916 and included one bridge that was over seven miles (11 km) long. In 1935 much of the railroad was destroyed by a terrible hurricane. A few years later a road followed literally in the tracks of the railroad, and the Ocean Highway — Route 1 — remains to this day the

world's longest ocean-going road. The Ocean Highway is lined with green mile-markers (MMs), and as it is the only major road through the Keys most hotels, restaurants, and shops have the number of the nearest mile-marker as their address (*e.g.*, The Caribbean Club, Route 1, MM 104). The MMs start on Route 1 — a mile (1.6 km) south of Florida City with MM 126 — and end with MM 0 in Key West. If an address falls between two mile-markers, the designation of .5 is used.

Nowadays the Keys are extremely popular holiday destinations, offering all kinds of fishing, diving, and water sports facilities. You can also enjoy the uniquely romantic experience of watching the sun rise over the Atlantic and later, after you have wandered over to the other side of the Key, watching the sun set into the Gulf of Mexico. Added to this, at the tip of the Ocean Highway, is America's southernmost city, with one of the most evocative names on the entire continent: Key West, once the home of Ernest Hemingway, Tennessee Williams, Wallace Stevens, and a host of other great American writers.

KEY LARGO TO LONG KEY

The string of islands from Key Largo to Long Key are known as the Upper Keys. Touristically, they are the busiest of the Keys as they are within a few hours' drive of Miami and Palm Beach. Key Largo is the starting point of the 113-mile (182-km) journey along the Ocean Highway to Key West, and is perhaps best known as the setting for the Bogart-Bacall film of that name. As it is the nearest island to the John Pennekamp Coral Reef State Park — the world's first underwater park — it is also the area's premier diving site.

Further south are the Upper and Lower Matecumbe Keys, whose name derives from the Spanish *matar* ("to kill") and *hombre* ("man"), which is a self-explanatory reference to the welcome originally given to shipwrecked sailors by the islands' Indians. These Keys are particularly renowned for their fishing. Islamorada is known as the

A favorite local pastime; cruising the Keys.

"purple island" because of the color of the snails that once thrived on its shores; Indian Key is an island of lush tropical growth; Long Key is noted for the quality of its beaches and camping facilities.

GENERAL INFORMATION

The Upper Keys Chamber of Commerce ((305) 451-1414, is at 105950 Overseas Highway, Key Largo. The Islamorada Chamber of Commerce ((305) 664-4503, can be found at MM 82.5, Islamorada.

found in the park, which is open from 8 AM to sunset every day. There is a small charge for admission and you pay extra for the diving and boat tours, for which you are urged to make reservations.

Fans of Bogart will be interested to know that the original boat used in the film, *African Queen*, is on display outside the Holiday Inn Dock, Route 1, MM 100.

In Islamorada you can take glass-bottom tours to the coral reefs from **Holiday Princess Cruises** ((305) 664-2321, Holiday Isle Marina, Route 1, MM 84.5, and visit the **The-**

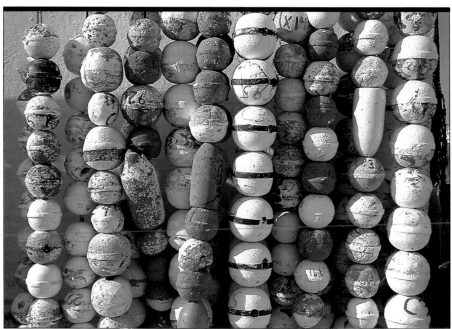

WHAT TO SEE AND DO

Sights

The main attraction in the Key Largo area is the **John Pennekamp Coral Reef State Park** ((305) 451-1202, Route 1, MM 102.5. It is 21 miles (34 km) long and eight miles (13 km) wide, covering over 2,000 acres (800 hectares) of land and over 178 sq miles (287 sq km) of water, and contains more than 40 types of coral and 650 species of fish. Scuba and snorkeling tours, as well as glass-bottom boat tours, are available for you to view the coral, fish, and shipwrecks in the park's waters. There are also beaches and nature trails on the park's coast. A gift shop, aquarium, and Visitor Center can be

ater of the Sea ((305) 664-2431, Route 1, MM 84.5, which is one of the nation's top marine parks; here you will find dolphin and sea lion shows, as well as collections of sharks and stingrays. The park is open from 9:30 AM to 4 PM daily, and admission is $14.75 for adults and $8.25 for children aged four to 12; for an extra $75 you can swim with the dolphins.

The **Indian Key State Historic Site** can be reached by taking a boat from MM 78, Indian Key Fill, between Upper and Lower Matecumbe Keys, to the 10-acre (four-hectare) **Indian Key**. Guides lead you on a tour of a reconstructed salvaging village and of the surrounding tropical vegetation. Boats also leave MM 78 for **Lignumvitae Key**, an uninhabited virgin hammock with tropical growth of the kind that once covered most of the Keys. On Long Key, the **Long Key State Park** ((305) 664-4815, Route 1, MM 67.5, is popular for its beaches and camping facilities.

Sports
Water sports, not surprisingly, are *the* sports on the Keys. **Fishing trips** are arranged in Key Largo at Miss Kitty Reef Fishing ((305) 451-2220, Route 1, MM 100, and in Islamorada at the Holiday Isle Resort Marina

There is also a **golf course** with nearby **tennis courts** open to the public at the Cheeca Lodge Hotel ((305) 644-4651, in Islamorada.

Shopping
Key Largo's streets are lined with department stores, groceries, hardware stores, gift shops, fishing shops, and shops selling everything you might need for the beach — in other words, here you will find the best selection of shops in the Upper Keys. In Islamorada, Irene and George's on Route 1 at MM 82 is a personalized emporium with

((305) 664-2321, Route 1, MM 84.5; the marina also offers **diving courses**, wreck trips, equipment for rent, as well as boats and yachts. The John Pennekamp Coral Reef State Park ((305) 451-1621, on Route 1, MM 102.5, has a water sports center, which has **snorkeling tours** three times a day for $25, **scuba diving** trips twice a day for $35, and a **combined sailing and snorkeling** trip for $50 a day. The center's dive shop also rents all sorts of equipment, sailboats, canoes, and **windsurfing boards**.

Windsurfing of the Florida Keys ((305) 451-3869, Route 1, MM 104, Key Largo, rents boards and offers lessons. All along Route 1 in the Key Largo area you will find shops catering to fishermen and water sportsmen.

nine departments, and the Bimini Town Shops alongside the Holiday Isle Resort, Route 1, MM 84, have beach and swimwear.

Nightlife
At the **Caribbean Club** ((305) 451-9970, Route 1, MM 104, you can sit on the verandah with a drink and watch the sun fall into the Gulf of Mexico. This, by the way, is the club where part of the film *Key Largo* was shot. Bogart would have liked the place now, as it is open 24 hours a day. The liveliest night spot in Key Largo is **Coconuts** ((305) 451-4107, MM 100 at Marina del Mar,

OPPOSITE: Crab floats. ABOVE: Sportfishing boats at Key West.

which features disco music and live reggae bands. In Islamorada, the nightlife centers around the Holiday Isle Resort ((305) 664-2321, Route 1, MM 84, where you can find the **Tiki Bar**, the **Bilge Bar**, the **Kokomo Beach Bar**, and the **Horizon Restaurant** at the top of the hotel, which has mellow, but nonetheless live, music for dancing.

WHERE TO STAY

Luxury
Offering some of the best facilities in Key

Largo, the **Marina del Mar** ((305) 451-4450 TOLL-FREE (800) 253-3483, Route 1, MM 100, has a marina with water sports equipment, several tennis courts, a fitness center, a swimming pool, a night club, and spacious, well-equipped rooms, some of which are efficiencies. The hotel is also in an excellent position near the offshore diving areas. The other top hotel in Key Largo is the **Sheraton Key Largo** ((305) 852-5553, Route 1, MM 97, which faces the Gulf.

In Islamorada there is a hotel that has just about everything: seven lounge bars, five restaurants, beachside shops, two swimming pools, a famous marine park next door, and accommodation ranging from luxurious rooms to fully-equipped

suites and apartments. The hotel is the **Holiday Isle Resort** ((305) 451-2121, and it's off Route 1 at MM 84. Two markers down Route 1 at MM 82 in Islamorada, is the **Cheeca Lodge** ((305) 327-2888, an old fishing lodge which has recently been renovated. It has a health spa, tennis courts, and a nine-hole golf course in its 25-acre (10-hectare) grounds. A pier poking out into the Atlantic affords fishing, diving, and snorkeling facilities.

Mid-range
There are six delightful two- or three-bedroom cottages set in tropical gardens at **Largo Lodge** ((305) 451-0424, on Route 1, MM 101.5, next to the beach; and at the stucco-style **Stone Ledge Lodge** ((305) 852-8114, Route 1, MM 95–96, you can have a simple room or a studio apartment overlooking a small beach. Very similar accommodation can be found at the **Drop Anchor** ((305) 664-4863, Route 1, MM 85, Islamorada, which also has a swimming pool. One of the best bargain hotels — considering the quality of its rooms and amenities — is **The Islander** ((305) 664-2031, in Islamorada at Route 1, MM 82, which is built on 25 acres (10 hectares) of beach, and has saltwater and freshwater swimming pools, as well as a fishing pier. Most of the hotel's 114 rooms have a kitchen.

Inexpensive
There are not many cheap hotels in the Keys, especially the nearer one gets to Key West, but in Key Largo there is the charming **Rock Reef Resort** ((305) 852-2401, which offers efficiency cottages and one- or two-bedroom suites, on Route 1 at MM 98.

WHERE TO EAT

Expensive
There is a natural ambiance at **The Quay** ((305) 451-0943, Route 1, MM 102, Key Largo, which overlooks the Gulf and features alligator meat sauteed in garlic lemon butter. Such is the reputation of **Marker 88** ((305) 852-9315, that you should book well in advance if you are to have any hope of getting a table. The reputation is well-deserved, and the address is predictable: MM 88,

Route 1, Plantation Key. Atop the Holiday Isle Resort in Islamorada at MM 84 is the **Horizon Restaurant**, with wonderful views over the ocean; and in the Cheeca Lodge Hotel at MM 82 there is the **Atlantic Edge** ((305) 664-4651, where George Bush once had a meal and said it was real swell.

Moderate

The very popular **Ziggy's Conch Restaurant** ((305) 664-4590, Route 1, MM 33, Islamorada, offers some of the best seafood in the Keys. Some of the rest of the best is

available at the **Italian Fisherman** ((305) 451-4471, Route 1, MM 104, Key Largo, where you should definitely try the *linguini mareciaro* clams, scallops, and shrimps in a garlic butter sauce and served with linguini. Steaks and excellent prime rib are on offer along with the seafood at the **Green Turtle Inn Restaurant** ((305) 394-6248, Route 1, MM 81.5, Islamorada. The two-level **Coral Grill** ((305) 664-4803, Route 1, MM 83.5, Islamorada, has a gourmet buffet upstairs and a seafood-soup-and-salad bar downstairs.

Inexpensive

It doesn't specialize in seafood and it's not elegant, but it's still worth a visit: **Mrs. Mac's**

The Florida Keys

Kitchen at MM 99.5 in Key Largo has good steaks, sandwiches, homemade soups, and a wide selection of beers. In Islamorada there are two places you might want to check out: **Lor-e-lei on the Gulf** ((305) 664-4657, at MM 82, which overlooks a small harbor and specializes in lamb and ribs; and **Papa Joe's** ((305) 664-8109, at MM 80, where the seafood is Italianate.

HOW TO GET THERE

Some national airlines have regular flights out of Miami International Airport into Marathon Regional Airport, which is about 20 miles (32 km) southwest of Long Key. Most people, however, drive from Miami down Route 1.

GRASSY KEY TO STOCK ISLAND

The islands between Grassy Key and Stock Island constitute the chain known as the Middle and Lower Keys (Key West is considered as being distinct from the other Keys). The population centers here are Marathon in the Middle Keys and Big Pine in the Lower Keys. Marathon, on Vaca Key, is a resort and fishing center, and the start of the Seven Mile Bridge, the country's longest, which reaches all the way to Sunshine Key, next to Bahia Honda Key. Bahia Honda has some of the best beaches between Key Largo and Key West.

The vegetation is more lush in the Lower Keys, due to the slightly warmer, slightly more tropical climate, but the activities are the same as anywhere else in the Keys: water sports, fishing, beachcombing, swimming. On Big Pine Key, and the surrounding islands, you can see a unique and wonderful sight: the tiny, endangered Key deer, which you are frequently reminded by road signs to watch out for. From Big Pine Key the highway passes over various wild-looking Keys with wide expanses of beach. Roadside motels, resorts, and restaurants begin to increase in number as you approach Key West.

OPPOSITE: The southernmost house in the United States. ABOVE: A typical old Key West residence.

GENERAL INFORMATION

The Greater Marathon Chamber of Commerce ((305) 743-5417, is at 12222 Overseas Highway, Marathon, FL 33043, and the Lower Keys Chamber of Commerce ((305) 872-2411, is in Big Pine.

WHAT TO SEE AND DO

Sights

Grassy Key is the home of the **Dolphin Research Center** ((305) 289-1121, Route 1, MM 59, which — I am not joking — rehabilitates show dolphins suffering from stress-related conditions brought on by over-work, pressure to perform, and cramped pools. You can swim with one of these sweet, long-suffering creatures if you like. In the town of Marathon is the 63-acre (25.2-hectare) **Crane Point Hammock** ((305) 743-3900, on Route 1, MM 50, an important nature reserve with exotic plants, trees, mangroves, and hardwoods. There are also archaeological sites and renovated conch-style houses in its grounds.

The **Seven Mile Bridge** between Vaca Key and Sunshine Key is a wonder to behold, as indeed is the vastness of the seas to either side of it.

On Bahia Honda Key at the **Bahia Honda State Park**, MM 37, you can find white sand beaches, tropical plants and birds, a nature trail, picnic areas, and a marina. Big Pine Key — which is covered in pines and cacti — contains the **National Key Deer Refuge**. In 1954 there were only 50 deer left, but protection and careful management of the park have enabled their numbers to reach something approaching 400, despite well-meaning tourists feeding them often-lethal snacks. (If you see a deer, please don't feed it anything: if you do the deer might die and you might be caught and heavily fined.)

Guided canoe tours of the Big Pine Key region run from **Canoeing Nature Tour** ((305) 872-2620, at MM 29. The final sight before reaching Key West is the **Perky Bat Tower** at MM 17, built in 1929 by one Richard C. Perky as a residence for the bats he brought in to decimate the swarms of mosquitoes plaguing his resort. The bats, alas, didn't take to their new accommodation, leaving Perky's tower to stand as an amusing folly.

Sports

You can go on **fishing trips** out of Marathon from The World Class Angler ((305) 743-6139, at the Faro Blanco Resort, MM 48.5; and in the Lower Keys out of Big Pine ((305) 872-3200, from Fantasy Charters at MM 28. For offshore trips, instruction, and rental of **diving equipment**, go to Seaview

Ocean Divers ((305) 743-8514, MM 50.5, in Marathon; and Cudjoe Gardens Marina and Dive Shop ((305) 745-2357, MM 21, in the Lower Keys. You can rent boats in Marathon at Clyde's Seven Mile Marina ((305) 743-7712, MM 47.5, and in the Lower Keys at Dolphin Marina ((305) 872-2685, on Little Torch Key at MM 28.5.

Sailing enthusiasts can rent a yacht from the Sailmaster Charters ((305) 743-4200, at Nº 1000 15th Street, Boot Key Marina, in Marathon, and from Amantha ((305) 743-9020, at the Faro Blanco Resort, MM 48.5, in the Lower Keys. The Key Colony Beach ((305) 289-0821, in Marathon, has a **golf course** and **tennis courts** open to the public.

Shopping

The only choice of shops in the Middle and Lower Keys is in Marathon, which has several shopping malls, and a selection of shops selling gifts, souvenirs, sportswear, and swimwear.

Nightlife

In the Middle Keys you might want to sample the atmosphere at **The Ship's Pub** ((305) 743-7000, MM 61 on Duck Key, which has live bands and a dance floor. At 19 Sombrero Boulevard, in Marathon, is

cleverly echoed in the decor and furnishings of the rooms and suites. The resort has its own Atlantic lagoon, with beach, where you can swim or windsurf or take your boat out to sea. Tennis courts and a golf course are also in the grounds. At **The Buccaneer** ((305) 743-9071 TOLL-FREE (800) 237-3329, MM 48.5, Marathon, there are rooms, cottages, and villas — not to mention the marina with windsurf boards, powerboats, yachts, and charter boats.

On Key Colony Beach at 351 Ocean Drive East, is the **Ocean Beach Club** ((305)

Good Times ((305) 743-4108, which features live music and even livelier cocktails. Rock bands perform at the **Looe Key Reef Resort** ((305) 872-2215, at MM 27.5, on Ramrod Key. At the **No Name Pub** ((305) 872-9115, on Big Pine Key at the north end of Watson Boulevard, you can play darts and pool, hear live bands, eat hearty pub grub, and choose from over 70 beers.

WHERE TO STAY

Luxury

Occupying its own 60-acre (24-hectare) island, the **Hawk's Cay Resort** ((305) 743-7000 TOLL-FREE (800) 432-2242, at MM 61 in Marathon, is in a tropical setting which is

289-0525, with its own beach, a swimming pool, and efficiency apartments. One of the most pleasant residences in the Lower Keys is the **Little Palm Island** ((305) 872-2524, at MM 28.5 on Little Torch Key, which features 14 two-suite villas in beautiful grounds, plus a full range of water sports facilities.

Mid-range

In Marathon there is the moderately-priced **Hopp-Inn Guest House** ((305) 743-4118, at Five Man o' War Drive, which is family-run and very comfortable. The **Conch Key Cottages** ((305) 289-1377, off Route 1 at MM 62.5, occupy their own lovely island, which

OPPOSITE: One form of transport in Key West. ABOVE: Another form — the Conch Tour Train.

is reached by a causeway. The delightful wooden cottages are fully-fitted and are near a small private beach.

Inexpensive

There are 12 rooms, some of them efficiencies, at the **Valhalla Beach Motel** ((305) 289-0616, which is by the ocean in Marathon at MM 56.5. On Ramrod Key in the Lower Keys, the **Looe Key Reef Resort and Dive Center** ((305) 872-2215, at MM 27.5, runs diving and charter trips to the distant Tortugas Islands from their own

872-2524, where the gorgeous seafood is only an accompaniment to the gorgeous before- and after-dinner drinks on the beach.

Moderate

The **Little Bavaria** ((305) 743-4833, in the Gulfside Village Shopping Center, MM 50, serves up your basic wienerschnitzel and some interesting Hungarian variations. **Monte's Restaurant and Fish Market** ((305) 745-3731, at MM 25 on Summerland Key, has lovely conch chowders and frit-

dock. Further southwest on **Sugarloaf Key**, the **Sugarloaf Lodge** ((305) 745-3211, at MM 17, has a marina and swimming pool.

WHERE TO EAT

Expensive

Overlooking a marina, **Kelsey's** ((305) 743-9018, is the restaurant of the Faro Blanco Resort at MM 48.5, and offers some wonderful seafood dishes. **Chef's** ((305) 743-4108, at the Sombrero Resort, 19 Sombrero Boulevard, Marathon, is as unpretentious as its name, and good. A boat will take you from MM 28.5 on Little Torch Key to the restaurant of **Little Palm Island** ((305)

ters. And then there's **Cousin Joe's Supper Bar** ((305) 745-1646, which is good for Caribbean food on Drost Drive off Route 1 at MM 21.

Inexpensive

The intimate **Grassy Key Dairy Bar** ((305) 743-3816, at MM 58.5, has a different menu — Italian, Mexican, etc. — every night. Seafood and salads are predictably popular at **Shuckers Raw Bar & Grill** ((305) 743-8686, 1415 15th Street, Marathon. On Big Pine Key there are two good budget restaurants: **Island Jim's** ((305) 872-2017, at MM 31.5, which specializes in steaks and prime ribs; and **Dr. Feelgood's BBQ** ((305) 872-4752, at MM 31.

KEY WEST

Key West, the southernmost city in the United States, has a permanent population of 24,000 on a sub-tropical island four miles (six and a half kilometers) long and two miles (three kilometers) wide. The inhabitants are a mixed bunch: retired military personnel and their families, a black community whose ancestors came from the West Indies, writers, artists, Cuban exiles — and the Conchs (pronounced "konks") who are

per-capita income in the country. By 1850 the Conch community (pop. 600) was earning a million dollars a year from wrecking. Then came a cigar-making factory set up by Cuban immigrants, and then a United States naval station. By 1880 Key West had a population of 10,000 and was the biggest city in the state.

But the cigar business packed up and moved to Tampa, which together with the Depression meant that by 1934 80 percent of Key West's inhabitants were on welfare. Economic aid from the state eventually bailed the city out and enabled it to survive

the descendants of the island's original settlers. Only genuine Conchs are permitted to call themselves Conchs, although if you live there for seven years you can become an honorary "freshwater Conch".

The original Conchs came to the island from the Bahamas late in the eighteenth century. It became a part of the future state of Florida in 1822 when one of the settlers, John Simonton, bought it in a Cuban bar for $2,000. Also around this time a United States Navy commodore named David Porter cleared the Keys of all the pirates, enabling the settlers to establish their own form of *ex post facto* piracy: shipwreck-plundering, or "wrecking". So profitable was wrecking that by 1830 the Conchs of Key West could claim the highest

even the hurricane that destroyed Flagler's railway. And when the Ocean Highway reached the Keys, so did the tourists.

GENERAL INFORMATION

The Greater Key West Chamber of Commerce ((305) 294-2587, is at 402 Wall Street, Key West, FL 33040. The Florida Keys Visitor's Bureau TOLL-FREE (800) FLA-KEYS, which covers all the Keys, is at 416 Fleming Street, Key West, FL 33040. *Key West* magazine will give you comprehensive information on local events and attractions.

OPPOSITE: Diners enjoy a Key West sunset.
ABOVE: A Key West Memorial to Cubans who fled the 1959 revolution.

The Florida Keys   237

WHAT TO SEE AND DO

Sights

A good way to see Key West and many of its sights is to take a ride on the **Conch Tour Train**, which has boarding points at Mallory Square, Roosevelt Avenue, and Duval and Angela Streets. It runs at regular intervals from 9 AM to 4 PM daily. On the tour you will pass through the restored Old Town centered around **Duval Street**, which is lined with Spanish, Southern, and old

James Audubon, who painted the local birdlife and also made engravings and prints; many of his works are on display in the **Audubon House** ((305) 294-2116, at 205 Whitehead Street. The house is open from 9:30 AM to 5 PM daily, and admission is $5 for adults and $1 for children.

The world's largest display of treasure from shipwrecks is at the **Mel Fisher Museum** ((305) 294-2633, (named after the man who found the wreck of the *Atocha*, a seventeenth-century Spanish ship which carried treasure with a modern value of $400

Conch buildings (including the city's oldest house), and several old bars, among them **Sloppy Joe's**, where Hemingway used to drink and, occasionally, write.

Hemingway's House ((305) 294-1575, at 907 Whitehead Street, is where the great man lived and worked during the 1930s. Here he wrote, among other works, *The Green Hills of Africa* and *To Have and Have Not*. You can see some of Hemingway's possessions in the study where he wrote, which is open from 9 AM to 5 PM daily, for $6 adults and $1.50 children. **Tennessee Williams'** House is not open to the public, but you can see the outside of it at 1431 Duncan Street. Another of Key West's famous citizens was the painter and naturalist John

million). The ship's gold and silver bullion, coins, diamonds, and precious stones are on display in the museum at 200 Greene Street. It's open from 9:30 AM to 5 PM, and admission is $5 for adults and $1 for children.

At **The Wrecker's Museum** ((305) 294-9502, 322 Duval Street, you can learn all about the city's earliest industry. There are model ships and sundry maritime artifacts on display at the Key West **Lighthouse Museum** ((305) 294-0012, 938 Whitehead Street, as well as such military peculiarities as a two-man Japanese submarine captured at Pearl Harbor. The view from the top of the lighthouse alone is worth the $4 entrance charge ($1 for children). It is open from 9:30 AM to 5 PM.

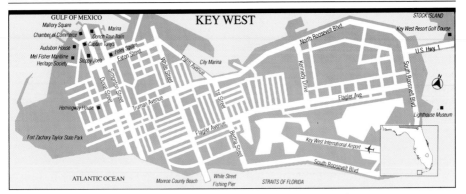

For more military history, go to the **Fort Zachary Taylor State Historic Site** ((305) 292-6713, at the western end of Southard Street. This museum has much historic weaponry, including the nation's largest collection of Civil War cannons. Here you can also learn the story of the fort, which was occupied by Union troops during the Civil War and re-armed in 1898 for the Spanish-American War. The park around the fort has picnic sites and one of the finest beaches on the island.

If you are feeling adventurous, you should go to Key West Seaplane Service ((305) 294-6978, at 5603 West Junior College Road, and arrange to fly the 68 miles (109 km) west to the **Fort Jefferson National Monument** in the Dry Tortugas, a group of small coral islands. The plane passes over the Marquesas Keys atoll and a number of coral reefs, sandbars, and shipwrecks before landing at the Dry Tortugas, where you can explore both the fort and the island.

Sports

For **fishing trips** out of Key West to both Gulf and Atlantic waters, or to the Dry Tortugas, try the Garrison Bight Marina ((305) 294-3093, at 711 Eisenhower Drive, or Sea Breeze Charters ((305) 294-6027, at 25 Arbutus Drive. **Scuba diving** and **snorkeling trips** and lessons can be arranged and equipment rented at the Key West Pro Dive Shop ((305) 296-3823, 1605 North Roosevelt Boulevard; and at the Reef Riders Dive Shop ((305) 294-3635, 109 Duval Street. **Boating** enthusiasts should point themselves at Key West Boat Rentals ((305) 294-2628, 617 Front Street.

There is a **golf course** on Stock Island at the Key West Resort ((305) 294-5232, and there are public **tennis courts** at Island City Tennis ((305) 294-1346, on Truman Avenue.

Shopping

Most of the shopping in Key West is done in the Old Town area around Duval Street, where you will find numerous souvenir and gift shops, boutiques, designer outlets, and artsy-craftsy shops. For the best selection of merchandise under one roof, go to Fast Buck Freddies at 500 Duval Street. There are also several galleries in the Old Town with quite decent works by resident and visiting artists.

Nightlife

Key West offers the most colorful and varied nightlife in the Keys. You mustn't miss, for example, **Sloppy Joe's** ((305) 294-8585, at 201 Duval Street, Hemingway's favorite watering hole. On the wall there is a sailfish that Hemingway is reputed to have caught. Short drinks and tall stories still abound here, as well as live rhythm and blues bands. Another Key West landmark is **Captain Tony's Saloon** ((305) 294-1838, at 428 Greene Street, where many of the town's bohemian characters hang out. Those who prefer to dance the night away to disco music have a good choice of venues, such as **The Copa** ((305) 296-8521, at 623 Duval Street; the **Havana Docks Bar** ((305) 294-9541, at Pier House, One Duval Street; and **Delmonico's** ((305) 294-4383, at 218 Duval Street, all in the Old Town district.

OPPOSITE: A seaside bar at Key West provides plenty of maritime atmosphere.

For a dinner-and-cabaret evening you can try **Jan McArts Cabaret Theatre** ((305) 296-2120, at 410 Wall Street. The **Tennessee Williams Fine Arts Center** ((305) 294-6232, at 5901 Junior College Road, presents concerts, plays, and dance performances all year round. For one of the most enchanting and romantic experiences of your life go to Mallory Square at the northwest end of Duval Street and lose yourself in the nightly crowd watching the sun set into the Gulf while local musicians play gentle folk music.

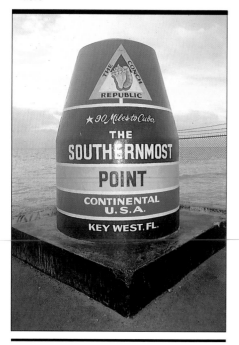

WHERE TO STAY

Luxury

Among the destinations for travelers on Flagler's railway was the **Marriott's Casa Marina Resort** ((305) 296-3535 TOLL-FREE (800) 626-0777, at 1500 Reynolds Street, which is still one of the city's most elegant hotels. It has its own beach with extensive water sports facilities, lighted tennis courts, a swimming pool, and a fishing pier.

There are some exceptional old Victorian guest houses in Key West, including **Eaton Lodge** ((305) 294-3800, at 511 Eaton Street, where every room has a balcony overlooking a central tropical garden. Another fine guest house, with rooms facing the ocean, is

La Mer Hotel ((305) 296-6577, at 506 South Street. At the edge of the Old Town at 901 Front Street, you can find the **Hyatt Key West** ((305) 296-9900 TOLL-FREE (800) 228-9000, which has a beach, a marina, a swimming pool, Jacuzzis, and an exercise room among its amenities, as well as rooms offering magnificent views of Key West's famous sunsets.

Mid-range

The **South Beach Motel** ((305) 296-5611, with a small pier for swimming and fishing, in addition to its bright and neatly furnished rooms, is at 500 South Street. At the 130-year-old **Duval House Historic Inn** ((305) 294-1666, the 22 antique-furnished rooms surround a garden and swimming pool in the heart of the Old Town at 815 Duval Street. Another small and friendly guest house, **Eden House** ((305) 296-6868, at 1015 Fleming Street, has Twenties decor and furnishing, efficiency rooms, and a swimming pool. Amenities offered by the **Best Western Key Ambassador** ((305) 296-3500, 3755 South Roosevelt Boulevard, include a pool with a bar, a fitness center, and shuffleboard courts.

Inexpensive

On Simonton Street there is the **Santa Maria** ((305) 296-5678, at N° 1401, and the **Hibiscus** ((305) 296-6711, at N° 1313, both of which are very comfortable. Also good value is the **Atlantic Shores** ((305) 296-2491, at 510 South Street, which has its own pier and swimming pool.

For complete information on accommodation in Key West, get in touch with the Key West Chamber of Commerce, which will be happy to supply you with a guide to hotels and guest houses, or the Key West Reservation Service ((305) 294-7713, at 628 Fleming Street, Key West, FL 33040.

WHERE TO EAT

Expensive

Louie's Backyard ((305) 294-1061, located at 700 Wadell Street, is a Revival Conch House listed in the National Register of Historic Places. Chef Norman Van Aken's fascinating menu features barbecued duck with Oriental noodles and Sichuan dressing, and Dijoncrusted rack of lamb with rosemary and roast garlic. It's probably the best restaurant in town. A close competitor is **Henry's** ((305) 296-3535, in the Casa Marina Resort at 1500 Reynolds Street, where you can get the best Cajun cooking in the Keys. The **Café des Artistes** ((305) 294-7100, at 1007 Simonton Street, specializes in Provençal cooking and spicy Haitian food.

Moderate

Lovers of sushi, sashimi, teriyaki, sukiyaki, and other Japanese delights should try

Inexpensive

La Crêperie ((305) 294-7677, at 124 Duval Street, specializes in very reasonably priced French food. If you prefer Mexican, **El Loro Verde** ((305) 296-7298, serves the usual burritos, tacos, tostadas, and salsas, as well as the odd Bahamian dish, at 404 Southard Street. All the Cuban food served at **El Siboney** ((305) 294-2721, 900 Catherine Street, comes with black beans, rice, and plantain or yucca. At the pleasantly bohemian **Full Moon Saloon** ((305) 294-9090, 1202 Simonton Street, the last orders —

Kyushu ((305) 294-2995, at 921 Truman Street. You can eat outside under a straw roof or in a traditional tatami dining room. **La-Te-Da** ((305) 294-8435, is the restaurant inside the La Terrazza de Marti Hotel at 1125 Duval Street, and offers mostly continental cuisine. **Antonia's** ((305) 294-6565, at 615 Duval Street, has masterfully prepared northern Italian food, and cleverly offers half-servings of various pasta dishes. **The Bagatelle** ((305) 294-7195, is in a restored Conch house at 115 Duval Street, and serves a mixture of local seafood and more exotic Bahamian cooking. For good old Southern-fried cooking go to **Pepe's Café** ((305) 294-7192, down near the old waterfront at 806 Caroline Street.

usually for conch or smoked fish — are taken around 3 AM.

HOW TO GET THERE

Delta Airline has regular flights to Key West. Motorists will take Route 1, which ends at the Key West Lighthouse. If you get this far, you have gone as far south as it is possible to go in the continental United States.

OPPOSITE: Self-captioning landmark in Key West.
ABOVE: A watering hole near the water.

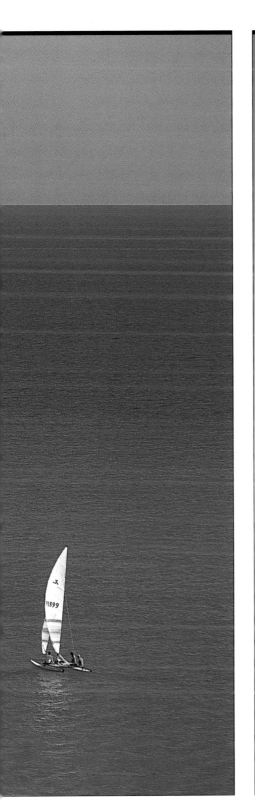

Travelers' Tips

THE BEST TIP of all: Find a good travel agent. How? Ask the same questions of several different agents — questions that can't be answered out of a brochure. You can answer those questions yourself. The point of the exercise is not to find a travel agent who has all the answers — nobody does — but to find one who is willing to take the time and trouble to get the answers for you.

GETTING THERE

BY AIR

All major cities in Florida are served daily (often many times daily) by airlines from all corners of the United States. Likewise, many international airlines have regularly-scheduled flights to Florida. These include, from Europe: British Airways, Continental, Virgin Atlantic, Lufthansa, Delta, American Airlines, KLM, Air France, and Icelandair. In addition, charter flights are available from Britain through Brittania, Virgin Atlantic, Novair, Airtours, Intasun, and Thomson; from Germany through Condor and LTU; from Holland through Martinair; from Scandinavia through Sterling Air and Tower Air; from Switzerland through Balair.

There are, too, an infinite variety of special discount fares and package deals. Every airline has at least one, as does American Express and other travel companies. In London, The American Dream ((081) 470-1181, will create a package specifically to suit your requirements.

BY RAIL

Not to be outdone by the airlines, Amtrak now offers a variety of special fares (and much improved food and service) to try to bring more Florida-bound travelers back to earth. In particular, ask your travel agent about the "All Aboard America" fares. If you are coming from overseas, ask about the USA Railpass, which allows unlimited train travel for varying periods of time. Information about timetables and special fares, including tour packages, is available directly from Amtrak TOLL-FREE ((800) USA-RAIL, P.O. Box 311, Addison, Illinois 60101.

BY BUS

The two main American coach companies, Greyhound and Trailways, both now offer special cut-rate fares to Florida from all over the United States. Greyhound's "Money-saver" tickets, bookable 30 days in advance, are an especially good bargain.

BY CAR

Living as they do in a car-oriented, high-way-blessed society, Americans do not need to be told of the pleasures or advantages of motoring. But visitors from abroad may be surprised to learn that these pleasures are not only available but extremely affordable as well. This is due to the recent and rap-

idly growing phenomenon of "driveaway" companies acting on behalf of clients who are in a hurry to get to Florida and who would like their cars to join them there later.

This means that there are companies in New York and elsewhere in the United States who are eager not to rent you a car but to *give* you a car (and free insurance and a free tank of gasoline!) so long as you deliver it to the car's owner in Florida within an agreed period of time. I have spoken to several people who took driveaway cars to Florida and they were unanimous in their opinion that this is the most delightful as well as economical way to get there from other parts of America. Of the driveaway companies in New York I would recommend All America Transport ((212) 766-

0700; Dependable Transport ((212) 840-6262; Transporters Inc. ((212) 594-2690; and Boutell Driveaway ((212) 227-1230.

TOURIST INFORMATION

All you need do to find yourself caught in a blizzard of facts and figures, maps and pictures, brochures and pamphlets, is to contact one of the following:

In the United States
Florida Division of Tourism
126 West Van Buren Street
Tallahassee, FL 32399-2000
((904) 487-1462

The seaside at Seaside, Florida.

Florida Chamber of Commerce
P.O. Box 11309
Tallahassee, FL 32302
((904) 222-2831

Florida Department of
Natural Resources
Division of Recreation and Parks
3900 Commonwealth Boulevard
Tallahassee, FL 32303
((904) 488-7326

Florida Attractions Association
P.O. Box 833
Silver Springs, FL 32688
((904) 694-5444

Florida Tourist Information Center
2801 East Oakland Park
Fort Lauderdale, FL 33306
((305) 566-0700

In Europe
United States Travel and Tourism
Administration
22 Sackville Street
London W1X 2EA
((071) 439-7433

Florida Division of Tourism
18–24 Westbourne Grove
London W2 5RH
((0171) 727-1661

This is not to mention the 200 or so Chambers of Commerce scattered around the state, each one of which will be happy to answer any queries or supply any information about the area in which it is located. There are also many tourist bureaus and information agencies designed to deal with specific enquiries; these you will find listed on the following pages under the appropriate categories.

CONSULATES

IN FLORIDA

BRITISH
Suite 2110
Brickell Bay Office Tower
1001 South Bayshore Drive
Miami, FL 33131
((305) 374-1522

IN NEW YORK

AUSTRALIAN
636 Fifth Avenue
New York, NY
((212) 245-4000

CANADIAN
1251 Avenue of the Americas
New York NY
((212) 586-2400

IRISH
515 Madison Avenue
New York, NY
((212) 319-2555

TRAVEL DOCUMENTS

Canadians need only prove that they are Canadian; British need only a valid passport. Everybody else had better check with a travel agent, as the requirements are constantly changing (and usually for the better).

CUSTOMS

You may bring in, duty-free, 200 cigarettes or 50 cigars or three pounds (1.4 kg) of tobacco. I should add, however, that you would be stark raving mad to bring tobacco (especially cigars) into a state where you can buy all kinds of excellent tobacco products for a fraction of their price in the duty-free shops of the world's airports. The same goes for alcohol: you can bring in one United States quart (a liter), but it would be wiser and more economical to buy it when you get there. You may also bring in gifts up to $100 in value.

WHEN TO GO

Most people, like most birds, tend to flock to Florida in the winter. In the coldest month, January, the average daytime temperatures in the southern part of the state are 74°F (23°C) on land and 72°F (22°C) in the water. It is cooler, of course, in the evenings, but pleasantly so.

The summers are hot — but not *that* hot; it seldom gets over 90°F (32°C). It's the humidity that's bothersome, although the late afternoon showers tend to wring the moisture out the air. And the ubiquitous air conditioning blow-dries as it cools the air indoors.

As with most places in these latitudes, spring and autumn are the most agreeable times to visit.

WHAT TO TAKE

As always, the oldest advice is the best: take half the clothes and twice the money you

GETTING AROUND

The best way to get around Florida is by automobile. For one thing, Florida is the cheapest place in the world to rent a car. All the major car rental firms (Hertz, Avis, Budget, *et al*) offer special deals, and the others don't need to. For another thing, fuel is astonishingly cheap by European standards. And lastly, of course, American roads and highways and highway signs are a motorist's dream.

think you will need. This applies especially in Florida's case because everything you could possibly need or want is available there, at prices — here's the good news — that are much cheaper than you might expect.

Having said that, let me list a few of the things I personally would never travel without: a Swiss Army knife, nail clippers, tissues, plastic knife, fork and spoon, a plastic beaker, toothpicks, "wet wipes", sewing kit, eyedrops, aspirin, glue, antiseptic ointment, insect repellent, batteries for what ever battery-powered objects you take with you, and a flask for non-battery-powered situations. And by all means, don't forget the sunscreen.

If you prefer to travel by train, Amtrak serves 22 cities in the state. Your travel agent can provide the details, or you can phone Amtrak General Information and Reservations TOLL-FREE (800) 872-7245. Greyhound and Trailways have buses going to every nook and cranny of the state, and Greyhound also has several package tours. For details write to Greyhound, 901 Main Street, Dallas, TX 75202.

For air travel within Florida, ask your travel agent about the availability of specially-priced Visit USA tickets and the many domestic shuttle flights between cities.

Pelicans wait for the return of the fishing boats at Cedar Key on the Gulf Coast.

BASICS

The language spoken in Florida is English, right? Wrong, if you're in those parts of south Florida where Spanish (or, occasionally, Yiddish) is the *lingua franca*. And even the English that is spoken is very different from the British version; however, the differences are either so well-known or so easily decipherable (*e.g.*, "elevator" for "lift") that it would be a waste of time to catalogue them.

The electric current is 110–115 volts AC. Unless you buy your electrical appliances in America you will need an adaptor.

Except for the extreme western part of the Panhandle, Florida is on Eastern Standard Time, which is five hours behind Greenwich Mean Time (*i.e.*, when it is noon in London it is 7 AM in Miami). If for some reason you feel the need to know the precise time, to the second, you can call ((305) 324-8811.

HEALTH

The health care is excellent, as you would expect, but unbelievably expensive, so don't even *think* about going to Florida

without some kind of short-term medical insurance. The best overseas insurer, in my opinion, is Europ Assistance Ltd. ((081) 680-1234, 252 High Street, Croydon, Surrey CR0 1NF, England, but your travel agent or private health insurance company will be able to advise you on the insurance you will need while visiting Florida.

The only other general advice I can offer is: don't underestimate the capacity of the local insects to ruin your holiday. Mosquitoes, ants (especially fire ants), flies (especially sand flies), and other tiny pests are abundant and obnoxiously happy to welcome you unless you have some kind of insect repellent with you.

MONEY

The old joke about the American tourist who asks, "How much is that in real money" is not so funny when a bank teller in America looks at your foreign currency as if it were a bank robber's note demanding cash. The dollar may occasionally fall on hard times, but it is still the only currency that Americans understand and trust. Therefore you should only travel with dollars or travelers' checks in dollars. Also, in the land that invented plastic money, it's a very good idea to have a Visa Card or MasterCard or some other internationally recognized credit card with you. A *very* good idea, in fact, because many American firms prefer cards to cash — and some even insist on plastic rather than cash.

ACCOMMODATION

The good news is that Florida has accommodation to suit every taste, every need, and every budget. The bad news is that it may already be taken unless you have booked well in advance.

The best news of all is that Florida has the most efficient system of matching visitors to their desired accommodation of any tourist destination in the world. If your travel agent can't find exactly what you want, try the Florida Hotel/Motel Association ((904) 224-2288, P.O. Box 1529, Tallahassee, FL 32302. They will send you a free guide and any other specific information you may require. Or you can write to the local Chamber of Commerce in the area you intend to visit and they will happily circulate your request to all the hotels and motels and rental agencies in the area (but be prepared for an avalanche of letters and brochures in return).

If you are elderly and would prefer a package holiday that provides all of the fun without all of the hassle, you should contact Senior Vacation Hotels of Florida ((813) 345-8123, 7401 Central Avenue, St. Petersburg, FL 33710.

PRICES

Florida hotel and restaurant prices can fluctuate enormously depending on a number of factors (see WELCOME TO FLORIDA, page 67 for additional commentary). For the purposes of this guide, I have therefore divided hotels and restaurants into three categories according to the *range* of prices you can expect.

Rates for accommodation fall into the following price categories:

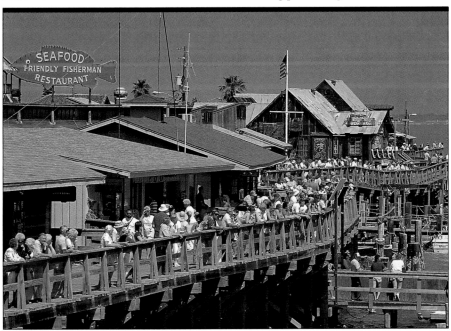

If you will be traveling on a restricted budget I would suggest patronizing the chain motels — Days Inn, Motel 6, Best Western, TraveLodge, Econo Lodge, Scottish Inns, and Red Carpet Inns are the ones I have found to be the best value for the money. If you will be traveling on very restricted budget, you can get a listing of campsites from the Florida Department of Natural Resources, Bureau of Education and Information, 3900 Commonwealth Boulevard, Tallahassee, FL 32303. A listing of youth hostels — you don't have to be a youth stay in one — is available from the American Youth Hostel Association, National Campus, Delaplane VA 22025.

Luxury: over (sometimes way over) $120 for a double room;
Mid-range: between $60 and $120;
Inexpensive: under (sometimes way under) $60 for a double room.

Price categories for restaurants are:
Expensive: over $50 per person, excluding wine;
Moderate: between $20 and $50;
Inexpensive: below $20, often well below.

EATING OUT

There are many fine restaurants in Florida featuring continental cuisine, and indeed I

OPPOSITE: The Columbia restaurant in Tampa's Ybor City. ABOVE: The boardwalk at Madeira Beach.

have already recommended quite a few of them, but as a general rule, to enjoy the best meals in Florida you should stick to what is uniquely — or at least distinctively — Floridian. (See YOUR CHOICE, GALLOPING GOURMET pages 57–59).

TANNING

As the difference between a suntan and a sunburn can be the difference between a happy holiday and an unhappy one, it is important to remember that the Florida sun

is very strong and should be not be taken lightly if you want to go dark pleasantly. To begin with, in Noel Coward's memorable phrase, only mad dogs and Englishmen go out in the midday sun: from 11 AM to 2 PM you are well advised to stay inside.

Secondly — and this is the hard — part you must wear a sunscreen, at least for the first few days, and you must be patient, increasing your exposure to the sun only gradually. Depending, of course, on the type of skin you have, you should only be out in the sun for half an hour (or less) the first few days, slowly increasing your exposure time to a couple of hours by the end of the first week. After that you should be ready for some serious sunbathing.

Another point to bear in mind is that some parts of the body are more sensitive to the sun's rays than others. Your nose, knees, and the tops of your feet should be particularly well protected by sun lotion, and your eyes should be protected by "proper" sunglasses. By proper sunglasses I mean ones that are UV-coated to keep out the harmful ultraviolet rays, and preferably also have Polarized filters if you are planning to spend much time on the water, where your eyes are vulnerable to the reflected light.

TIPPING

Because a tip is an acknowledgment of a service rendered, the size of the tip depends ultimately on your opinion of the quality of the service. However, assuming that the service performed was at least adequate, and that no service charge has already been included in your bill (which it only rarely is in Florida), you should give tips of about 15 percent in restaurants and for room service. Porters and doormen who help with your bags should get 50 cents to a dollar per bag, depending on the size and weight; taxi drivers will expect a tip of 10 to 15 percent; and chambermaids should be tipped about $10 a week, or more for specially attentive service. Remember that almost everyone employed in a service industry in Florida is on the minimum wage — $200 a week before tax — and so they rely heavily on, and work hard at earning a tip.

DRIVING

The most frustrating thing — in fact, about the *only* frustrating thing — about driving in Florida, or in the United States generally, is that the nation with the best roads in the world has the lowest speed limits in the world: 55 mph (88 kph) on many highways and 20 to 40 mph (32 to 64 kph) in cities and residential areas. Speed limits, which are clearly marked, have recently been raised to 65 mph (105 kph) or 70 mph (113 kph) but only on some main highways in some rural areas. Obey the signs, for the speed limits are strictly enforced.

It is legal to turn right at red rights in Florida, provided that you come to a full stop first and there is no sign prohibiting a right turn. Two other laws with which visitors may not be familiar require all drivers to carry proof of personal injury insurance coverage, and all drivers to secure children five years old and younger in safety belts or child restraint seats.

For more detailed information contact the Florida Highway Safety and Motor Vehicles Department ((904) 488-3144, Neil Kirkman Building, Tallahassee, FL 32399. For help or travel information while on the road call the American Automobile Association ((305) 573-6911.

Of the sights you can expect to see while motoring, perhaps the most remarkable are to be seen on the roads themselves, for Florida probably has more "customized" cars than any other state except California. The funniest one I saw when I was there was a yellow Volkswagen beetle with mouse ears, nose and tail. You also see a lot of amusing personalized license plates. My favorite: L8 4 WORK.

CAMPING

There are more than 100 state parks in Florida, as well as campsites for recreational vehicles and wilderness areas, all of which provide camping facilities. Two essential guides, the *Florida State Parks Guide* and the *Florida State Parks Camping Reservation Procedures*, are available from the Florida Department of Natural Resources, Bureau of Education and Information ((904) 488-7326, 3900 Commonwealth Boulevard, Tallahassee, FL 32399. In addition, there is the valuable *Florida Camping Directory* published by the Florida Campground Association ((904) 656-8878, 1638 North Plaza Drive, Tallahassee, FL 32308.

You can expect to pay about $6 a night (slightly more in the Keys) for a campsite in a state park, and the maximum permitted stay is two weeks. You can reserve a site up to two months in advance by calling the park where you would like to camp. You will pay an extra $2 for an electrical connection and $2 more for a second car on your site.

TENNIS

If Florida had an official state sport, it would undoubtedly be tennis. It is no accident that the queen of American tennis, Chris Evert, and stars like Jennifer Capriati, are both products of Florida tennis courts.

These courts — both public and private — are everywhere, including at all the larger hotels. The local recreation department can give you details of all the courts in the area you are visiting, or you can contact the Florida Tennis Association ((305) 757-8568, 9620 Northeast Second Avenue, Room 200, Miami Shores, FL 33138.

GOLF

Golf is a close second to tennis as the most popular pastime in Florida. Accordingly, the acreage given over to golf courses would be sufficient to accommodate your average banana republic. Not only are there splendid public courses in every corner of the state, especially near the more popular resort areas, but most of the private courses admit visitors for a nominal fee. Again, the local recreation department can provide you with a list of the courses in your area. Alternatively, you can get in touch with the Florida State Golf Association ((813) 921-5695, P.O. Box 21177, Sarasota, FL 33585.

If your interest in golf is spectatorial, you should plan on visiting Florida in February, March, or October, the months in which the major PGA tournaments are held. In February the Doral Eastern Open is held in Miami, in March the Tournament Players Championship is held in Jacksonville, and in October you have both the Pensacola PGA Open and the Walt Disney World National Team Championship Golf Classic.

FISHING

With 8,000 miles (12,800 km) of tidal coastline, 30,000 lakes, and countless rivers and streams, it is hardly surprising that Florida is a fisherman's paradise. You will need a

---

Florida's police officers are trained to assist the state's 47 million annual visitors.

non-resident's license for freshwater fishing — which costs $16 for 7 days and $31.50 for a year — but no license is required for saltwater fishing. Licenses can be bought from any marina or tackle shop.

There are more than 600 different species of saltwater fish off the Florida coast, and there are almost as many species of boats for charter in every port to take you out to fish for them. For landlubbers, there are many public fishing piers from which one can fish in the ocean without going *deep* sea fishing. And for those fishermen who are

CRUISES

There are so many ocean cruises from Florida ports that the peninsula could almost be considered one giant dock. There are morning cruises and afternoon cruises, sunlight and starlight cruises, half-day and one-day cruises, two-day and two-night cruises, week-long and longer cruises, cruises to the Bahamas and the Virgin Islands, to the West Indies and Mexico, even through the Panama Canal to Los Angeles and San Francisco.

not particularly good at sitting and waiting, there are ample opportunities for shell-fishing among Florida's offshore population of crabs, scallops, and lobsters.

For a complete guide to fishing in Florida, write to the Florida Game and Freshwater Fish Commission ((904) 488-1960, Farris Bryant Building, Tallahassee, FL 32399. The *Orlando Sentinel* also publishes two excellent books by its fishing correspondent, Max Branyon: *Florida Freshwater Fishing Guide* and *Florida Saltwater Fishing Guide*. They are available from P.O. Box 6512, Surfside, FL 33154. Both cost $9.95, including postage and handling, in the United States; overseas readers should enquire before ordering.

Likewise, there are so many cruise lines operating out of so many port cities and catering for so many different tastes that it would be pointless to try to list them all. The one offering the most cruises, out of the most ports, is SeaEscape Ltd. ((305) 379-0000, 1080 Port Boulevard, Miami, FL 33132. If they can't provide what you want, your travel agent can.

PUBLIC HOLIDAYS

New Year's Day	January 1
Martin Luther King, Jr. Day	January 15
President's Day	February 20
Memorial Day	Last Monday in May
Independence Day	July 4

Labor Day   First Monday in September
Columbus Day Second Monday in October
Veterans' Day   November 11
Thanksgiving Day   Fourth Thursday in November
Christmas Day   December 25

During these holidays, federal, state and city offices close, and more importantly the banks. Whether shops and restaurants are open during public holidays depends on the region, but anywhere you go, shopping malls are likely to be open seven days a week, including holidays.

Other holidays such as St. Patrick's Day (March 17), Easter Sunday (late March or early April), Mother's Day (May), Father's Day (June), and Halloween (October 31) may be celebrated in various ways by different communities. (See YOUR CHOICE, FESTIVE FLINGS for statewide and regional celebrations.)

MAIL

Post offices in Florida are generally open from 8 AM to 5 PM weekdays, and from 8 AM to noon on Saturday. If you do not know what your address will be, you can have your mail sent to you ℅ General Delivery at the main post office in the town where you will be staying. You must collect such mail personally and have with you some form of identification. You can also have mail sent to you, marked "Client's Mail", ℅ American Express.

If the post offices are closed or inconveniently located, there are vending machines selling stamps all over the place. However, as there is an iniquitous mark-up on stamps sold through these machines, you will be better off paying your hotel or motel to send your mail for you.

Telegrams and telex messages are handled by Western Union and International Telephone and Telegraph, private companies that you will find listed in the yellow pages of the telephone directory. Having dictated your message over the telephones, you can have the charge billed to your hotel room.

TELEPHONES

Most foreign visitors find the American telephone system a revelation. It is cheaper and more efficient by far than any other telephone system in the world; British visitors, in particular, are overcome by the experience of using telephones that actually work — and relatively cheaply. Public telephones are located on all major urban streets, as well as in hotel lobbies, restaurants, service stations, drugstores, shopping malls, and public buildings. At this writing, local calls are 25 cents everywhere in Florida. For information on local telephone numbers dial 411; for information on long-distance numbers call 1-555-1212. Rates for long-distance calls drop after 5 PM, and drop further after 11 PM.

Florida is in the process of adding new area dialing codes. If the area code has changed when you dial, an automated message will give you the new number. To place a long-distance call within the same area code, you dial 1 + the number you are calling. To place a call outside your area code you dial 1+ area code + telephone number. If for any reason you need operator assistance, you dial 0 instead of 1 before dialing the rest of the number; an operator will come on the line before your call is connected. For direct dialing of international calls you dial 011 + country code + area code + telephone number.

RADIO AND TELEVISION

Like the rest of the United States Florida is media-intensive. And that's putting it mildly. The airwaves are a Babel of voices and a blizzard of images that will delight the media junkie and dismay those not similarly addicted. The radio dial features end-to-end music — classical, pop, rock, reggae, and a *lot* of country and western — interspersed with dozens of mind-numbing phone-in talk shows ("Hi Debbie, my name is Marcia and I live in Coral Gables and I would just like to ask if you think foreplay is…"). Still, Larry King, whose networked program from Washington comes on at 11 PM on stations all around the state, is well worth listening to.

Florida's golf courses are among the most beautiful in the world.

Travelers' Tips

As for television, I'll start with some numbers. There are 34 television channels in Miami alone — 11 regular broadcast stations and 23 cable. In one week I counted 60 hours of soap operas. In one day I counted 22 talk shows. On CNN there is news 24 hours a day. Get the picture?

To help you wade through this avalanche of faces and voices, all I can do is report my personal choices. In my considered opinion, the best newscast is the MacNeil-Lehrer Newshour at 6 PM on PBS (the non-commercial Public Broadcasting

The funniest talk show — the funniest show, period — is *Late Night with David Letterman* on CBS at 12:30 AM. All the other programs worth watching will already be familiar to overseas viewers.

Although I am not a great fan of American television, I have to admit that a television station in Miami has come up with an idea of such wit that I would commend it to television producers anywhere in the world. The idea comes from the 10 PM news on Channel 7. During the sports segment of the program, there are all the usual interviews

Service), although the main evening newscasts on the three major commercial networks (ABC, CBS, and NBC) are very good, despite being carved up into bite-size chunks to accommodate the advertisements. They air at either 6:30 PM or 7 PM, depending on which network station you are watching.

The best early-morning show is *Today* on NBC. The best early-morning weekend program is *CBS Sunday Morning*, hosted by the estimable Charles Kuralt — a delightful, gentle program to wake up to. In fact, CBS owns Sunday as far as I'm concerned, because after the NFL football games are over, the best magazine program on television, *60 Minutes* on CBS, comes on at 7 PM.

with players and coaches about yesterday's game or next week's game or the prospects for the seasons, etc. What is not usual about these interviews is that the moment they begin, a Cliché Meter appears in the bottom left-hand corner of the screen. Thus you still hear the usual rubbish — "the boys really want this one" and "will give it their best shot" and they "will take the game to them" because they will "come to play" and hope to "control the line of scrimmage" and "shut down their big guns" and "take them out of their offense" because after all "it's a game of inches" and "the best defense is a good offense" and vice versa and *(fill in the blank)* — and all the while the cliché meter in the corner is clicking away. Brilliant.

NEWSPAPERS AND MAGAZINES

With a very few exceptions — the *Wall Street Journal*, the *Christian Science Monitor*, the *International Herald Tribune* — American newspapers are all local newspapers. Even the great papers like the *New York Times*, the *Washington Post*, and the *Los Angeles Times* carry more local news than global news. And the one avowedly national newspaper, *USA Today*, is referred to derisively in the States as the McNewspaper, because its

zine, with comprehensive listings of upcoming events, entertainments, and exhibitions.

BUYING PROPERTY

Perhaps the greatest compliment that one can pay to Florida is to note the fact that a huge proportion of the people who go there for a holiday want to go back for good.

It is not only easy to buy property in Florida, but surprisingly inexpensive by current international standards. It is still

relationship to serious journalism is approximately the same as McDonald's is to serious food.

The local papers, as well as *USA Today* and, occasionally, the *New York Times*, are available from sidewalk vending machines in every major city, as well as from news agents and drugstores. One- or two-day old foreign newspapers are available in all the main tourist areas but are expensive.

Drugstore and supermarket racks groan under the overwhelming weight of magazines published in America on every conceivable subject, and for every conceivable taste (and some inconceivable). Worth bearing in mind, however, is that virtually every Florida city has its own city maga-

possible, for example, to find luxurious accommodation, often right on the beach, for under $100,000. Considering that the down payments are low (20 percent), and the mortgage rates are extremely attractive to overseas buyers (an average eight percent on a 30-year fixed mortgage at the time of writing), you could do a lot worse than put your money into a holiday or retirement home in Florida.

Whatever appeals to you, the local Chamber of Commerce will be eager to help you with information and introductions.

OPPOSITE: Fishing boats at Tarpon Springs.
ABOVE: Whatever kind of fishing you want, Florida has it.

Recommended Reading

BARTRAM, WILLIAM. *Travels*. Penguin Books, New York 1988.

BENNETT, CHARLES E. *Settlement of Florida*. University of Florida Press, Gainesville 1968.

BIRNBAUM, STEVE. *Walt Disney World: The Official Guide*. Houghton Mifflin, Boston 1989.

BURNETT, GENE M. *Florida's Past*. Pineapple Press, Sarasota 1986.

DASMAN, RAYMOND F. *No Further Retreat: The Fight to Save Florida*. Macmillan, New York 1971.

DIDION, JOAN. *Miami*. Pocket Books, New York 1987.

DOUGLAS MARJORY STONEMAN. *Florida: The Long Frontier*. Harper and Row, New York 1967.

FICHTER, GEORGE S. *Birds of Florida*. E.A. Seamann, Miami 1971.

Florida Outdoor Guide. The Miami Herald, Miami 1989.

HATTON, HAP. *Tropical Splendor: An Architectural History of Florida*. Alfred A. Knopf, New York 1987.

HEMINGWAY, ERNEST. *Islands in the Stream*. Scribner's, New York 1970. *To Have and Have Not*. Scribner's, New York 1937.

JAHODA, GLORIA. *Florida: A Bicentennial History*. W.W. Norton, New York 1976.

Kennedy Space Center Story. NASA, Cape Canaveral 1986.

LUMMUS, JOHN N. *The Miracle of Miami Beach*. Teacher Publishing, Miami 1940.

MACDONALD, JOHN D. *Condominium*. Lippincott, New York 1977.

MCGUANE, THOMAS. *Ninety-two in the Shade*. Farrar, Straus, New York 1973.

MCLENDON, JAMES. *Papa Hemingway in Key West*. E. A. Seamann, Miami 1972.

MARTH, DEL and MARTHA. *Florida Almanac*. A.S. Barnes, St. Petersburg 1988.

MORRIS, ALLEN. *The Florida Handbook*. Peninsula Publishing, Tallahassee 1989.

NEY, JOHN. *Palm Beach*. Little, Brown, Boston 1966.

RABKIN, RICHARD and JACOB. *Nature Guide to Florida*. Banyan Books, Miami 1978.

SMILEY, NIXON. *Florida: Land of Images*. E.A. Seamann, Miami 1977. *Yesterday's Florida*. E.A. Seamann, Miami 1974.

STACHOWITZ, JIM. *Diver's Guide to Florida and the Florida Keys*. Windward Publishing, Miami 1976.

WILLIAMS, TENNESSEE. *Memoirs*. Doubleday, New York 1975.

Quick Reference A–Z Guide
to Places and Topics of Interest with Listed Accommodation, Restaurants and Useful Telephone Numbers

Star ratings for accommodation and restaurants indicate price relationships only. Refer to text for rates, facilities and recommendations.

A access, general 244
accommodation
general 248
luxury 37
airlines, domestic 247
airlines, international 244
alligators 28
Amelia Island 31, 127, 145
Apalachicola
attractions
John Gorrie Museum 43
Apalachicola River 24
archaeological sites 43
Atlantic Coast 127–145
history 127

B backpacking 34
Bahia Honda Key *See under* Florida Keys
Bahia Honda Wildlife Reserve 28
Big Pine Key *See under* Florida Keys
birdwatching 60
Biscayne National Park 24
Blue Spring State Park 18, 26
boating 29
Boca Raton *See* Palm Beach and Baca Raton
Bradenton
festivals and events
Manatee Heritage Week (March) 54
British colonial presence 72
Bulow Creek 26
Bunnel
festivals and events
Flagler County Bluegrass Festival (May) 54

C Cabot, John 71
Caladesi Island 27
camping 251
Canaveral National Seashore and Merritt Island 23, 127
canoeing 29
car rental 247
Cayo Costa barrier island 27
Central Florida 32, 38, 50, 151–173
history 153
children, traveling with 40
citrus fruits 59
Civil War 73
Clearwater *See* St. Petersburg–Clearwater
Clermont
attractions
Lakeridge Winery and Vineyards 60
climate 76
Collier-Seminole Park 28
colonization 71
communications 253
consulates 246

Creek Indians 72
cruises 252
Cuban influence 82
Cypress Gardens
festivals and events
Chrysanthemum Festival (November) 55

D **Daytona** 132–137
access 137
accommodation
***Daytona Hilton ((904) 767-7350 135
***Indigo Lakes Resort ((904) 258-6333 135
**Daytona Sands ((904) 767-2551 136
**Nautilus Inn ((904) 254-8600 136
**Perry's Ocean Edge ((904) 255-0581 136
**St. Regis Hotel ((904) 242-8743 136
**Sun Viking Lodge ((904) 252-6252
TOLL-FREE (800) 874-4469 136
**Treasure Island ((904) 255-8371
TOLL-FREE (800) 874-7420 136
*Captain's Quarter Inn ((904) 767-3119 136
*Del Aire Motel ((904) 252-2563 136
*Econo Lodge ((904) 255-3661 136
attractions
Casements ((904) 676-3216 134
Daytona Beach 20–21
Daytona International Speedway 21, 133
Daytona Playhouse 21
Daytona USA 21
Dixie Queen II ((904) 255-1997 134
Main Street Pier 21
Museum of Arts and Sciences
((904) 255-0285 134
Ormond Beach 21, 26, 133
Peabody Auditorium 21
Seaside Music Theater 21
Tomoka State Park 134
festivals and events
Greater Daytona Beach Striking Fish
Tournament (May) 55
Speed Week (February) 53
general information
Daytona Beach Chamber of Commerce
((904) 255-0415 132
Daytona National Airport
((904) 255-8441 133
Dental service ((904) 734-1355 133
Ormond Beach Chamber of Commerce
((904) 677-3454 132
Volusia County Medical Association
((904) 258-1611 133
history 132
nightlife
Clarendon Plaza Hotel
((904) 255-4471 135
Club Mocambo ((904) 258-9413 135
Finky's ((904) 255-5059 135
Oyster Pub ((904) 255-6348 135
P.J.'s ((904) 258-5222 135

restaurants
***King's Cellar   *137*
***La Crêpe en Haut ((904) 673-1999   *136*
***St. Regis Hotel Restaurant
((904) 252-8743   *136*
***The Chart House ((904) 255-9022   *137*
**Aunt Catfish's ((904) 767-4768   *137*
**Gene's Steak House ((904) 255-2059   *137*
**Hungarian Village ((904) 253-5712   *137*
**Inlet Harbor   *137*
**Down the Hatch ((904) 761-4831   *137*
*Duff's Smörgasbord ((904) 788-0828   *137*
*Piccadilly Cafeteria ((904) 258-5373   *137*
shopping
Seabreeze Boulevard   *135*
sports, active
golf   *134*
tennis   *135*
water sports   *135*
Depression Era   *74*
Destin   *15*
festivals and events
Billy Bowlegs Festival (June)   *55*
Fishing Rodeo (September)   *55*
dolphins   *32, 42, 110, 141, 158, 165, 222*
Disney World   *See* Walt Disney World
diving   *See also under* place names
Florida Association of Dive Operators
((904) 222-6000   *29*
Drake, (Sir) Frances   *72*
driving   *31, 250*
Duck Key   *See under* Florida Keys

E early development   *73*
eating out   *56, 249*
Egmont Key Wildlife Refuge   *27*
electricity   *248*
Emerald Coast   *15*
entering the United States   *246*
Everglades National Park   *13, 23, 217–224*
access   13, 224
Tamiami Trail   *13*
accommodation
camping   *223*
**Captain's Table Resort ((941) 695-4211   *223*
**Flamingo Lodge Marina and
Outdoor Resort ((305) 253-2241   *223*
**Greenstone Motel ((305) 247-8334   *222*
**Holiday Inn ((305) 247-7020   *222*
**Knights Inn ((305) 245-2800   *222*
**Park Royal Inn ((305) 247-3200   *222*
attractions
Back Country Tour ((305) 253-2241   *221*
birdwatching, Chokoloskee Bay   *221*
E. J. Hamilton Observation Tower   *13*
Everglades National Park Boat Tours
((941) 695-2591   *221*
Florida Bay Cruises ((305) 253-2241   *221*
Miccosukee Indian Village
((305) 223-8380   *221*
Royal Palm Interpretive Center   *13*
Shark Valley ((305) 221-8455   *221*
Tamiami Trail   *221*
Wilderness Waterway   *222*
general information
Everglades City Chamber of Commerce
((813) 695-3941   *220*
Everglades National Park Visitor Center
((813) 695-3311   *221*

Greater Homestead-Florida City
Chamber of Commerce ((305) 247-2332   *220*
history   220
restaurants
***Le Kir ((305) 247-6414   *223*
**Captain Bob's ((305) 247-8988   *223*
**El Toro Taco ((305) 245-5576   *223*
**Flamingo Restaurant ((941) 695-3101   *224*
**Miccosukee Restaurant
((305) 223-8388   *223*
*Potlikker's ((305) 248-0835   *223*
**Rod and Gun Club ((941) 695-2101   *224*
shopping
Flamingo Marina   *222*
Homestead   *222*
sports, active
water sports   *222*
exploration   *71*

F fauna   *19–20, 23, 25, 27–29, 32–33, 35, 37, 40,
60, 76, 127, 165, 172, 195–196, 208, 211, 220*
See also flora
Fernandina Beach
attractions
Fort Clinch State Park   *43*
festivals and events
Isle of Eight Shrimp Festival (May)   *54*
Victorian Seaside Christmas (December)   *56*
festivals   *51, 252   See also under* place names
fishing   *29, 89, 251   See also under* place names
Flagler Beach
festivals and events
Miss Flagler County Pageant (June)   *55*
Flagler, Henry *74, 82, 105, 115, 117, 127, 132, 138, 229*
flea markets   *46*
flora   *60, 76, 87, 115, 160, 218, 220   See also* fauna
Florida Caverns   *24*
Florida Keys   *227–241*
general information
Florida Keys Visitors Bureau
TOLL-FREE ((800) FLA-KEYS   *237*
history   229
KEY WEST   *16, 229–241*
access   241
accommodation
***Eaton Lodge ((305) 294-3800   *240*
***Hyatt Key West ((305) 296-9900   *240*
***La Mer Hotel ((305) 296-6577 *240*
***Marriott's Casa Marina Resort
((305) 296-3535   *240*
**Best Western Key Ambassador
((305) 296-3500   *240*
**Duval House Historic Inn
((305) 294-1666   *240*
**Eden House ((305) 296-6868   *240*
**South Beach Motel
((305) 296-5611   *240*
*Atlantic Shores ((305) 296-2491   *240*
*Hibiscus ((305) 296-6711   *240*
*Santa Maria ((305) 296-5678   *240*
attractions
Audubon House and Gardens
((305) 294-2116   *16, 238*
Conch Tour Train   *238*
Curry Mansion   *16*
Duval Street   *238*
Fort Jefferson National Monument *239*
Fort Zachary Taylor State Historic Site
((305) 292-6713   *239*

Hemingway's House
 ((305) 294-1575 *16, 238*
Key West Lighthouse Museum
 ((305) 294-0012 *238*
Key West Seaplane Service
 ((305) 294-6978 *239*
Mallory Market *16*
Mel Fisher Museum
 ((305) 294-2633 *16, 238*
Old Customs House *16*
Sloppy Joe's *238*
Tennessee Williams' House *238*
Wrecker's Museum ((305) 294-9502 *238*
festivals and events
Hemingway Days (July) *55*
general information 237
Greater Key West Chamber of
 Commerce ((305) 294-2587 *237*
Key West Reservation Service
 ((305) 294-7713 *240*
history 237
nightlife
Captain Tony's Saloon
 ((305) 294-1838 *239*
Copa ((305) 296-8521 *239*
Delmonico's ((305) 294-4383 *239*
Havana Docks Bar ((305) 294-9541 *239*
Jan McArts Cabaret Theatre
 ((305) 296-2120 *240*
Mallory Square *240*
Sloppy Joe's ((305) 294-8585 *239*
Tennessee Williams Fine Arts Center
 ((305) 294-6232 *240*
restaurants
***Café des Artistes ((305) 294-7100 *241*
***Henry's ((305) 296-3535 *241*
***Louie's Backyard ((305) 294-1061 *240*
**Antonia's ((305) 294-6565 *241*
**Bagatelle ((305) 294-7195 *241*
**Kyushu ((305) 294-2995 *241*
**La-Te-Da ((305) 294-8435 *241*
**Pepe's Café ((305) 294-7192 *241*
*El Loro Verde ((305) 296-7298 *241*
*El Siboney ((305) 294-2721 *241*
*Full Moon Saloon ((305) 294-9090 *241*
*La Crêperie ((305) 294-7677 *241*
shopping
Duval Street *239*
Fast Buck Freddies *239*
Old Town *239*
sports, active
boating
 Key West Boat Rentals
  ((305) 294-2628 *239*
fishing
 Garrison Bight Marina
  ((305) 294-3093 *239*
 Sea Breeze Charters
  ((305) 294-6027 *239*
golf
 Key West Resort ((305) 294-5232 *239*
tennis
 Island City Tennis
  ((305) 294-1346 *239*
water sports
 Key West Pro Dive Shop
  ((305) 296-3823 *239*
 Reef Riders Dive Shop
  ((305) 294-3635 *239*

MIDDLE AND LOWER KEYS *233*
accommodation 235
 **Conch Key Cottages
  ((305) 289-1377 *235*
attractions
 Canoeing Nature Tour
  ((305) 872-2620 *234*
 Perky Bat Tower *234*
 Seven Mile Bridge *233*
general information
 Greater Marathon Chamber
  of Commerce ((305) 743-5417 *234*
 Lower Keys Chamber of Commerce
  ((305) 872-2411 *234*
Bahia Honda Key *233–234*
attractions
 Bahia Honda Wildlife Reserve *28, 234*
Big Pine Key *55, 233–236*
attractions
 National Key Deer Refuge *234*
nightlife
 No Name Pub
  ((305) 872-9115 *235*
restaurants
 *Dr. Feelgood's BBQ
  ((305) 872-4752 *236*
 *Island Jim's
  ((305) 872-2017 *236*
Duck Key *235*
nightlife
 Ship's Pub
  ((305) 743-7000 *235*
Grassy Key *234, 236*
attractions
 Dolphin Research Center
  ((305) 289-1121 *234*
restaurants
 *Grassy Key Dairy Bar
  ((305) 743-3816 *236*
Key Colony Beach *235*
accommodation
 ***Ocean Beach Club
  ((305) 289-0525 *235*
Little Torch Key *234–236*
accommodation
 ***Little Palm Island
  ((305) 872-2524 *235*
restaurants
 ***Little Palm Island
  ((305) 872-2524 *236*
sports, active
 boating
  Dolphin Marina ((305) 872-2685 *234*
Ramrod Key *235–236*
accommodation
 *Looe Key Reef Resort
  ((305) 872-2215 *236*
festivals and events
 Underwater Music Festival (July) *55*
nightlife
 Looe Key Reef Resort
  ((305) 872-2215 *235*
restaurants
 ***Kelsey's ((305) 743-9018 *236*
 ***Little Bavaria
  ((305) 743-4833 *236*
 **Cousin Joe's Supper Bar
  ((305) 745-1646 *236*
Stock Island *233*

Sugarloaf Key 236
accommodation
  *Sugarloaf Lodge
    ((305) 745-3211 236
Summerland Key 236
restaurants
  **Monte's Restaurant and
    Fish Market ((305) 745-3731 236
Sunshine Key 233
Vaca Key 233–236
accommodation
  ***Buccaneer
    ((305) 743-9071 235
  ***Hawk's Cay Resort
    ((305) 743-7000 235
  **Hopp-Inn Guest House
    ((305) 743-4118 235
  *Valhalla Beach Motel
    ((305) 289-0616 236
attractions 234
  Crane Point Hammock 234
  Marathon 233
festivals and events
  Seven Mile Bridge Run (April) 54
nightlife
  Good Times ((305) 743-4108 235
restaurants
  ***Chef's ((305) 743-4108 236
  *Shuckers Raw Bar & Grill
    ((305) 743-8686 236
shopping 235
sports, active
  boating
    Clyde's Seven Mile Marina
      ((305) 743-7712 234
  diving
    Cudjoe Gardens Marina and
      Dive Shop ((305) 745-2357 234
    Seaview Ocean Divers
      ((305) 743-8514 234
  fishing
    World Class Angler
      ((305) 743-6139 234
  golf
    Key Colony Beach
      ((305) 289-0821 234
  sailing
    Amantha (Faro Blanco Resort)
      ((305) 743-9020 234
    Sailmaster Charters
      ((305) 743-4200 234
  tennis
    Key Colony Beach
      ((305) 289-0821 234
Upper Keys 229–233
access 233
accommodation
  **Largo Lodge
    ((305) 451-0424 232
  **Stone Ledge Lodge
    ((305) 852-8114 232
general information
  Islamorada Chamber of Commerce
    ((305) 664-4503 230
  Upper Keys Chamber of Commerce
    ((305) 451-1414 230
Indian Key 230
attractions
  Indian Key State Historic Site 230

Islamorada 229–233
accommodation
  ***Cheeca Lodge ((305) 327-2888 232
  ***Holiday Isle Resort
    ((305) 451-2121 232
  **Drop Anchor ((305) 664-4863 232
  **Islander ((305) 664-2031 232
attractions
  Holiday Princess Cruises
    ((305) 664-2321 230
  Theater of the Sea
    ((305) 664-2431 230
nightlife
  Holiday Isle Resort
    ((305) 664-2321 232
restaurants
  ***Atlantic Edge ((305) 664-4651 233
  ***Horizon Restaurant (Holiday Isle
    Resort) ((305) 451-2121 233
  **Coral Grill ((305) 664-4803 233
  **Green Turtle Inn Restaurant
    ((305) 394-6248 233
  **Ziggy's Conch Restaurant
    ((305) 664-4590 233
  *Lor-e-lei on the Gulf
    ((305) 664-4657 233
  *Papa Joe's ((305) 664-8109 233
shopping
  Bimini Town Shops 231
  Irene and George's 231
sports, active
  diving and fishing 231
    Holiday Isle Resort Marina
      ((305) 664-2321 231
  golf and tennis
    Cheeca Lodge Hotel
      ((305) 644-4651 231
Key Largo 229–233
accommodation
  ***Marina del Mar
    ((305) 451-4450 232
  ***Sheraton Key Largo
    ((305) 852-5553 232
  *Rock Reef Resort
    ((305) 852-2401 232
attractions
  African Queen 230
  John Pennekamp Coral Reef
    State Park 229
nightlife
  Bimini Town Shops 231
  Coconuts ((305) 451-4107 231
restaurants
  ***Quay ((305) 451-0943 232
  **Italian Fisherman
    ((305) 451-4471 233
  *Mrs. Mac's Kitchen 233
shopping 231
sports, active
  fishing
    Miss Kitty Reef Fishing
      ((305) 451-2220 231
  water sports
    John Pennekamp Coral Reef
      State Park 231
  windsurfing
    Windsurfing of the Florida Keys
      ((305) 451-3869 231
Lignumvitae Key 230

Long Key *230–231*
attractions
Long Key State Park
((305) 664-4815 *231*
Lower Matecumbe Key *229*
Plantation Key *232*
restaurants
***Marker 88 ((305) 852-9315 *232*
Upper Matecumbe Key *229*
food and drink *56*
Fort Caroline *71*
Fort Lauderdale *106–115*
access *115*
accommodation
***Bahia Mar Resort and Yachting Center
((305) 764-2233
TOLL-FREE (800) 327-8154 *112*
***Bonaventure Resort and Spa
((305) 389-3300 *112*
***Hyatt Regency Pier 66 Hotel and Marina
((305) 525-6666
TOLL-FREE (800) 327-3796 *112*
***Marriott's Harbor Beach Resort
((305) 525-4000 *112*
***Riverside ((305) 467-0671 *112*
**DiVito by the Sea ((305) 929-7227 *112*
**Holiday Inn Hotel and Conference Center
((305) 739-4000 *113*
**Lago Mar Hotel ((305) 523-6511 *112*
*Sea Chateau ((305) 566-8331 *113*
*Sea View Resort Motel
((305) 564-3151 *113*
attractions
Butterfly World ((305) 977-4434 *110*
Davie Pro Rodeo Complex
((305) 434-7062 *110*
Flamingo Gardens ((305) 473-2955 *110*
Gondolas of America ((305) 522-3333 *108*
Jungle Queen (riverboat cruise)
((305) 462-5596 *108*
Lolly the Trolley ((305) 768-0700 *110*
Museum of Art ((305) 763-6464 *110*
Museum of Discovery & Science
((305) 467-6673 *42, 110*
Ocean World ((305) 525-6611 *110*
Seminole Okalee Indian Village *110*
Stranahan House ((305) 524-4736 *110*
Young at Art Children's Museum *42*
festivals and events
film festival (November) *55*
Sistrunk Historical Festival (February) *53*
general information
24-Hour Doctors' House Calls
((305) 748-5900 *108*
Broward County Dental Association
((305) 772-5461 *108*
Broward County Hotel/Motel Association
((305) 462-0409 *108*
Broward County Medical Association
((305) 525-1595 *108*
Broward Parks and Recreation Division
((305) 563-PARK *108*
Checker Cabs ((305) 485-3000 *108*
Fort Lauderdale/Hollywood International
Airport ((305) 357-6100 *108*
Greater Fort Lauderdale Chamber
of Commerce ((305) 462-4000 *108*
Greater Fort Lauderdale Convention
and Visitors Bureau ((305) 765-4466 *108*

Physician Information Service
((305) 966-DOCS *108*
events information (recorded)
((305) 765-8068 *108*
Sastel International Ltd. ((071) 630-5995 *108*
Yellow Cabs ((305) 527-8600 *108*
history *106*
nightlife
Bootlegger ((305) 563-4337 *112*
Casey's Comedy Club ((305) 491-4423 *112*
Comic Strip ((305) 565-8887 *112*
Do-Da's ((305) 791-1477 *112*
Durty Nelly's ((305) 564-0720 *112*
Musician Exchange Café *112*
Pier Top Lounge ((305) 525-6666 *112*
Shirttail Charlie's ((305) 463-3474 *112*
Shooter's ((305) 566-2855 *111*
restaurants
***Casa Vecchia ((305) 463-7575 *113*
***La Coquille ((305) 467-3030 *113*
***La Ferme ((305) 764-0987 *113*
***Le Dôme ((305) 463-3303 *113*
***Left Bank ((305) 462-5376 *113*
**Café de Paris ((305) 467-2900 *113*
**Down Under ((305) 563-4123 *113*
**Lagniappe Cajun House *113*
**Sea Watch ((305) 781-2200 *113*
*Bobby Rubino's Place for Ribs
((305) 561-5305 *113*
*Ernie's Bar-B-Que ((305) 523-8636 *113*
*Southport Raw Bar ((305) 525-2526 *113*
shopping
Anhinga Indian Museum and Art Gallery
((305) 581-8411 *111*
Flying Bird Gift Shop ((305) 792-3445 *111*
Galleria *111*
Las Olas Boulevard *111*
Thunderbird Trading Post
((305) 585-2281 *111*
sports, active
golf *110–111*
jai alai *110*
tennis *111*
water sports *111*
sports information
Fort Lauderdale Parks and Recreation
Department ((305) 761-2621 *111*
sports, spectator
baseball *110*
Fort Myers *20, 211–215*
access *215*
accommodation
***Seawatch-on-the-Beach
((941) 481-3636 *214*
***Sheraton Harbor Place
((941) 337-0300 *214*
**Fountain Motel ((941) 481-0429 *214*
**Outrigger Beach Resort
((941) 463-3131 *214*
*Beacon Court Motel ((941) 463-5264 *214*
*Ta Ki Ki Motel ((941) 334-2135 *214*
attractions
Adventure Sailing Escape Flotilla
((941) 489-0344 *212*
Thomas Edison Winter Home and Museum
((941) 334-7419 *20, 212*
Fort Myers Beach *20*
Henry Ford Home *20*
Shell Factory ((941) 995-2141 *212*

environs
  Eden Vineyards Winery and Park   61
festivals and events
  Edison Festival of Light (February)   53
  Shady Hills Arts and Crafts Festival
    (December)   56
general information
  Fort Myers Beach Chamber of Commerce
    ((941) 454-7500   211
  Fort Myers Chamber of Commerce
    ((941) 332-3624   211
nightlife
  Beach Club ((941) 939-2582   214
  Edison's Electric Lounge
    ((941) 482-2900   214
  Norma Jean's ((941) 275-9997   214
restaurants
  ***La Tiers ((941) 337-0300   214
  ***Snug Harbor Restaurant and Lounge
    ((941) 463-4343   215
  **Mucky Duck ((941) 463-5519   215
  **Prawnbroker ((941) 489-2226   215
  **Riverwalk Fish and Ale House
    ((941) 263-2734   215
  *Pelican Restaurant and Inn
    ((941) 463-6139   215
  *Woody's Bar-B-Q ((941) 997-1424   215
shopping
  Royal Palm Square Shopping Center   213
sports, active
  golf   213
  tennis   213
  water sports   213
Fort Walton   15
festivals and events
  Billy Bowlegs Festival (June)   55
  Fort Walton Beach Seafood Festival (April) 54
  Hog's Breath Hobie Regatta (May)   54
French and Indian Wars   72

G Gainesville
festivals and events
  Downtown Festival and Arts Show
    (November)   55
  Gatornationals (March)   53
gardens   44
geography   75–77
Gold Coast   105–115
  history   105
golf   30, 89, 251   See also under place names
Grassy Key   See under Florida Keys
Grayton Beach
festivals and events
  Arts Festival (May)   54
Gulf Coast   193–211
  history   195
Gulf Islands National Seashore   24

H Haines City   172
general information
  Haines City Chamber of Commerce
    ((813) 422-3751   172
health   248
Highlands Hammock State Park   26
hiking trails   34
Hillsboro River State Park
attractions
  Fort Foster   44
history   71–75
Homosassa Springs State Park   27

attractions
  Florida Nature Museum   27
Hontoon Island Indian settlement   26
horseback riding   26
Huguenots   71
hurricanes   77

I Ichetuckee Springs   25
Indian Key   See under Florida Keys
insects   248
Islamorada   See under Florida Keys

J Jacksonville   145–148
access   148
accommodation
  ***Adeeb's Sea Turtle Inn ((904) 279-7402
    TOLL-FREE ((800) 279-7402   147
  ***Amelia Island Plantation ((904) 261-6161
    TOLL-FREE ((800) 261-6161   147
  ***Lighthouse ((904) 261-5878   147
  ***Omini Hotel ((904) 355-6664
    TOLL-FREE (800) 228-2121   147
  **Bailey House ((904) 261-5390   147
  **Jacksonville Hotel ((904) 398-8800   147
  **Seaside Inn ((904) 261-0954   147
  **Seaside Studios ((904) 241-7000   147
attractions
  Amelia Island Museum
    ((904) 261-7378   146
  Cumner Gallery of Art and Gardens
    ((904) 356-6857   146
  Fort Caroline National Memorial
    ((904) 641-7111   146
  Jacksonville Art Museum
    ((904) 398-8336   146
  Jacksonville Landing   146
  Jacksonville Museum of Science and History
    ((904) 396-7062   146
  Jacksonville Zoo ((904) 757-4463   146
  Kingsley Plantation ((904) 251-3537   146
  Riverwalk   146
  Seashore Stable ((904) 261-4878   146
environs
  Crystal River   44
  Fort George State Cultural Site   44
  Little Talbot Island   26
festivals and events
  Heritage Days (May)   54
  Outback Steakhouse Gator Bowl (January) 51
  World's Greatest Free Jazz Concert
    (October)   55
general information
  Amelia Island-Fernandina Beach
    Chamber of Commerce   146
  Dental Information and Referral Service
    ((904) 356-6642   146
  Duval County Medical Society
    ((904) 335-6561   146
  Jacksonville Chamber of Commerce
    ((904) 366-6000   146
  Jacksonville International Airport
    ((904) 741-2000   146
  Yellow Cabs ((904) 354-5511   146
history   145
nightlife
  57 Heaven ((904) 721-5757   147
  Einstein-A-GoGo ((904) 249-4646   147
  Juliette's ((904) 355-6644   147
  Metropolis ((904) 355-6410   147
  Palace Saloon ((904) 261-9068   147

restaurants
***Brett's ((904) 261-2660 *147*
***Florida Café ((904) 737-2244 *147*
***Olive Tree ((904) 249-1300 *147*
***Wine Cellar ((904) 398-8989 *147*
**1878 Steak House ((904) 261-4049 *148*
**Crawdaddy's ((904) 396-3546 *148*
**Homestead ((904) 249-5240 *148*
**Salud! ((904) 241-7877 *148*
*Chiang's Mongolian Bar-B-Q
  ((904) 241-3075 *148*
*Ieyasu of Tokyo ((904) 353-0163 *148*
*Patti's ((904) 753-1662 *148*
*Slightly Off Center Bakery and Deli
  ((904) 277-2100 *148*
shopping
Center Street *147*
Jacksonville Landing ((904) 353-1188 *147*
sports, active
golf *146*
tennis *146*
water sports *146*
jai alai *See under* place names
**John Pennekamp Coral Reef
Underwater Park** *28*

K **Kennedy Space Center** *128*
Key Colony Beach *See under* Florida Keys
Key Largo *See under* Florida Keys
Key West *See under* Florida Keys
Kissimmee
attractions
Green Meadows Children's Farm *42*
festivals and events
Bluegrass music festival (March) *54*
Florida State Air Fair (October) *55*
Silver Spurs Rodeo (February) *53*
Warbird Weekend (January) *51*
general information
Kissimmee–St. Cloud Convention
  and Visitors Bureau ((813) 696-1112 *172*

L **Lake City**
camping
O'Leno camping area *26*
festivals and events
Battle of Olustee reenactment (February) *53*
Festival of Lights (November) *55*
Lake Kissimmee State Park *27*
attractions
Kissimmee Cow Camp *44*
Lake Wales *172*
general information
Lake Wales Area Chamber of Commerce
  ((813) 676-3445 *172*
language *248*
Lignumvitae Key *See under* Florida Keys
Little Torch Key *See under* Florida Keys
Long Key *See under* Florida Keys
Lower Matecumbe Key *See under* Florida Keys
Lower Wekiva River State Reserve *35*

M **Madeira Beach**
festivals and events
John's Pass Seafood Festival (October) *55*
mail *253*
major league sports *30*
Manatee Springs *24*
manatees *13, 18, 24, 26–27, 222*
Marco Island *213*
media

broadcast *254*
print *255*
medical insurance *248*
Menéndez de Avilés, Pedro *71*
Merritt Island Wildlife Reserve *23, 127*
Miami *16–17, 81–94*
access *94*
accommodation
***Crowne Plaza Miami ((305) 374-0000 *92*
***Doral Resort and Country Club
  ((305) 592-2000 *90*
***Grand Bay Hotel ((305) 858-9600
  TOLL-FREE (800) 327-2788 *92*
***Hotel Inter-Continental Miami
  ((305) 577-1000 *92*
***Mayfair House ((305) 441-0000
  TOLL-FREE (800) 433-4555 *92*
***Sonesta Beach Resort ((305) 361-2021
  TOLL-FREE (800) 343-7170 *92*
**Biltmore Hotel ((305) 445-1926
  TOLL-FREE (800) 727-1926 *92*
**Biscayne Bay Marriott Hotel and Marina
  ((305) 374-3900 *92*
**Doubletree Hotel ((305) 858-2500
  TOLL-FREE (800) 222-8733 *93*
**Economy Inn ((305) 633-6916 *93*
**Everglades Hotel ((305) 379-5461 *92*
**Hotel Place St. Michel ((305) 444-1666 *93*
**Hotel Sofitel Miami ((305) 264-4888 *92*
**Inn on the Bay ((305) 865-7100 *92*
*Bay Point Motel ((305) 573-4444 *93*
*Best Western Marina Park Hotel
  ((305) 372-2862 *93*
*Mardi Gras Motel Apartments
  ((305) 573-7700 *93*
*Sunnyside Motel ((305) 266-1727 *93*
attractions
Barnacle State Historical Site
  ((305) 448-9445 *86*
Bill Baggs Cape Florida State
  Recreation Area *86*
Cape Florida Lighthouse *86*
Center for Fine Arts ((305) 375-3000 *84*
Coral Gables House *86*
Fairchild Tropical Garden ((305) 667-1651 *87*
Greater Miami Opera ((305) 854-7890 *90*
Gusman Center for the Performing Arts
  ((305) 372-0925 *90*
Historical Museum of Southern Florida
  ((305) 375-1492 *84*
Lowe Art Museum ((305) 284-3536 *87*
Metrozoo ((305) 251-0400 *87*
Miami City Ballet ((305) 532-7713 *90*
Miami Museum of Science and Space
  Transit Planetarium ((305) 854-4247 *84*
Miami Seaquarium ((305) 361-5705 *86*
Miami Youth Museum *42*
Monkey Jungle ((305) 235-1611 *87*
Old Town Trolley Tours of Miami
  ((305) 374-8687 *88*
Parrot Jungle ((305) 666-7834 *87*
Philharmonic Orchestra of Florida
  ((305) 945-5180 *90*
President Nixon's Home *86*
Sea Escape cruises ((305) 379-0000 *88*
Silver Bluff *86*
Tropicana/Sea Venture cruises
  ((305) 477-5858 *88*
Venetian Pool ((305) 442-6483 *87*

Vizcaya Museum and Gardens
((305) 250-9133 *84*

districts
Coconut Grove *81, 86*
Coral Gables *74, 81–82, 86*
Key Biscayne *81, 86*
Little Havana *18, 81*
Miami Riviera *81*
Virginia Key *81, 86*
festivals and events
Calle Ocho Festival (March) *54*
Miami Film Festival ((305) 372-0925 *90*
Renaissance Faire *53*
general information
Bal Harbour Chamber of Commerce
((305) 573-5177 *84*
Central Taxicab Service ((305) 534-0694 *84*
Coconut Grove Chamber of Commerce
((305) 444-7270 *84*
Coral Gables Chamber of Commerce
((305) 446-1657 *84*
Dental Referral Service ((305) 285-5470 *84*
Greater Miami Convention and
Visitors Bureau ((305) 539-3000 *83*
Greater Miami Hotel and Motel Association
((305) 371-2030 *83–84*
Key Biscayne Chamber of Commerce
((305) 361-5207 *84*
Metro Taxicabs ((305) 944-4422 *84*
Miami International Airport
((305) 876-7077 *84*
Physician Referral Service
((305) 326-1177 *84*
South Miami Chamber of Commerce
((305) 238-7192 *84*
Weather–Surf Information
((305) 661-5065 *84*
Yellow Cabs ((305) 885-5555 *84*
history 81
nightlife
Biscayne Baby ((305) 445-3751 *90*
Cacharrito's Place ((305) 643-9626 *90*
Copacabana Supper Club ((305) 443-3801 *90*
Hungry Sailor ((305) 444-9359 *90*
Jardin Brasilien ((305) 374-4748 *90*
La Tranquera ((305) 856-9467 *90*
Regine's ((305) 858-9600 *90*
Tobacco Road ((305) 374-1198 *90*
restaurants
***Café Sci Sci ((305) 446-5104 *38*
***Chez Maurice ((305) 448-8984 *94*
***El Bodegon de Castilla ((305) 649-0863 *93*
***Il Tulipano ((305) 893-4811 *93*
***Malaga ((305) 858-4224 *93*
***Mayfair Grill ((305) 441-0000 *94*
***Monty's Seafood Restaurant
((305) 858-1431 *38*
***Pavillion Grill ((305) 372-4494 *93*
***Veronique's ((305) 374-3900 *93*
***Victor's Café ((305) 445-1313 *38*
**Bangkok, Bangkok ((305) 444-2397 *94*
**Centro Vasco ((305) 643-9606 *94*
**Grand Café ((305) 858-9600 *94*
**House of India ((305) 444-2348 *94*
**La Choza ((305) 361-0113 *94*
**La Lupa ((305) 893-9531 *94*
**La Parilla ((305) 553-4419 *94*
**Las Tapas ((305) 372-2737 *94*
**Señor Frog's ((305) 448-0999 *94*

*Big Fish ((305) 372-3725 *94*
*English Pub ((305) 361-5481 *94*
*Granny Feelgood's ((305) 358-6233 *94*
*Monty Trainer's Bayshore ((305) 858-1431 *94*
*Nick and Maria's ((305) 891-9232 *94*
shopping
Aventura Mall *89*
Bayside Marketplace *89*
Little Havana *89*
Mayfair Shops *90*
Miracle Center *90*
Miracle Mile *90*
sports, active
diving *89*
fishing *89*
golf *89*
sailing *89*
tennis *89*
windsurfing *89*
sports information
Florida Tennis Association
((305) 757-8568 *89*
sports, spectator 18
baseball *88*
basketball *88*
football *88*
horse racing *88*
jai alai *89*
soccer *89*
stock car races *88*
Miami Beach *81, 96–101*
access 101
accommodation
***Alexander Hotel ((305) 865-6500 *100*
***Doral Ocean Beach Resort
((305) 532-3600 *100*
***Eden Roc ((305) 531-0000 *100*
***Fontainebleau Hilton ((305) 538-2000 *100*
***Hotel Cavalier ((305) 531-6424 *100*
**Chateau by the Sea ((305) 931-8800 *100*
**Desert Inn ((305) 947-0621
TOLL-FREE (800) 327-6362 *101*
**Edison Hotel ((305) 531-0461 *100*
**Hawaiian Isle ((305) 932-2121
TOLL-FREE (800) 327-5275 *100*
**Park Central Hotel ((305) 538-1611 *100*
*Beach Motel ((305) 861-2001 *101*
*Beachcomber Hotel ((305) 531-3755 *101*
*Ocean Roc ((305) 931-7600 *101*
attractions
Art Deco district *97–98*
Bass Museum of Art ((305) 673-7533 *98*
Boardwalk *98*
Miami Beach Garden Center
and Conservatory *98*
festivals and events
Miami Beach Street Festival (January) *53*
general information
Miami Beach Chamber of Commerce
((305) 672-1270 *97*
Miami Beach Resort Hotel Association
((305) 531-3553 *97*
nightlife
Café des Arts ((305) 534-6267 *100*
Chevy's on the Beach ((305) 868-1950 *100*
Club Bamboo ((305) 538-5803 *100*
Irish House Bar ((305) 672-9626 *100*
Joseph's on the Beach ((305) 673-9626 *100*
Penrod's ((305) 538-1111 *100*

Tropics International ((305) 531-5335   100
Wet Paint Café ((305) 672-3287   100
restaurants
***Café Chauveron ((305) 866-8779   101
***Carlyle Grill ((305) 534-2135   101
***Dominique's ((305) 865-6500   101
***Forge ((305) 538-8533   101
***Joe's Stone Crab ((305) 673-0365   101
**Gino's Italian Restaurant
  ((305) 532-6426   101
**Pineapples ((305) 532-9731   101
**Strand ((305) 532-2340   101
**Tiramesu ((305) 532-4538   101
*News Café   101
*Palace ((305) 531-9077   101
*Pumperniks ((305) 891-1225   101
*Wolfie Cohen's Rascal House
  ((305) 947-4581   101
shopping
Bal Harbour Shops   100
Chocolate   100
Española Way   100
Lincoln Road Mall   100
Tommy at the Beach   100
sports, active
boating   98
diving   98
fishing, deep-sea   98
golf   98
surfing   98
tennis   98
sports information
Miami Beach Recreation Department
  ((305) 673-7700   98
money   248
museums   42
Myakka River Park   28

N Naples   211–215
access   215
accommodation
***Ritz-Carlton ((941) 598-3300   214
**La Playa ((941) 597-3123   214
*Fairways Motel ((941) 597-8181   214
attractions
Corkscrew Swamp Sanctuary
  ((941) 657-3771   212
Frannie's Teddy Bear Museum   42
Jungle Larry's Zoological Park
  ((941) 262-5409   212
festivals and events
Fifth Avenue Oktoberfest   55
general information
Naples Chamber of Commerce
  ((941) 262-6141   211
restaurants
***Chef's Garden ((941) 262-5500   215
*Venetian Café ((941) 261-4050   215
shopping
Periwinkle Way   213
Royal Palm Square Shopping Center   213
Old Marine Market Place   213
sports, active
diving   213
golf   213
tennis   213
national parks   23
Canaveral National Seashore and Merritt Island   23
Everglades National Park   23
Gulf Islands National Seashore   24

Key Biscayne National Park   24
Ocala National Forest   35
Soto National Memorial   23
Navarre   15
Niceville
festivals and events
Boggy Bayou Mullet Festival (October)   55

O Ocala
festivals and events
Florida Horse and
  Agricultural Festival (October)   55
Ocala National Forest   35
Orlando   164–172
access   96, 164
accommodation
***Harley Hotel ((407) 841-3220
  TOLL-FREE (800) 321-2323   169
***Colonial Plaza Inn ((407) 896-9858   169
***Norment-Parry Inn ((407) 648-5188   169
***Park Plaza Hotel ((407) 647-1072   169
**Fugate House ((407) 423-8382   169
**Howard Johnson's ((407) 841-8600   169
**Langford Hotel ((407) 644-3400   169
*Econo Lodge Orlando Central
  ((407) 293-7221   169
*Howard Vernon Motel ((407) 422-7162   169
*TraveLodge Downtown Orlando
  ((407) 423-1671   169
attractions   168
Balloon Flights of Florida ((407) 422-2434   168
Cartoon Museum ((407) 273-0141   168
Fun 'n' Wheels ((407) 351-5651   165
Jungleland Zoo ((407) 396-1012   165
Lake Eola Park Centennial Fountain   168
Museum of Woodcarving ((407) 396-4422   165
Mystery Fun House ((407) 351-3355   165
Old Town ((407) 396-4888   165
Orlando Science Center
  ((407) 896-7151   42, 168
Scenic Boat Tours ((407) 644-4056   168
Sea World ((407) 351-3600   165
Toy Train Museum   42
Wet 'n' Wild ((407) 351-1800   165
general information
Emergency Dental Care ((407) 425-1616   165
Greater Orlando Tourist Information Center
  ((407) 351-0412   165
Orange County Medical Society
  ((407) 898-3338   165
Orlando International Airport
  ((407) 826-2001   165
Orlando-Orange County Convention and
  Visitors Bureau ((407) 363-5800   165
Town and Country Cabs ((407) 828-3035   165
Yellow Cabs ((407) 423-4455   165
history   164
nightlife   168
Apple Annie's Courtyard   169
Cheyenne Saloon   169
Church Street Station ((407) 422-2434   38, 169
Little Darlin's Rock 'n' Roll Palace
  ((407) 396-6499   169
Mardi Gras ((407) 351-5151   168
Phileas Phogg's Balloon Works   169
Rosie O'Grady's   169
restaurants
***Catham's Palace ((407) 345-2992   38
***Christini's ((407) 345-8770   171
***Gran Cru ((407) 859-1500   38

***Hemingways ((407) 239-1234 38
***Hemisphere ((405) 825-1234 38
***Manuel's ((407) 246-6580 38
***Park Plaza Gardens ((407) 645-2475 169
***Ran-Getsu ((407) 354-0044 171
***Royal Orleans ((407) 352-8200 171
**Coq au Vin ((407) 851-6980 171
**Darbar ((407) 345-8128 171
**La Belle Verrière ((407) 645-3377 171
**La Cantina ((407) 894-4491 171
*British Tearoom ((407) 677-0121 171
*Gary's Duck Inn ((407) 843-0270 171
*Greek Place ((407) 352-6930 171
*Skeeter's ((407) 298-7973 171
shopping
    Mercado Shopping Village 168
    Park Avenue 168
sports, active
    boating 168
    golf 168
    tennis 168
    water sports 168
sports, spectator
    baseball 168

P Palm Beach and Boca Raton 74, 116–122
access 122
accommodation
    ***Boca Raton Resort and Club
        ((407) 395-3000
        TOLL-FREE (800) 327-0101 121
    ***Breakers ((407) 655-6611
        TOLL-FREE (800) 833-3141 120
    ***Brazilian Court Hotel ((407) 655-7740 121
    ***Colony ((305) 655-5430 121
    **Beachcomber Apartment Motel
        ((407) 585-4648 121
    **Best Western Seaspray Inn ((407) 844-0233
        TOLL-FREE (800) 528-1234 121
    **Best Western University Inn
        ((407) 395-5255 121
    **Howard Johnson Motor Lodge
        ((407) 582-2581 TOLL-FREE (800) 654-2000 121
    **Rutledge Resort Motel ((407) 848-6621 121
    *Boca Raton Motel ((407) 395-7500
        TOLL-FREE (800) 453-4511 121
    *Harbor Lights Apartments
        ((407) 844-5377 121
    *Shore Edge Motel ((407) 395-4491 121
attractions
    Dreher Park Zoo ((407) 547-9453 117
    Henry M. Flagler Museum
        ((407) 655-2833 117
    Lion Country Safari ((407) 793-1084 117
    Norton Gallery of Art ((407) 832-5196 117
    Star of Palm Beach (sightseeing cruises)
        ((407) 848-7827 116
    Steamboat Landing (sightseeing cruises) 116
general information
    Boca Raton Chamber of Commerce
        ((407) 395-4433 116
    Chamber of Commerce of the Palm Beaches
        ((407) 833-3711 116
    Doctor Referral Service ((407) 433-3940 116
    Palm Beach County Convention and
        Visitors Bureau ((407) 471-3995 116
    Palm Beach International Airport
        ((407) 471-7400 116
    Travel Markets International
        ((081) 688-1451 116

    Yellow Cabs ((407) 689-4222 116
history 115
nightlife
    Colony 120
    Royal Palm Dinner Theater
        ((407) 392-3755 120
    Ta-Boo ((407) 655-5562 120
    Top of the Bridge Lounge
        ((407) 368-9500 120
    Tugboat Annie's ((407) 394-9900 120
    Wildflower ((407) 426-0066 120
restaurants
    ***Chez Marcel ((407) 368-6553 122
    ***Dining Room ((407) 655-7740 122
    ***La Vieille Maison ((407) 391-6701 121
    ***Le Monegasque ((407) 585-0071 122
    **Chuck & Harold's Café
        ((407) 659-1440 122
    **Doherty's ((407) 655-6200 122
    **Harpoon Louie's ((407) 744-1300 122
    **Siam Garden ((407) 368-9013 122
    *Hamburger Heaven ((407) 655-5277 122
    *Original Grandma Sarah's
        ((407) 833-6369 122
    *Tom's Place ((407) 997-0920 122
    *Toojay's ((407) 659-7232 122
shopping
    Worth Avenue 120
sports, active
    diving 118
    golf 118
    polo 118
    tennis 118
sports, spectator
    baseball 118
    jai alai 118
    polo 118
Panama City 181–186
access 186
accommodation
    ***Edgewater Beach Resort ((904) 235-4044
        TOLL-FREE (800) 874-8686 184
    ***Marriott's Bay Point Resort ((904) 234-3307
        TOLL-FREE (800) 874-7105 184
    **Cobb's Gulfview Inn ((904) 234-6051 184
    **Flamingo Motel ((904) 234-2232 184
    **Rendezvous Inn ((904) 234-8841 184
    **Sugar Sands Hotel ((904) 234-8802 184
    *Bikini Beach Motel ((904) 234-3392 184
    *Howard's Motor Lodge ((904) 763-4998 184
    *La Brisa Motor Inn ((904) 871-2345 185
    *Silver Sands Motel ((904) 234-2201 184
attractions 181
    Captain Anderson's Marina
        ((904) 234-5940 181
    Dead Lakes State Recreation Area
        ((904) 639-2702 181
    Gulf World ((904) 234-5271 181
    Junior Museum of Bay County
        ((904) 769-6128 181
    Miracle Strip Amusement Park
        ((904) 234-5810 181
    Museum of Man and the Sea
        ((904) 235-4101 181
    St. Andrews State Recreation Area
        ((904) 233-5140 181
festivals and events
    Beach Fishing Classic (August) 55
    Elgin Air Show (April) 54

Indian Summer Seafood
   Festival (September) 55
PGA Classic for Young
   Professionals (April) 54
general information
   Bay Walk-In Clinic
      ((904) 234-8442 181
   Beach Taxi ((904) 234-5202 181
   Panama City Beach Convention and
      Visitors Bureau ((904) 233-5070 181
   Panama City-Bay County Regional Airport
      ((904) 763-6751 181
   Tallahassee Regional Airport
      ((904) 574-7800 181
nightlife
   Captain Anderson's Dinner Cruise
      ((904) 234-5940 184
   Ocean Opry ((904) 234-5464 184
   Pineapple Willie's ((904) 235-8928 183
   Southern Elegance ((904) 785-3006 184
   Spinnaker III ((904) 234-7882 183
restaurants
   ***Boar's Head ((904) 234-6628 185
   ***Sylvia's ((904) 234-0184 185
   **Caporelli's ((904) 763-2245 185
   **Claudio's ((904) 769-8722 185
   **Greenhouse ((904) 763-2245 185
   **Harbour House ((904) 785-9053 185
   *Cajun Inn ((904) 235-9987 186
   *Cheese Barn ((904) 769-3892 186
   *Gulf Cafeteria ((904) 234-6457 186
   *Los Antojitos ((904) 769-7081 186
shopping
   Field's Plaza 182
   Galleria 183
   Olde Towne Mini Mall 183
sports, active
   diving 182
   golf 181
   tennis 181
   water sports 182
Panama City Beach 16
Pánfilo de Narváez 71
Panhandle, The 15, 181–191
   history 177
Pensacola 15, 186–191
   access 191
   accommodation
      ***Dunes ((904) 932-3526 190
      ***New World Landing ((904) 432-4111
         TOLL-FREE (800) 258-1103 190
      ***Pensacola Grand Hotel
         ((904) 433-3336 190
      **Days Inn ((904) 238-4922
         TOLL-FREE (800) 874-071 190
      **Residence Inn ((904) 479-1000
         TOLL-FREE (800) 331-3131 190
      **Sandpiper Inn ((904) 932-2516 191
      *Days Inn ((904) 477-9000 191
      *Gulf Aire Motel ((904) 932-2319 191
      *Motel 6 ((904) 477-7522 191
      *Two Tom's Bed and Breakfast
         ((904) 939-2382 191
   attractions
      Big Lagoon State Recreation Area 187
      Blackwater River State Park
         ((904) 623-2363 187
      Gulf Island National Seashore 187
      Historic Pensacola Village 186

Naval Aviation Museum
   ((904) 452-3604 187
Pensacola Beach 15
Pensacola Historical Museum
   ((904) 433-1559 186
Perdido Key 15
San Carlos de Barrancas 187
West Florida Museum of History
   ((904) 444-8905 186
Zoo and Botanical Gardens
   ((904) 9832-2229 186
festivals and events
   Arts Festival (November) 55
   Blue Angels Homecoming Show
      (November) 55
   Fiesta of the Five Flags (June) 55
   jazz festival (April) 54
general information
   Blue and White Cab ((904) 438-1497 186
   Escambia County Health Department
      ((904) 438-8571 186
   Pensacola Area Chamber of Commerce
      Visitor Information ((904) 434-1234 186
   Pensacola Regional Airport
      ((904) 435-1746 186
history 186
nightlife
   Flounder's Ale House ((904) 932-2003 190
   McQuire's Irish Pub ((904) 433-6789 190
   Red Garter Saloon ((904) 433-9229 190
   Seville Inn ((904) 433-8331 190
restaurants
   ***Driftwood ((904) 433-4559 191
   ***Jamie's ((904) 434-2911 191
   ***Jubilee ((904) 934-3108 191
   **Angus Steak Ranch ((904) 432-0539 191
   **Beignet's ((904) 434-7225 191
   **Dainty Del ((904) 438-1241 191
   **Scotto's Ristorante Italiano
      ((904) 434-1932 191
   *Captain Joe Patti's ((904) 434-3193 191
   *Coffee Cup ((904) 432-7060 191
   *E.J.'s Food Company ((904) 432-5886 191
   *Hopkin's Boarding House
      ((904) 438-3979 191
shopping
   Harbourtown Shopping Village 190
   Quayside Thieves Market 190
   Seville Square 190
sports, active
   golf 187
   tennis 187
   water sports 187, 190
Pensacola Beach
   festivals and events
      Seafood Festival (September) 55
Perry
   attractions
      Forest Capital 43
Plantation Key *See under* Florida Keys
Plant City
   festivals and events
      Floral City Strawberry Festival (March) 53
Ponce de León, Juan 71, 74, 127, 141, 229
porpoises 181
Port St. Joe
   attractions
      Constitution Convention 43
post World War II development 74

postal services *See* mail
prices *67, 249*
public holidays *252*

R **Ramrod Key** *See under* Florida Keys

real estate *255*
Ribault, Jean *71*

S **Sandestin**
festivals and events
Great Southern Gumbo Cook-Off
(January) *51*
St. Augustine *11, 51, 138–145*
access 145
accommodation
***Casa de Solano ((904) 824-3555 *144*
***Conch House Marina Resort
((904) 829-8646
TOLL-FREE (904) 432-6256 *144*
***Westcott House ((904) 824-4301 *144*
**Casa de la Paz ((904) 829-2915 *144*
**Kenwood Inn ((904) 824-2116 *144*
**St. Francis Inn ((904) 824-6068 *144*
**Victorian Inn ((904) 824-5214 *144*
*Monsoon Motor Lodge ((904) 829-2277 *144*
*Park Inn ((904) 824-4352 *144*
attractions
Basilica Cathedral of St. Augustine *139*
Castillo de San Marcos *11, 139*
Colee's Carriages *139*
Fort Matanzas *11*
Fort Mose *11*
Fountain of Youth Discovery Park *141*
Government House Museum *11*
Lighthouse Tower and Museum *11*
Lightner Museum ((904) 824-2874 *11, 141*
Marineland of Florida ((904) 471-1111 *141*
Oceanarium *13*
Old City Gate *139*
Oldest House *11, 139*
Oldest Store Museum ((904) 829-9729 *11, 141*
Oldest Wooden Schoolhouse *11, 139*
Ponce de León Hotel *11*
Ripley's Believe It or Not
((904) 824-1606 *141*
St. Augustine Alligator and Crocodile Farm
((904) 824-3337 *11, 141*
St. Photios Chapel *139*
San Augustin Antiguo *139*
Sightseeing Trains ((904) 829-6545 *139*
Webb Museum *139*
festivals and events
Easter Parade (April) *54*
Grand Illumination (December) *56*
general information
St. Augustine Chamber of Commerce
((904) 829-6477 *139*
St. Augustine Visitor Information Center
((904) 829-3334 *139*
Spanish Heritage Tours ((904) 829-3726 *139*
history 138
nightlife
Conch House Marina Lounge
((904) 829-8646 *141*
El Caballero ((904) 824-2096 *141*
Mario & Chickies ((904) 824-2952 *141*
Sister Sally's ((904) 471-2555 *141*
White Lion ((904) 829-2388 *141*
restaurants
***Columbia ((904) 824-3341 *144*

***Le Pavillon ((904) 824-6202 *144*
***Raintree ((904) 824-7211 *144*
**Captain Jim's Conch Hut
((904) 829-8646 *145*
**Gypsy Cab Company ((904) 824-8244 *145*
**Monk's Vineyard ((904) 824-5888 *145*
**Scarlett O'Hara's ((904) 824-6535 *145*
*Café Alcazar ((904) 824-2618 *145*
*O'Steens ((904) 829-6974 *145*
*Panama Hattie's ((904) 471-2255 *145*
shopping
Lightner Antique Mall *141*
San Augustin Antiguo *141*
sports, active
golf *144*
tennis *144*
water sports *144*
St. George Island *24*
St. Johns River *18, 26, 71*
St. Joseph Peninsula *25*
St. Petersburg–Clearwater *18–19, 202–206*
access 206
accommodation
***Don CeSar Beach Resort ((813) 360-1881
TOLL-FREE (800) 237-8789 *205*
***Heritage ((813) 822-4814 *204*
***Tradewinds ((813) 367-6461
TOLL-FREE (800) 282-5553 *204*
**Bayboro House ((813) 823-4955 *205*
**Colonial Gateway Resort Inn
((813) 367-2711
TOLL-FREE (800) 282-5245 *205*
**Dolphin Beach Resort ((813) 360-7011 *205*
**Edgepark Hotel ((813) 894-9435 *205*
**Long Key Beach Resort
((813) 360-1748 *205*
*Avalon Hotel ((813) 822-4783 *205*
*Beach Park Motor Inn ((813) 898-6325 *205*
*Carlida Apartments and Motel
((813) 360-7233 *205*
attractions
Boatyard Village *19*
Clearwater Beach *19*
Clearwater Marina *19*
Clearwater Marine Science Center *19*
Great Explorations Childrens Museum *19*
Largo Heritage Park and Museum *19*
Marine Science Center *19*
Museum of Fine Arts ((813) 896-2667 *19, 202*
Pier ((813) 821-6164 *19, 202*
Ruth Eckerd Hall *19*
Salvador Dali Museum
((813) 823-3767 *19, 202*
SeaEscape ((813) 432-0900 *202*
Sunken Gardens ((813) 896-3187 *202*
festivals and events
Caribbean Calypso Carnival (August) *55*
Sunsational Museums Month (September) *55*
general information
Pinellas County Tourist Development Council
((813) 530-6132 *202*
St. Petersburg and Clearwater Convention
and Visitors Bureau ((813) 582-7892 *202*
nightlife
Alessi Café at the Pier ((813) 804-4659 *204*
Bayfront Center ((813) 893-3367 *204*
Beach Place ((813) 596-5633 *204*
Cadillac Jack's ((813) 360-2099 *204*
Cha Cha Coconuts at The Pier *40*

Coconuts Comedy Club at Barnacle Bill's
  ((813) 360-4575   204
Coliseum Ballroom   40
Crow's Nest Supper Club   40
Don's Beach Bar ((813) 360-5531   204
Grog Shoppe   40
Studebaker's ((813) 799-4147   204
Tierra Verde Resort Ballroom   40
Woody's Waterfront   40
restaurants
  ***Girard's ((813) 576-7076   206
  ***King Charles ((813) 360-1881   205
  ***Palm Court ((813) 360-0061   206
  ***Pelican Diner ((813) 363-9873   206
  ***Peter's Place ((813) 822-8436   206
  **Bahama Bill's ((813) 821-4931   206
  **Crab Market ((813) 360-4656   206
  **Ted Peters ((813) 381-7931   206
  *Big Tim's Bar-B-Que ((813) 327-7388   206
  *Carol's Seafood and Steak House
    ((813) 522-9907   206
  *China City ((813) 822-3713   206
shopping
  John's Pass Village and Boardwalk   204
  Pier   204
  St. Petersburg Arts and Crafts Emporium   204
sports, active
  golf   203
  tennis   203
  water sports   203
Sanibel Island   19, 211
accommodation
  ***Sanibel Beach and Tennis Resort
    ((941) 472-4151   214
  **Kon Mai Motel ((941) 472-1001   214
attractions
  Bailey-Matthews Shell Museum   20
  Bowman's Beach   212
  J.N. "Ding" Darling National Wildlife Refuge
    ((941) 472-1100   20, 212
  Lighthouse Beach   212
  Old Schoolhouse Theater   19
  Pirate Playhouse   20
  Sanibel-Captiva Conservation Foundation   20
festivals and events
  Shell Fair (March)   54
general information
  Sanibel-Captiva Chamber of Commerce
    ((941) 472-1080   211
restaurants
  ***Jean-Paul's French Corner
    ((941) 472-1493   215
  **Thistle Lodge ((941) 472-9200   215
  *Island Pizza ((941) 472-1518   215
shopping
  Periwinkle Way   213
sports, active
  golf   213
  tennis   213
  water sports   213
Sarasota   206–211
access   211
accommodation
  ***Colony Beach Resort ((941) 383-6464
    TOLL-FREE (800) 426-5669   210
  ***Harley Sandcastle Hotel
    ((941) 388-2181   210
  ***Hyatt Sarasota ((941) 233-1234
    TOLL-FREE (800) 228-9000   210

  **Crescent House ((941) 346-1786   210
  **Days Inn Sarasota ((941) 924-4900   210
  **Golden Host   210
  *Econo Lodge ((941) 355-8867   210
  *Hampton Inn ((941) 351-7734   210
  *Our Hacienda ((941) 951-1920   210
attractions   208
  Asolo Performing Arts Center
    ((941) 359-5700   209
  Asolo Theater ((813) 355-8000   208
  Bell's Cars and Music of Yesterday
    ((941) 355-6228   208
  Ca'd'Zan, Ringling estate   208
  Circus Galleries   208
  Florida Studio Theater
    ((941) 366-9796   209
  Florida Symphonic Band
    ((941) 955-6660   209
  Marie Selby Botanical Gardens
    ((941) 366-5730   208
  Mote Marine Science Center
    ((941) 388-4441   208
  Myakka River State Park   208
  Oscar Sherer Recreation Area   208
  Players of Sarasota ((941) 365-2494   209
  Ringling Museum of Art ((941) 359-5700   208
  Sarasota Jungle Gardens ((941) 355-5305   208
  Sarasota Opera ((941) 953-7030   209
  Siesta Beach   208
  South Lido beach   208
festivals and events
  French Film Festival (November)   55
  Medieval Faire (March)   54
general information
  Airport Taxi ((941) 365-1360   208
  Sarasota Chamber of Commerce
    ((941) 955-8187   206
  Sarasota Convention and Visitors Center
    ((941) 957-1877   206
  Sarasota County Health Clinic
    ((941) 365-2020   208
  Sarasota-Bradenton Airport
    ((941) 355-5200   208
  Yellow Cabs ((941) 955-3341   208
history   206
nightlife
  Beach Club ((941) 349-6311   209
  Club Paradise ((941) 366-3830   209
  Hemingway's ((941) 388-3948   210
  Pub ((941) 383-2391   209
restaurants
  ***Café L'Europe ((941) 388-4415   210
  ***Marina Jack's and Marina Jack II (paddle
    wheel dinner boat) ((941) 365-4232   210
  ***Michael's on East ((941) 366-0007   210
  ***Osteria ((941) 388-3671   210
  **Charley's Crab ((941) 388-3964   210
  **Indian Cuisine ((941) 953-5102   210
  **Poki Joe's Greatest Hits
    ((941) 922-5915   210
  **Ristorante Bellini ((941) 365-7380   210
  *Der Dutchman ((941) 955-8007   210
  *Old Salty Dog Pub ((941) 349-0158   211
  *Walt's Fish Market, Raw Oyster Bar
    and Restaurant   210
  *Wildflower ((941) 349-1758   210
shopping
  St. Armand's Circle   209
  Sarasota Square Mall   209

sports, active
  golf 209
  tennis 209
  water sports 209
sports, spectator
  baseball 209
sea lions 86, 110, 165, 181
Seminoles 72
sharks 141, 222, 230
Shell Coast 211–215 *See also* Fort Myers
  access 215
shelling 60
shopping 44 *See also under* place names
  antiques 14, 46, 84, 100, 141, 190, 199
  crafts 45, 53–54, 89, 110–111, 239
  factory outlets 46, 204, 209
  malls 47
  specialty 46
Soto National Memorial 23
South Walton 15
Southwest Florida
  access 215
souvenirs 45
Space Coast 127–131
  access 131
  accommodation
    ***Cocoa Beach Hilton ((407) 799-0003
      TOLL-FREE (800) 445-8667 130
    ***Inn at Cocoa Beach
      ((407) 799-3460 130
    **Crossway Inn and Tennis Resort
      ((305) 783-2221 130
    **Polaris Beach Resort Inn ((305) 783-7621
      TOLL-FREE (800) 962-0028 130
    **Surf Studio Beach Apartments
      ((305) 783-7100 130
    *Brevard Hotel ((407) 636-1411 131
    *Luck's Way Inn ((305) 269-7110
      TOLL-FREE (800) 228-2000 130
    *Ocean Suite Hotel 131
  attractions
    Black Point Wildlife Drive 129
    Kennedy Space Center 128
    Lone Cabbage Fish Camp (airboat cruises)
      ((407) 632-4199 129
    Merritt Island National Wildlife Refuge
      bus tour ((407) 867-0677 129
    Spaceport USA 128
  general information
    Cocoa Beach Tourism and Convention
      Council ((407) 459-2200 128
    NASA TOLL-FREE (800) 432-2153
      (information) 128
    NASA ((305) 452-2121 (reservation) 128
  history 127
  nightlife
    Cocoa Banana ((407) 799-3700 130
    Coco's ((407) 799-0003 130
    Dino's Jazz Piano Bar ((407) 784-5470 130
  restaurants
    ***Bernard's Surf ((305) 783-2401 131
    ***Black Tulip ((407) 631-1133 131
    **Dixie Crossroads ((407) 268-5000 131
    **Kountry Kitchen ((407) 459-3457 131
    **Victor's Family Restaurant
      ((407) 459-1656 131
    *Desperadoes ((407) 784-3363 131
    *Pasta Garden ((407) 639-8343 131
    *Peking Garden ((407) 459-2999 131

    *Village Ice Cream and Sandwich Shop
      ((407) 632-2311 131
  shopping
    Cocoa Village 129
    Handwerk House 129
    Indian River Pottery 129
    Ron Jon Surf Shop 129
    Wine Experience 129
Spanish Armada 72
sports, active *See under* place names
sports, spectator 30 *See also under* place names
state parks and recreation areas 24, 37
statehood 73
stingrays 230
Stock Island *See under* Florida Keys
Sugarloaf Key *See under* Florida Keys
Summerland Key *See under* Florida Keys
Sunshine Key *See under* Florida Keys
Stock Island *See under* Florida Keys
Suwanee River 26

T Tallahassee 177–181
  access 181
  accommodation
    ***Governor's Inn ((904) 681-6855 179
    ***Radisson Hotel ((904) 224-6000 179
    ***Tallahassee Sheraton ((904) 224-5000 179
    **Capital Inn Parkway ((904) 877-3141 179
    **Holiday Inn University Center
      ((904) 222-8000 179
    **Leisure Inn ((904) 877-4437 179
    *Days Inn South ((904) 877-6121 179
    fishing camps and lodges (information)
      ((904) 681-9200 180
  attractions
    Aeronauts & Balloons ((904) 893-1282 178
    Alfred B. Maclay Gardens 44
    Apalachicola National Forest 178
    Edward Ball Wakulla Springs State Park
      ((904) 222-7279 178
    Florida Capitol 177
    Lake Jackson Indian Mounds
      ((904) 562-0042 44, 178
    LeMoyne Art Foundation
      ((904) 222-8800 178
    Museum of Florida History
      ((904) 488-1484 178
    Old Capitol 177
    Old Union Bank ((904) 487-1902 178
    Tallahassee Museum of History and
      Natural Science ((904) 575-8243 178
    University Gallery and Museum
      ((904) 644-2098 178
  festivals and events
    1865 Natural Bridge Battlefield
      Reenactment (March) 53
    Fourth of July 55
    Southern Accents of Winter (December) 56
  general information
    Capital Medical Society
      ((904) 877-9018 177
    Tallahassee Area Convention and
      Visitors Bureau ((904) 413-9200 177
    Tallahassee Regional Airport
      ((904) 574-7800 177
  history 177
  nightlife
    Flamingo Café Lounge 179
    Moon ((904) 222-6666 179
    Studebaker's ((904) 656-2191 179

restaurants
   ***Andrew's Second Act ((904) 222-2759 *180*
   ***Golden Pheasant ((904) 222-0241 *180*
   **Anthony's ((904) 224-1477 *180*
   **Brothers Three ((904) 386-4193 *180*
   **Melting Pot ((904) 386-7440 *180*
   **Ms. Lucy's Bamboo Gardens
     ((904) 878-3366 *180*
   *Adams Street Café ((904) 222-3444 *180*
   *Julie's Place ((904) 368-7181 *180*
   *Mom and Dad's ((904) 877-4518 *180*
shopping
   Market Square *179*
   Outdoors Shop ((904) 368-4180 *179*
sports, active
   golf *178–179*
   tennis *179*
   water sports *179*
Tampa *195–201*
access *201*
accommodation
   ***Hyatt Regency ((813) 225-1234
     TOLL-FREE (800) 228-9000 *200*
   ***Radisson Bay Harbour Inn
     ((813) 281-8900 *200*
   ***Saddlebrook Golf and Tennis Resort
     ((813) 973-1111 *200*
   ***Sheraton Grand Hotel ((813) 286-4400 *200*
   ***Wyndham Harbour Island Hotel
     ((813) 229-5000 *200*
   **Days Inn ((813) 884-2000 *200*
   **Holiday Inn Ashley Plaza Hotel
     ((813) 223-1351 *200*
   **Holiday Inn Busch Gardens
     ((813) 971-4710 *200*
   **Howard Johnson's Busch Gardens
     Main Gate ((813) 988-9191 *200*
   *Expressway Inn ((813) 837-1971 *200*
   *Garden View Motel ((813) 933-3958 *200*
   *Tahitian Inn ((813) 877-6721 *200*
attractions
   Adventure Island ((813) 987-5000 *197*
   Anclote Keys *15*
   Busch Gardens The Dark Continent
     ((813) 971-5082 *196*
   Clearwater Beach *197*
   Dunedin Beach *197*
   Florida Center for Contemporary Art *14*
   Henry Plant Museum ((813) 254-1891 *197*
   José Gasparilla pirate ship *197*
   Konger Coral Sea Aquarium *14*
   La Casita (Ybor City) *14*
   Las Novedades *14*
   Sand Key Beaches *197*
   Seminole Culture Center
     ((813) 623-3549 *197*
   Spongeorama Exhibit Center *14*
   St. Nicholas Greek Orthodox Church *14*
   Tampa Museum of Art ((813) 223-8130 *197*
   Tampa Rico Cigars *197*
   Tarpon Springs *14, 204*
   Villazon & Co. *14*
   Ybor City *13, 195, 197*
   Ybor City State Museum *14, 197*
   Ybor City Visitors Center ((813) 248-3712 *197*
   Ybor Square *197*
festivals and events
   Florida State Fair (February) *53*
   Gasparilla Pirate Fest Weekend (February) *53*

general information
   Emergency clinic ((813) 877-8450 *196*
   Greater Tampa Chamber of Commerce
     ((813) 228-7777 *196*
   Tampa International Airport
     ((813) 870-8700 *196*
   Tampa–Hillsborough Convention and
     Visitors Association ((813) 223-2752 *196*
   Tampa–St. Petersburg Reservations Center
     ((813) 596-9944 *196*
   Yellow Cabs ((813) 253-0121 *196*
history *195*
nightlife
   Dallas Bull ((813) 985-6877 *199*
   Killians Backbeat Lounge
     ((813) 884-8965 *200*
   MacDinton's Tavern ((813) 254-1661 *199*
   Parker's Lighthouse ((813) 229-3474 *199*
   Skipper's Smokehouse
     ((813) 971-0666 *200*
   Stingers ((813) 968-1515 *200*
restaurants
   ***Bern's Steak House ((813) 251-2421 *200*
   ***Columbia ((813) 248-4961 *201*
   ***Coyotes ((813) 831-9759 *201*
   ***J. Fitzgerald's ((813) 873-4400 *200*
   ***Lauro Ristorante ((813) 884-4366 *201*
   ***Monte Carlo ((813) 879-6245 *200*
   **Café Pepe ((813) 253-6501 *201*
   **Colonnade ((813) 839-7558 *201*
   **Don Quixote *14*
   **Jasmine Thai ((813) 968-1501 *201*
   **Kaoribana ((813) 968-3801 *201*
   **Selena's ((813) 251-2116 *201*
   *Bella Trattoria ((813) 254-3355 *201*
   *Club Key West ((813) 832-4115 *201*
   *La Tropicana *201*
   La Segunda Central Bakery *14*
shopping
   Harbour Island Market *199*
   Interbay Antique Row District *199*
   Tampa Bay Center *199*
   Ybor City *48*
   Ybor Square *199*
sports, active
   golf *199*
   tennis *199*
sports, spectator
   baseball *197, 199*
   football *199*
   soccer *199*
tanning *250*
Tarpon Springs *See under* Tampa
tennis *30, 251* *See also under* place names
   International Tennis Center
     ((305) 361-5252 *89*
tennis, professional *89*
tipping *250*
Tomoka Indian settlement *26*
Torreya nature area *25*
tourist information *245*
tours, organized *62*
transportation *247*
travel documents *246*
Tristán de Luna *71*
tropical fish *24*
Tuttle, Julia *81*

U United States territory *73*
Upper Matecumbe Key *See under* Florida Keys

V   **Vaca Key**   *See under* Florida Keys

W   **Wakulla Springs**   *25*
Walt Disney World   *153–164*
  access   *164*
  accommodation
    ***Buena Vista Palace ℂ (407) 827-2727
      TOLL-FREE (800) 327-2990   *162*
    ***Club-Suite Villas   *162*
    ***Contemporary Hotel   *161*
    ***Disney Inn   *162*
    ***Grand Floridian Beach Resort   *162*
    ***Grosvenor Resort ℂ (407) 828-4444
      TOLL-FREE (800) 624-4109   *162*
    ***Hilton Hotel ℂ (407) 827-4000
      TOLL-FREE (800) 445-8667   *162*
    ***Hotel Royal Plaza ℂ (407) 828-2828
      TOLL-FREE (800) 248-2424   *162*
    ***Pickett Suite Resort ℂ (407) 934-1000
      TOLL-FREE (800) 742-5388   *162*
    ***Pleasure Island   *38*
    ***Polynesian Village   *161*
    ***Resort Villas   *161*
    ***Treehouses   *162*
    ***Two-Bedroom Villas   *162*
    ***Vacation Villas   *161*
    **Colonial Motor Lodge
      ℂ (407) 847-6121   *162*
    **Days Inn Orlando Lakeside ℂ (407) 351-1900
      TOLL-FREE (800) 777-3297   *162*
    **Gemini Motel ℂ (407) 396-2151   *162*
    **Hawaiian Village Inn ℂ (407) 396-1212   *162*
    **Hilton Inn Florida Center ℂ (407) 351-4600
      TOLL-FREE (800) 327-1363   *162*
    **Holiday Inn International
      ℂ (407) 351-3500   *162*
    **Orlando Marriott Inn ℂ (407) 351-2420
      TOLL-FREE (800) 351-9290   *162*
    **Radisson Inn Maingate ℂ (407) 396-1400
      TOLL-FREE (800) 333-3333   *162*
    **Sheraton World ℂ (407) 352-1100
      TOLL-FREE (800) 325-3535   *162*
    **Spacecoast Motel ℂ (407) 933-5732
      TOLL-FREE (800) 654-8342   *162*
    *Casa Rosa Inn ℂ (407) 396-2020   *163*
    *Comfort Inn ℂ (407) 855-6060
      TOLL-FREE (800) 327-9742   *163*
    *Golden Link Motel ℂ (407) 396-0555   *163*
    *Knight's Inn Orlando Maingate West
      ℂ (407) 396-4200   *163*
    *Lakeside Cedar Inn ℂ (407) 396-1376   *163*
    *Quality Inn Plaza ℂ (407) 345-8585
      TOLL-FREE (800) 228-5151   *163*
  camping   *162*
  Walt Disney Central Reservation Office
    ℂ (407) 824-000   *161*
  Walt Disney Travel Company
    ℂ (407) 828-3232   *161*

  attractions
    Discovery Island   *160*
    Disney MGM Studio Tour   *158*
    Murphy's Vine Street Emporium Dance
      Palace ℂ (407) 396-6500   *160*
    River Country ℂ (407) 824-3737   *160*
    Epcot Center   *157*
      Future World   *158*
      World Showcase   *157*
    Magic Kingdom   *155*
  general information   *154*
    Walt Disney World (Vacation Guide)
      ℂ (407) 828-3481   *154*
    ticket information   *154*
  nightlife
    Biergarten   *160*
    Giraffe Lounge ℂ (407) 828-2828   *160*
    Laughing Kookaburra Good Time Bar
      ℂ (407) 827-2727   *160*
    Mickey's Tropical Revue (The Polynesian
      Revue) ℂ (407) 824-8000   *160*
  restaurants   *164*
    Epcot Center World Showcase restaurants
      ℂ (407) 824-4000   *163–164*
      Les Chefs de France   *164*
      San Angel Inn   *164*
      Alfredo's   *164*
      Rose and Crown Pub   *164*
      Marrakesh   *164*
    Victoria and Albert's ℂ (407) 824-3000   *38*
    Walt Disney World Village restaurants   *164*
      American Vineyards ℂ (407) 827-4000   *164*
      Arthurs 27 ℂ (407) 827-3450   *38, 164*
      Outback ℂ (407) 827-3430   *164*
      Planet Hollywood ℂ (407) 827-7827   *164*
  shopping
    Walt Disney World Village   *160*
water sports   *28*   *See also under* place names
West Palm Beach
  attractions
    Lion Country Safari   *42*
  festivals and events
    Sunfest (April)   *54*
whales   *165*
what to bring   *247*
when to go   *246*
wildlife   *See* fauna
wine   *60*
Winter Haven
  festivals and events
    Florida Citrus Festival (January)   *51*
    Polk County Fair (January)   *51*
Withlacoochee State Forest   *37*
Woodville
  attractions
    Natural Bridge Battlefield
    State Historic Site   *43*

Y   **Ybor City**   *See under* Tampa